The Sohbat Series

The Sohbat Series

This series captures the intensely personal journey of the spiritual wayfarer's path to wisdom and enlightenment. Encompassing everything from edifying lessons to powerful love poetry, these books explore the most intimate reflections and experiences of disciples at the hands of their spiritual masters.

Each volume is distinct in structure and form, mirroring the unique, extraordinary bond that exists between novice and sage. These personal recollections of both one-to-one and collective experiences will enable you, the reader, to savour the presence of the Shaykh who so enraptured the heart of the disciple.

Other books in the series:

Servant of the Loving One
Paul Abdul Wadud Sutherland
(Shaykh Nazim al-Haqqani)

~

The School of Celestial Fire
John Lindsay
(Shaykh Abdullah Sirr-Dan Al-Jamal)

THE Merciful Door

LIVING WITH A SUFI TEACHER IN INDIA

THE Merciful Door

LIVING WITH A SUFI TEACHER IN INDIA

Scott Siraj al-Haqq Kugle

First published in the UK by Beacon Books and Media Ltd
Earl Business Centre, Dowry Street, Oldham, OL8 2PF, UK.

Copyright © Scott Kugle 2022

The right of Scott Kugle to be identified as the author of this work has been asserted in accordance with the Copyright, Designs and Patents Act 1988. All rights reserved. This book may not be reproduced, scanned, transmitted or distributed in any printed or electronic form or by any means without the prior written permission from the copyright owners, except in the case of brief quotations embedded in critical reviews and other non-commercial uses permitted by copyright law.

First edition published in 2022

www.beaconbooks.net

ISBN: 978-1-912356-66-9 Paperback
ISBN: 978-1-912356-67-6 Hardback
ISBN: 978-1-912356-68-3 eBook

Cataloging-in-Publication record for this book is available from the British Library.

Cover photograph by Abdullah Lipton
Cover design by Raees Mahmood Khan

Chapter heading illustrations by Elliot Flynn

DEDICATION

This book comes through me but is not from me—though it is with me is not about me. It is dedicated to my Sufi teachers in the Kaleemi Order, may Allah mercify their souls and increase their light.

ACKNOWLEDGEMENTS

This book is a gift from Pir Rasheed Kaleemi. As a gift, I now pass it on to my friends, followers and fellow wayfarers. Many people helped to bring it into existence. Those who helped me along my meandering path toward the hands and heart of Pir Rasheed participated in giving it form and substance, some named in the book itself and many left unnamed. Pir Rasheed's wife and family always welcomed me into their home and nourished me with food and care. His community of disciples and followers, my siblings-on-the-path (*pir-bhaiyan*), never treated me as a stranger despite my curious ways.

Special thanks are reserved for Pir Zia Inayat Khan, who first prompted me to write the book, by urging me to publish a memorial for Pir Rasheed just days after his death. To do that, I opened a journal that I had been keeping of my conversations and interactions with Pir Rasheed, and from that point—from that hole of my grief into which Pir Zia planted a tiny seed—the impetus for this book took root and slowly grew. To Pir Zia and his community members who run Omega Publications, I am grateful.

I am also indebted to Tariq Ashfaq of Aligarh, who lovingly typeset Persian and Urdu poems using his deep knowledge of the literary tradition. He, along with many other members of my Kaleemi Sufi community—both in the USA and in India—encouraged me to write quickly and quench their thirst for Pir Rasheed's teachings. Many thanks go to my doctoral student at Emory, now Dr. Summar Shoaib, for proofreading the manuscript.

Many representatives of Sufi institutions in India have shown me exemplary kindness. Dr. Farida Ali (the custodian at the dargah of Pir Inayat Khan in Delhi) and Syed Waris Hussain (a *Gaddi-nasheen* at the dargah of Khwaja Muʿin al-Din Chishti at Ajmer) personify the best of Sufi ethics; they welcomed Pir Rasheed, and me too, at the institutions and events under their care. Syed Tahir Nizami (a *khadim* at the dargah of Hazrat Nizam al-Din Awliya) always looked after me during my sojourns in Delhi, with wholesome plates from the *langar* and heart-warming stories from his treasure-house of wisdom.

These Sufi leaders, who do not see themselves as leaders but rather as servants, keep qawwali music alive as patrons and skilled listeners. So many of the events and teachings related in this book are conveyed in and through qawwali music and its lyrics; the leaders of Sufi communities deserve my thanks for this service, including also Sayyid Khusro Husayni (the Sajjada-nasheen of the dargah of Hazrat Gesu Daraz in Gulbarga) and Mahbub Mian (the Sajjada-nasheen of the dargah of Shaykh Nizam al-Din in Aurangabad). Special thanks go to the Qawwals, the singers who translate the words of Sufi poetry into exquisite sonic fabric of melody, rhythm and improvisation, to clothe spiritual ideals in the beauty of sensory forms. I have benefited greatly from their labor of love during *sama'* sessions in Hyderabad, Gulbarga, Aurangabad and Khuldabad, Delhi and Ajmer and Pakpattan. May Allah protect their bodies and voices, refine their skills and extend their tradition into the future.

TABLE OF CONTENTS

Acknowledgements ix
List of Photographs and Maps xiv

Introduction 1

I. The Wall 11
    1. Circuitous Journeys 11
    2. Influence 19

II. The Door's Threshold 21
    3. Initiation 21
    4. Instruction 25
    5. Love 29
    6. Ancestors in Aurangabad 29
    7. Controlling the Senses 32
    8. Inner Worship and Outer Worship 35
    9. Eternal Garden 37
    10. Nature in the Potter's Hands 41
    11. The Gold Giver 43
    12. Generosity 46

III. The Door's Jamb 51
    13. Submission's Knife 51
    14. Allah Always Gives 54
    15. The Kaleemi Alms Bowl 60
    16. The Kaleemi Astana in Hyderabad 66
    17. Advancing Along the Road 73
    18. Back to the Past and Into the Future 74
    19. Appearances that Deceive 80
    20. Beggars About Town 85
    21. Going West 87

	22.	Coming East.. 88
	23.	A Westerly Breeze 96
	24.	Worship Through Song.. 98
	25.	Oneness Between Faith and Heresy 101
IV.	The Door's Leaf 105	
	26.	Play 105
	27.	Marriage 109
	28.	Confession.. 114
	29.	Gender... 117
	30.	I Became You and You Became Me 123
	31.	The Unstruck Sound 128
	32.	Song of Endurance 132
	33.	A Friend Most Rare.. 137
	34.	Skin, String and Wood.. 142
	35.	Forgiving and Forgetting 150
	36.	Begging 151
V.	The Door's Handle.. 157	
	37.	Echoes of a Distant Melody 157
	38.	Negligence 159
	39.	Power 163
	40.	Prestige.. 164
	41.	Zakat—Giving of Oneself 167
	42.	Separation 174
	43.	Concurrence 178
	44.	Purifying the Heart 179
	45.	Reeling in the Senses 184
	46.	Healing.. 186
	47.	Please Write Our Book 189
VI.	The Door's Lock 193	
	48.	Heart Attack... 193
	49.	Climax of a Lifetime 195
	50.	Counting 199
	51.	Dancing to the Execution Ground 202
	52.	Before Birth and Beyond Death 206
	53.	One Great Spirit 209
	54.	Ending and Beginning 210

VII.	The Door's Hinge		217
	55.	Tying Continuity	217
	56.	Emptiness	222
	57.	Shifting Ground	224
	58.	The Ka'ba of the Heart	225
	59.	Dream Guides	227
	60.	Night of Union	230
	61.	Peace be Upon You	233
VIII.	The Door's Key		239
	62.	Being	239
	63.	Awareness	240
	64.	Purity	240
	65.	Unity	241
	66.	Insight	241
	67.	Respect	242
	68.	Love	243
	69.	Listening	244
	70.	Remembrance	245
	71.	Intimacy	245
	72.	Mercy	246

Appendix	251
Glossary	253
Endnotes	267

LIST OF PHOTOGRAPHS AND MAPS

Photo 1, pg. 2: Portrait of Pir Rasheed Kaleemi (photography by Scott Kugle)

Map 1, pg. 15: Map of India

Map 2, pg. 18: Map of the Islamic World with tombs of the Founders of Major Sufi Orders

Photo 2, pg. 19: Pir Rasheed and Pir Zia at the Dargah of Nizam al-Din Awliya in Delhi (photograph by Pir Zia)

Photo 3 A B and C, pg. 23: Pir Rasheed in ecstasy during Qawwali in the ʿurs of his grandfather, Sayyid Zia al-Hasan Jeeli Kaleemi, at his home called the Khanqah Kaleemi (photography by Mohammed Mubeen)

Map 3, pg. 24: Map of Hyderabad

Map 4, pg. 31: Map of the Deccan

Photo 4, pg. 37: Tomb of Shaykh Nizam al-Din Aurangabadi (photography by Salim Logtmeijer)

Map 5, pg. 47: Map of Khuldabad

Photo 5, pg. 52: Pir Inayat Khan and his daughter Noor-un-Nisa, the eldest of his three children, followed by his sons Hidayat and Vilayat Inayat Khan (anonymous archival photo with permission of Pir Zia Inayat Khan)

Photo 6, pg. 56: Astana Kaleemi, a Dargah housing the tombs of Pir Rasheed's great-grandfather, grandfather and father who were Pirs of the Kaleemi Order before him, in addition to other family members in the open courtyard (photography by Salim Logtmeijer)

Photo 7, pg. 61: The Dargah of Shaykh Kaleemullah Shahjahanabadi in Delhi (photography by Salim Logtmeijer)

Map 6, pg. 69: Map of Delhi

Photo 8, pg. 71: Tomb of Sayyid Muhammad Hasan Jeeli Kaleemi, the great-grandfather of Pir Rasheed, inside the Astana Kaleemi (photography by Salim Logtmeijer)

Photo 9, pg. 78: Pir Rasheed praying at the doorway of the Dargah of Husayn Shah Wali (photograph by Scott Kugle)

Photo 10 A B C, pg. 90: A and B Pir Rasheed sweeping the tomb of Abu Hashim Madani the restoration of which he oversaw in 2008 (photographs by Scott Kugle). C restored tomb of Abu Hashim Madani in 2018 (photograph by Salim Logtmeijer)

Photo 11, pg. 95: Pir Vilayat Khan and Pir Rasheed and his father, Sayyid Fakhr al-Hasan Jeeli Kaleemi in Hyderabad circa 1950 (anonymous archival photo with permission of Pir Zia Inayat Khan)

Photo 12, pg. 96: Pir Zia receiving successorship from his father, Pir Vilayat Khan, with Pir Rasheed and Syed Waris Hussain

Photo 13, pg. 120: The Dargah of Hazrat Nizam al-Din Awliya; in the crowd are Pir Rasheed, Pir Zia Inayat Khan, and the author who were in Delhi for the ʿurs of Hazrat Inayat Khan (photograph by Mikko Viitamaki)

Photo 14, pg. 158: The Dargah of Hazrat Gesu Daraz at Gulbarga (photography by Scott Kugle)

Photo 15, pg. 164: Pir Rasheed and his grandson Madani in qawwali (photography of Mubeen)

Photo 16, pg. 232: Mujahid Baba Kaleemi, his family, and followers standing in prayer over the tomb of Pir Rasheed on the occasion of his ʿurs in 2014 (photograph by Scott Kugle)

Photo 17, pg. 248: Tomb of Pir Rasheed at the Astana Kaleemi in 2018 (photography by Scott Kugle)

INTRODUCTION

On the day of judgement, those who are hypocrites will say to those who believe, "Look at us that we might acquire some of your light!" It will be said to them, "Return from whence you came to seek light." Thus, a wall will be erected between them in which there is a door whose outer aspect is pain but within which is mercy.

~ Qur'an (Surat al-Hadid 57:13)

People often wonder about heaven and hell. The Qur'an seems to vehemently uphold the absolute separation between those who are saved on the day of judgment and those who are damned. The saved will enjoy the gardens of felicity forever, while the damned will suffer the fires of torment forever. Yet that is merely the surface. The Qur'an hints that this dire scenario is merely apparent and not absolute. In the wall of eternal separation between the saved and the damned there is a mysterious door *whose outer aspect is pain but within which is mercy*. Perhaps that door can be opened such that those who suffer can find relief, if they develop the wisdom to see within their pain an inherent mercy.

Pain and torment are integrally related to mercy and felicity. One cannot find mercy without going through pain; that is a simple spiritual truth. As the Qur'an intones: *Inna maʿ al-ʿusrin yusran*—indeed with hardship there is ease (Surat al-Inshirah 94:6). The aspect of God that appears as punishment to those in pain is never absolutely thus. Between hell and heaven there is a wall. In that wall is a door. The door can open. Its apparent aspect seems like painful torment, while what lies within it and beyond it is mercy upon mercy. The trick is to find that door and accept the pain of grasping its handle and struggling to open it. As Maulana Rumi taught us:

You're in the realm of space now, but before
    You were beyond space—open up that door!
He gives your ears a share, as with your eyes
    of His glad tidings, music and deep cries

> This world has many remedies it stores
>   But, first, God has to open up the doors
> Though you're now unaware, He'll make you see
>   When you feel that you need it desperately
> The Prophet said, 'Our Noble God, who heals,
>   Has made a cure for every pain one feels.'[1]

Each person's life can become a painful hell when it is ringed around by arrogance and self-concern. Yet for each person, a door appears at a different place with a different frame in a different form. In my life, the merciful door appears in the form of Pir Rasheed Kaleemi.

I entitled this book *The Merciful Door* in his honor. Pir Rasheed is a Sufi master who teaches by example rather than by books. He teaches the Sufi path—Tasawwuf or Sufism, as it is sometimes called. This tradition is a way of practising Islam that is focused on overcoming the ego with its arrogance and selfishness. The Sufi path is about cultivating moral values and spiritual experience so that one can strive to encounter the presence of God personally, intimately interwoven with one's daily life and relationships. In this endeavor, Sufi masters follow the Prophet Muhammad's example when he said, "My mission is to bring to completion the best of virtues."[2] Sufis are not a cult or a sect, they are just Muslims who take their religion personally and try to dive deeper than mere ritual and communal loyalty. They highlight the universal spiritual teachings and moral values in Islam, and they invite like-minded people from other religions to join them in this striving. Increasingly, people who are not Muslims are also attracted to these Sufi teachings and values.

Photo 1: Portrait of Pir Rasheed Kaleemi

Sufism is deeply ingrained in the folk cultures of many Muslim communities. That is certainly the case in India, where the vast majority of Muslims integrate Sufi teachings and personalities into their devotional lives, even if journalists and political analysts ignore their quiet presence to run after loud self-proclaimed leaders and extremist rabble. The same is true in Pakistan and Bangladesh, which neighbor India and share a broad cultural affinity with it. This is also true of Turkey, Indonesia, many

African regions, and Arab-speaking parts of the Mediterranean. Even in Saudi Arabia, Sufis were boldly present in the holy cities of Mecca and Medina until very recently, when the Saudi ruling elite with their *Wahhabi* ideology attacked Sufi understandings of Islam and suppressed them. The Wahhabi and Salafi interpretation of Islam sees the world as corrupt and its Muslims as deficient or misled, and they believe that only their ideology can purify it; they are happy to coerce others into joining them and punishing or killing those who do not. On the other hand, Sufis see the world as still an enchanted realm, full of promise and possibility. Their mission is to cultivate moral values in whatever environment God places them, accepting people as they are and calling them to the quest to find *the signs of God on the horizons and in their own selves* (Surat al-Fussilat 41:53).

This quest is based on heart-to-heart teaching and cultivation of wisdom. It is not based on ideology that can be easily institutionalized. It can be written about in books, but books do not transmit its power to the heart. The internet expands the scope of words beyond conventional books, but the information it provides is shallow and often misguided, and it is a poor channel for conveying wisdom. Poems, music, litanies and prayers can convey signs of Sufism but, in reality, it can only be learned from a teacher. It can only be learned by taking a teacher's hand through initiation and learning from him or her, as the earliest Muslims learned from the Prophet Muhammad.

Finding such a teacher is a huge challenge, especially in today's environment. Sufi teachers tend not to advertise themselves, and those who do tend not to be real Sufi teachers. As the adage goes, "Those who really know don't speak, and those who speak really don't know." Finding a teacher and taking initiation with him as a Sufi master—called a Pir—is a great blessing. People often search for a Pir over years of travel and longing. But finding a teacher and becoming his disciple is only the beginning: the real test is facing the challenges of learning from him and living up to his example. Some disciples take to it naturally and excel. Most find it both frustrating and promising, and they stumble and fall... then rise up again and keep trying. Some find it useful to write about their Pir's teachings, to keep a record for themselves or perhaps to share with others.

Sharing with others is the heart of Sufism. In fact, the pith of it is not seeing "others" at all because one does not reify a self against which the other can be defined. In medieval India, the Sufi way that became most popular and widespread was the Chishti Order, and it achieved success because of its zealous promotion of sharing. It is named after Khwaja Muʿin al-Din Chishti who moved with the spread of the Islamic frontier, from a little town in Afghanistan called Chisht to the city of Ajmer in Rajasthan, India. He brought with him a Sufi lineage and teachings that were cultivated earlier in Syria, Iran, Iraq and Medina. From Ajmer, the Chishti Order spread to Delhi and Punjab and Nagaur, and from these centers to every region of India. Its early leaders renounced wealth and power, and made it a devotional practice to share with others whatever came to them. The Chishti Order embraced music and poetry as ways of spreading its message, so it pushed beyond the barriers of literacy and elite Islamic culture to attract the teeming population of India in all its diversity. The Chishti Order always valued giving and sharing with others over solitary worship or ritualistic purity. It spread so widely and influenced people so deeply because of its unique emphasis on storytelling, on sharing the oral teachings of its great masters through literary narratives. The book you are reading is a contemporary extension of this tradition.

The Chishti Order was elaborated and organized by a charismatic teacher in Delhi, Hazrat Nizam al-Din Awliya. When he was a youthful university student hoping to become an Islamic judge, he met the Chishti teacher Baba Farid Ganj-e Shakar in a remote village in Punjab, and his life changed completely. He abandoned worldly ambitions and took initiation into the Chishti Order. Baba Farid ordered him to return to Delhi and complete his studies, so that his knowledge of Qur'an and *hadees* traditions about the Prophet could benefit the common people. The Chishti teachers were not distracted by writing books themselves. But the young Nizam al-Din Awliya kept notes about the sayings of Baba Farid and his interactions with them. He later recalled,

> At the time that I entered the service of Shaykh al-Islam Farid al-Din—may God sanctify his lofty secret—I had the same idea in mind… from that day every time the Shaykh spoke, whatever I heard from him I wrote down. I kept on writing down what I heard till one day I informed him of this activity. After that, whenever he told a story or offered a guideline, he would check to see if I was present. If, on some occasion, I did not happen to be present, the directive which he had given in my absence he would repeat again later in my presence… I would record the discourse of the Shaykh as I heard it, and to this day that compilation is with me.[3]

Nizam al-Din Awliya kept these notes for himself and never formalized them into a book. However, later in life he found one of his disciples, Ameer Hasan Sijzi, taking similar notes from his own oral teaching sessions. Ameer Hasan said to him:

INTRODUCTION

> Every moment that I have obtained the blessing of kissing your feet, I have also derived counsels from your elegant words, what exhortation and advice and inducement to obedience, what stories about the saints and their spiritual states I have heard from you! Every kind of soul-inspiring discourse has fallen on my ears, and I wanted to make that the foundation for my own life—indeed, to use it as a guide on the Path for this broken person, at least to the extent that I could record with the pen what I understood... Since no collection has been made of the inspiring teachings of the master's predecessors, I have compiled those of your blessed words which I have heard and till now I have not shown them to anyone, awaiting your command, that I might do what you want in this regard.[4]

Hazrat Nizam al-Din Awliya was pleased, and told him how he took notes about the sayings of his own Sufi teacher. He encouraged Ameer Hasan to write down his spoken words. Ameer Hasan Sijzi was no routine disciple—rather, he was a court poet with masterful command of Persian and a sweet eloquence with words. So Nizam al-Din Awliya encouraged the poet to keep notes and further, then refine the notes into a detailed documentation of his own oral teachings, so that the written word could be widely shared with others in distant places and later times.

Ameer Hasan published this *malfuzat*, as the genre was later to be called, with the title *Morals for the Heart* (*Fawa'id al-Fu'ad*). After him, the genre gained rapid popularity. In the next generation, Hazrat Nizam al-Din Awliya was succeeded by Shaykh Naseer al-Din Chiragh-e Delli as the leader of the Chishti Order. One of his disciples, Hamid Qalandar, recorded his oral teachings. Hamid Qalandar was not of the literary caliber of Ameer Hasan, but he bumbles along recording for posterity Naseer al-Din Chiragh-e Delli's teachings, even as he does not fully understand them and humbly acknowledges his own struggle to live up to them. His malfuzat book, *Best of Gatherings* (*Khayr al-Majalis*) is published in Persian and in translation to Urdu and English. As Chishti Sufis moved from Delhi to the South, to the Deccan region of India, the tradition of recording malfuzat books grew deeper. One of Hazrat Nizam al-Din's oldest disciples, Burhan al-Din Ghareeb, settled in the Deccan. There he found able followers in the four Kashani brothers who each wrote a malfuzat of their spiritual master, each in his own style and according to his gifts of scholarly knowledge, poetic eloquence, and personal exposure. A generation later, Sayyid Muhammad Husayni Gesu Daraz also migrated to the Deccan. He was a successor to Shaykh Naseer al-Din Chiragh-e Delli but he left Delhi as it faced invasion and settled at Gulbarga, near Hyderabad. There,

Gesu Daraz started a new Chishti tradition in the South and his eldest son recorded his malfuzat entitled *Jawamiʿ al-Kalim* or *Most Comprehensive Speech*. Their family started the tradition of father succeeding son as Sufi master, and their ancestor's tomb is the largest *dargah* in the South of India; this tomb-shrine (literally, the "royal court" of a saint) attracting multitudes in pilgrimage for special occasions.

I visited that dargah when I first arrived at Hyderabad, and have had the blessing of returning there many times since. Like so many foreigners before me, I came to the Deccan to seek new opportunities and adventures. I found all that and more in Hyderabad. I ended up finding a Sufi master whom I love: he is fondly known as Pir Rasheed, but his full name is Sayyid Muhammed Rasheed al-Hasan Jeeli Kaleemi.[5] He was Hyderabad's most treasured gift to me and I took him with me in spirit whenever I left that city of the Deccan longing to return.

Coming to Hyderabad, I felt much like Rabindranth Tagore had expressed when he came to the city sixty years before me and found to his surprise an unexpected haven, which he praised in a poem.[6]

> From the distance, thou didst appear
> Barricaded in rocky aloofness
> Timidly I crossed the rugged path
> To find here all of a sudden
> An open invitation in the sky
> And friend's embrace in the air
> In an unknown land, the voice that
> Seemed ever known,
> Revealed to me a shelter of loving intimacy

During the decade that I spent with Pir Rasheed, I shared with him many conversations, interactions, teachings and questionings. Most of these occurred in Hyderabad when I lived there or beyond: in other places in India as we traveled to Sufi pilgrimage sites. I began to write down some of these conversations and interactions the day after they happened, as a personal journal of my spiritual journey under his guidance. I wrote down some events but not all events. I wrote some down word-for-word as I remembered them but others I merely sketched. This record began as a malfuzat which tried to capture the exact words of the Sufi master and the precise social setting in which questions were raised and answers were given. Yet my teacher did not hold regular meetings with his disciples, and he did not convene large gatherings in which to deliver lectures, as did Sufi masters in the past.

INTRODUCTION

As time went on, I found most of my meetings with Pir Rasheed were intensely personal, one-on-one interactions. Our conversations slipped from English to Urdu and back to English in ways that his other disciples found to be frustrating, accustomed as they were not merely to Urdu, but to the local Deccani dialect. That local lingo I had trouble catching as it coursed along at its typical sweet and sly style at a break-neck speed. Later, after I took permission from Pir Rasheed to return to the USA to teach at university, my interactions with him were less in conversation and more in doing practices and experiencing the fruit of these practices in dreams and visions. Pir Rasheed was nonetheless present in these experiences of mine, despite the distance between us. I began to record these also in my journal: the record began to look less like a classical malfuzat and more like a spiritual "autobiography" which is really not "auto" in that it does not refer to me myself, but rather to me as I was taking shape in relation to him. Even when I was based in the USA, life kept giving me opportunities to return to Hyderabad to visit him.

There is certainly a Sufi tradition for recording dreams and visions. The prodigious Sufi master named Ruzbihan Baqli of Shiraz wrote his spiritual autobiography in addition to poetry and a mystical commentary on the Qur'an. Such first-person narratives of spiritual experiences or visions were rare but persistent in the Sufi tradition. The patron saint of the region in which Hyderabad is located, Hazrat Banda Nawaz Gesu Daraz, also wrote one such text; among his many scholarly and ethical books, we find his *Asmar al-Asrar* or *Secret Evening Intimacies* which records his dream visions. These tell audaciously of the spirit's expansive experience beyond the realm of ordinary social reality. The malfuzat genre, in contrast, is careful and modest. In it, the author effaces himself to record his Sufi master's insights and extraordinary example, that is both limited by and made accessible through ordinary social conversation with all its delights. Between these extremes of outer polite conversation and inner individual spiritual flight, there is also the experience of listening to devotional music in a ritual setting, known as *mehfil-e sama'* in the wider Islamic tradition (or *qawwali* in the Indian context). Listening to music in a community ritual bridges the seemingly wide gulf between individual spiritual experience and the communal bonding of disciples being in the presence of their spiritual teacher.

I was unspeakably fortunate to have had the opportunity to listen to qawwali with Pir Rasheed and in gatherings presided over by other Sufi masters. Many insights came my way while listening to Sufi poetry sung through the art of the qawwali groups and families that keep this 800-year-old tradition thriving. I also began to record some experiences I had listening to qawwali, experiences entirely enabled by Pir Rasheed teaching me how to listen even if he was not present in the music assembly. These songs and poems are woven into this account, as are my reactions to them. This is also a feature of classical malfuzat literature, in which poetry is cited to clarify or intensify the points being discussed. Sometimes the Sufi master will quote poems, and sometimes the recorder will compose them. The difference here is that I translated the poems that were cited, quoted and sung, from their original Persian, Hindi and Urdu to convey their meaning to a wider audience in English. I beg the reader's forbearance and forgiveness if my translations do not live up to the verve and spiritual force of the originals.

The book in your hands is a hybrid of several genres of Sufi writing. It is not the story of Pir Rasheed's life nor is it the story of my life. It is a sequence of episodes about our living together which tries to convey something of the nature of Sufi teaching and listening. It records a disciple's questioning and doubt poised against a master's wisdom and humble confidence, along with experiences that seem to transcend them both. I had originally recorded the date and place of each event as malfuzat authors had always done. Yet as the record grew in complexity, I found such documentary detail to be irrelevant. The episodes given here are roughly in chronological sequence starting from one year after I had taken initiation with Pir Rasheed and continuing over a decade. But as I crafted these episodes into a narrative for others to read, rather than for myself to review, I found it necessary to reach back through memory to fill in episodes that were not originally recorded. I needed to explain how I ended up in India, how I met Pir Rasheed, and how I took initiation with him. Some retrospective narratives were added, which muddled the documentary chronology and eventually convinced me to jettison a strictly time-bound record.

When I was reviewing these episodes to savor the presence of Pir Rasheed that I find in their words, I stumbled across something that shocked me. In 2012, Pir Rasheed said to me, "I have one last request. Why don't you write a small book about our Sufi Order and your experiences in it? ... Write that small book, I ask of you." I had dutifully recorded this in my journal then forgot about it. In the tumult of travel and work, this small request got buried in my journal—but thank God it was still there. I read this several years later and realized that although I had not shared with Pir Rasheed that I was recording his teachings and sayings and my experiences of them, that he was already intending that I do this! I had been following his orders all along, without him having to give any order. Of course, in his radiant modesty, he couches his orders as humble requests. When I read this statement in my own record, I realized that I had already written the book that he was requesting from me. There in my notes were his sayings, teachings, travels and reactions to events.

INTRODUCTION

These records just needed to be cleaned up, fleshed out, and presented properly for others—whether Muslim or non-Muslim, whether Sufi or non-Sufi—to understand a bit of what Sufi teaching and learning is like.

Of course, the master-disciple relationship is intensely personal. It is different for each disciple even if they share the same master, and it differs from master to master. The same teachings are conveyed through different personalities, in diverse cultural contexts, in divergent eras. Like water in glasses of varying colors, it may appear different as you gaze from a distance at light passing through it; yet after tasting it, you find that water is water regardless of the color it appears through glass. To honestly convey what my Pir taught me, I had to reveal some aspects of my personality that are deeply personal and which some readers may find shocking or shameful. That cannot be helped and to apologize is useless—their reactions are theirs and my experiences are mine. I do not reveal things about myself to get the praise of others or to court their blame, but rather because without revealing these things about myself, one cannot understand the mercy and compassion of Pir Rasheed in dealing with me.

There is a wall between the torment of ego and peace of contentment. In that wall is a door, a door that appears in a different shape for each one who searches for it, taking on a human shape for a seeker who is human. At the foot of the doorway is its threshold. Bearing the passage is the door leaf set within the door jambs that frame it. On the door leaf is a handle, yet the door is locked. Hidden in its inner structure are the door's hinges, conveying hope that it can swing open if only one can find the door's elusive key.

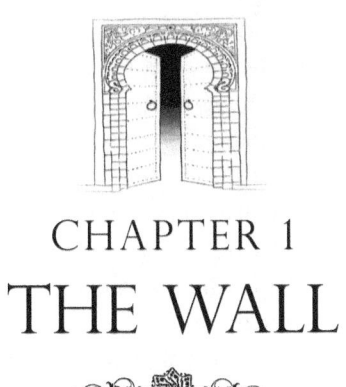

CHAPTER 1
THE WALL

CIRCUITOUS JOURNEYS

I cannot talk about Pir Rasheed directly, because I am the one who is talking. You must know something about me before you can hear of my experience of him. You see, it took me a long time to meet Pir Rasheed. I had met many Sufi teachers and scholars in my travels to Egypt, Pakistan, Morocco and also in the US. Some of them I recognized as Pirs and some of them I did not—for I saw in them only teachers or friends or kind strangers until, with hindsight, I realized who they really were. Perhaps the vision of my heart was obscured or perhaps fate was leading me away from one possibility toward another, but in my early travels, I was more obsessed with studying and learning. I thought that I needed to build myself up—to develop my personality with knowledge and skills—by my own efforts. The Sufi poet from Hyderabad, Watan, laughs at such people when he says...[7]

> Ask the seekers what they want to strive to do
>   When desire itself is sought, what's demanded of you?

The thought of taking initiation from a Pir did not really occur to me as an urgent need. How many powerful people did I just walk by or dismiss with a casual conversation? I thought that I could do what needed to be done by my own efforts. Like a person walking down a forest path intent on reaching my goal, I may have passed powerful lions crouching in the brush or majestic tigers lying in the tree branches while I remained unaware of them.

One of those I passed was Qazi Basheer al-Din, who lived in Karachi. I was fortunate to spend a year in Pakistan on a Fulbright Grant when I was young—just 22 years old. There I met the most wonderful family named Qambar with two sisters named Rubina and Rukhsana who, along with their mother, took me under their wing. They almost adopted me during the time that I spent in Pakistan, and I cannot even estimate what I learned in their care. Rukhsana had just come back from the USA where she was a Fulbright Scholar working in Latin American history, and her sister was starting a cattle ranch outside Rawalpindi after having studied animal husbandry in Texas. Two stronger and smarter women one could not hope to meet. The three of us together went to a conference about Andalusia held in Lahore. There we met Qazi Basheer al-Din, who was also attending the conference on behalf of the Motamar al-'Alam al-Islam or World Muslim Congress, where he had worked. He was a retired gentleman of great stature and regal bearing who proudly wore a tall cap of Chishti yellow. Some other delegates to the conference were from the International Islamic University in Islamabad, a primarily Salafi modernist institution, including a Polish fundamentalist who loved to give fiery speeches. He objected to my sitting with my two adopted sisters during the long bus drive to Lahore, because of gender norms. But Qazi Basheer al-Din, without really knowing me very well at all, stood up for me and kindly asked the Polish firebrand to keep his voice down and speak respectfully. It was my first witnessing to the quiet power of Chishti authority.

I later met Qazi Basheer al-Din at his home during a trip to Karachi. After lunch, I was ready to leave and he apologized profusely that he did not have a car to drop me back to downtown Karachi where I was staying. "You'll have to take an autorickshaw, I'm afraid. But at this hour, in the heat of the afternoon, there may not be any autos on hand. Our neighborhood is like that, very quiet and off the beaten path. We may have to walk some distance to find an auto, I'm very sorry for that." Qazi Basheer al-Din must have been over 70 years old then, and could not walk so well, so I wondered how this was going to work. He continued to talk as we put on our shoes and headed outside. "Now with the civic unrest in Karachi and strikes and general disorder, autos don't come regularly to our neighborhood. It can sometimes be really difficult! I just hope that you are not inconvenienced…" Before he could finish his sentence and we could reach the road in front of his house, a lone autorickshaw came buzzing down the entirely empty street. He smiled and waved it down. He sat me in the empty seat and explained to the driver exactly where to take me. Then he said goodbye and smiled, adding cryptically, "That is the power of *ikhlas*," meaning sincerity. To this day, I don't know if he meant Surat al-Ikhlas, the compact and powerful 112th chapter of the Qur'an, or just ikhlas in general as sincere purity of the heart's intent.

When my year in Pakistan was finished, I returned to the USA to begin my Ph.D. studies at Duke University, which included reading Sufi literature and Urdu *ghazals*. The next summer, during university holidays, I returned to Pakistan to keep learning Urdu while staying with the Qambar family, but I never met Qazi Basheer al-Din again. Yet his persona and his lessons I carried with me into the future. Occasionally he would post a greeting card to my mother, thanking her for bringing a son like me into the world. She would quizzically ask me who is the man who writes to her from Pakistan saying such absurd things! Twenty years later, I got a surprise phone call from him. He had moved to Canada to live with his daughter, and was in failing health. We had a fine chat and it turned out that his family was from Hyderabad before moving to Karachi, and he knew of Pir Rasheed quite well. I cannot help thinking that Qazi Basheer al-Din was looking out for me in my long and tangled journey.

At Duke University, I was studying with Prof. Bruce Lawrence, a leading expert on Islam in South Asia and Sufism especially. When I finished my college degree, I applied to graduate school at Duke University and three others. I had to choose one of the four and I really did not know which would be better for me. Professor Bruce Lawrence reached out to me in ways that no professor from the other universities did. By blessed coincidence, he happened to come to Honolulu for a conference at the East-West Center, just at the time when I was visiting my parents who lived there. He went out of his way to take me to lunch and gifted me his new book, an English translation of the oral discourses, or malfuzat, of Hazrat Nizam al-Din Awliya, entitled *Morals for the Heart* (*Fawa'id al-Fu'ad*). He signed the book with a very generous dedication to me, a young student he had never met before. I had no idea how famous Bruce Lawrence was in the field in Islamic Studies and no inkling of how influential he would be in my life from that point on. I also had absolutely no conception of how precious the book he handed to me would become for my spiritual life. All of that would unfold slowly in the future.

The next summer break from university, I decided that my Urdu studies needed to be more formal so I went to Aligarh Muslim University in India. Bruce Lawrence had done his translation of *Morals for the Heart* at Aligarh, in cooperation with Prof. Khaliq Ahmed Nizami, the leading expert in India on Sufism of the Chishti Order. Sadly, Prof. Nizami had passed away, but Bruce Lawrence still had friends at Aligarh and urged to me go. The father-in-law of a History professor there, who was a friend of Bruce Lawrence, was a retired journalist with long experience in Urdu literature. He offered to teach me

Urdu at his home, and his son-in-law secured me a room at the University guest house. The home of my teacher, Sayyid Mehdi, was simple but rich. I looked around the living room lined with books and pictures, then noticed something strange. Their Qur'an was on a book-holder in a respectful way, right next to a bronze bust of Lenin. Their ornate calligraphic copy of the poetic *Diwan of Ghalib* was on the shelf right next to Marx's *Das Kapital*. Sayyid Mehdi, it turns out, was an old time communist and member of the Urdu Progressive Writers Union. Coming from America, I found the juxtaposition of religious loyalty and political ideology jarring, but I got used to it fast enough. Sayyid Mehdi was a fine gentleman, a good Urdu stylist, and a very patient teacher. I made progress, which is what one can expect in the hands of a Muslim communist litterateur.

I was in Aligarh during the summer months of May and June. Aligarh lies in the heart of Uttar Pradesh, where the heat is intense and the hygiene less than perfect. The University guest house was simple but comfortable, yet it turned out that the food served there was not in the least clean. After a month, I came down with acute dysentery. Unable to keep down food of any kind, I ended up in the hospital, an IV in my arm. After three days, Sayyid Mehdi took me back to the university guest house, insisting that I eat or drink nothing there but rather come to his home for meals. I limped through my last few weeks of summer studies and got home safely. When my professors in the USA asked how my summer went, I replied that I learned lots of Urdu but lost lots of weight so I was never going back to India. Bruce Lawrence accepted this stubborn intransigence with grace. Perhaps he thought I could pursue research just as well in Pakistan.

Fortunately for me, I was learning not just from Prof. Bruce Lawrence but also from Prof. Carl Ernst. When he asked about my summer, I gave the same reply. He smiled slyly and asked, "Well, where in India did you go?" Aligarh, I answered. "Oh… in Uttar Pradesh, and during what month?" May and June, I replied. "Oh… in the middle of the hottest season—of course you got sick! It would be strange if you didn't. I totally agree with you—never go back to India if that means Uttar Pradesh in the summer." Then he added in a cryptic way, "Next time you might head to the Deccan instead." I ignored his reply. I didn't know much about the Deccan, but I knew it was even further into the interior of India and that was not where I was going.

As the year progressed, my attention kept getting drawn back to the Deccan. It nettled my brain, and I asked myself who would go to interior South India to learn Urdu? Isn't that where people are speaking Telugu and Kannada and a host of Dravidian languages that are rooted in a language family entirely different from Urdu? In one conversation, Carl Ernst mentioned that there were rich archives of old Islamic manuscripts in Hyderabad, a city in the Deccan. How is it possible, I wondered, for there to be Arabic and Persian manuscripts in a land-locked city in the heart of peninsular South

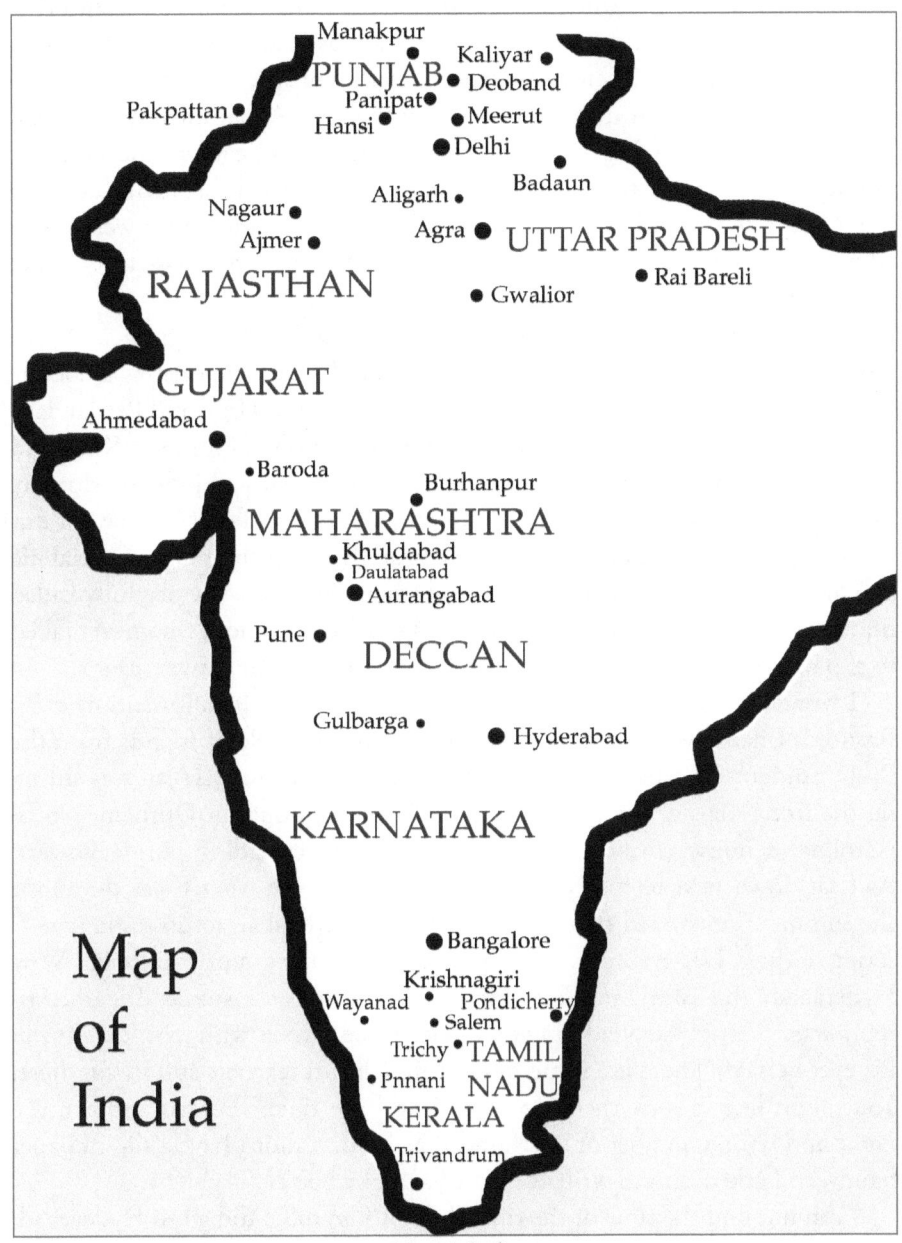

Map 1: India

India? The questions just would not leave my head, and I began to research about Hyderabad. Indeed, people there spoke Urdu, and the first modern university to teach in an Indian language was founded there, whose language of instruction was Urdu. The city was built by Muslim kings who ruled—first the Bahmanis, then the Qutb Shahis, then the Nizams—for over six centuries. Indeed, Urdu and Persian literature thrived there even after the Mughal empire up north, around Delhi and Agra and Aligarh, collapsed and was colonized by the British. My worldview got spun topsy-turvy. As summer approached, I applied for a research grant to go to Hyderabad and explore the libraries, hoping to get a tutor to read Persian manuscripts of Chishti malfuzat texts, like Nizam al-Din Awliya's *Morals for the Heart* and others that were never edited and published. When the grant came through, I purchased my ticket and prepared for my trip.

By that time, a new student had joined my Ph.D. program at Duke University. We knew Zia Inayat Khan as just another student earning a doctorate in Islamic Studies, though one particularly gifted in Urdu and Persian languages. The rest of the world knew him as the grandson of Pir Inayat Khan and the bearer of a rich tradition of Sufism from India that had influenced many in America and Europe. I did not inquire much into his family legacy, for our university program helpfully stripped away all the outer trappings of social life and let us focus intensely on learning together. Zia Jan, as we playfully called him, was a delightful friend and wonderful study companion, who never failed to slip bits of insightful and obscure information into our conversations.

I wonder why I did not pay closer attention when Zia Jan mentioned Pir Rasheed. I had hosted a lunch at my house for our circle of friends from the Ph.D. students to celebrate the end of the spring semester. Zia Jan was sitting on the front steps of the porch of my old wooden house in Durham, North Carolina, a house covered in wisteria vines with cascading purple flowers. As I sat down next to him on the stairs, he asked me what I was doing for the summer. I answered that I was heading to Hyderabad to do some manuscript reading. His eyebrows shot up and he gave me a quizzical look. "Why Hyderabad?" he asked, and I recounted my previous disaster at Aligarh. His reply was, "Yes, Hyderabad is a good place to be." Then with a little gleam in his eye, he said, "There are some interesting Chishti teachers still living there. You might like to look them up, if you find the time." He wrote down the name and phone number of Pir Rasheed Kaleemi. I didn't have a slip of paper handy, so I asked him to write it in the back of a book.

I did not find the time or the time did not find me. I did go to Hyderabad, but the paper with Pir Rasheed's name on it remained inside the back cover of a little book called *Sufis of Sindh*, the nearest paper to hand as Zia scribbled while sitting on my porch. The book ended up on my shelf. Since I was not researching Sufis of Sindh, it stayed on the shelf for a very long time. As it sat, waiting patiently, I left for Hyderabad. I found manuscripts, more than I could read in a lifetime. I fell in love, more with the city than with anyone in particular who lived there. I stayed healthy, more through a sort of constant happiness that buoyed me up even as little illnesses came and went. I found friends who ran a community-based organization doing grassroots HIV prevention education and I leapt headlong into that, meeting people from every walk of life and all levels of society. Hyderabad was vibrant and alive in a way that no other city had been for me.

I extended a two-month grant to six months, but eventually had to leave Hyderabad. I vowed to choose a Ph.D. dissertation topic that would bring me back to the city. Then two years later, I was back. I had spent the intervening years in Morocco completing my Arabic studies, all the while plotting how to return to Hyderabad. I found a research topic in a Sufi scholar from Burhanpur in the Deccan but who lived in exile in Mecca, and whose writings existed in some rare manuscripts found only in Hyderabad's libraries. I came back to Hyderabad for two more years, and still failed to follow the advice of Zia Jan. Occasionally I remembered him telling me about a Chishti teacher in Hyderabad, but I seemed to have lost the chit of paper with his name. Eventually, I ran out of fellowship money and my research visa expired. I moved on to Canada, where I had a fellowship at University of British Columbia in Vancouver to finish writing my dissertation. There I lived with the family of Seemi Ghazi, a dear friend of mine who had also studied for a time with Zia Jan and me at Duke University. I helped her care for her newborn daughter, Aliya, and she helped me to get through the rigors of writing a dissertation with songs, stories and wonderful meals.

Then in the year 2000, I finally finished my dissertation and was offered a job teaching Islamic Studies at Swarthmore College. This was rather strange, because one decade before that I had been a student at Swarthmore College. I did a B.A. there in Religious Studies, at a time when this small but fantastic liberal arts college had no professor teaching Islamic Studies at all. I took off my junior year to spend nine months in Egypt studying Islamic history and Arabic. When I returned to Swarthmore College, I began a petition with some other students to get the college to hire someone doing Islamic Studies. A decade later, I was the college's first permanent hire to teach the subject that I had campaigned for earlier. Our actions have consequences that we really can never foresee, sometimes bringing blessings and sometimes bringing disasters. As the Qur'an guides us, "If God should make harm touch you there is none to remove it except God, and if God wills benefit to come to you there is none to prevent its bounty. God brings this upon whomever God wills among his servants, for God is the forgiving One, the merciful One" (Surat Yunus 10:107).

I moved to Philadelphia, and began to teach. I lobbied Swarthmore College to hire an Arabic teacher and finally integrate Islamic Studies and Arabic language into the liberal arts curriculum of that fabulous college. But under the surface, more mundane things were unfolding that held greater significance ultimately. I finally had an apartment to call home. For six years, my books and music had been packed in boxes and locked in storage facilities, while I was traveling and learning. I finally had a place to unpack them. I finally had money to buy shelves. I took great delight in unboxing my books and arranging them on my new shelves. That is how I finally found a little book *Sufis of Sindh*, and two years later, for some reason, I opened it. There I found Zia Jan's message. Since then, he had become Pir Zia, the delegated leader of the Sufi Order International (now called the Inayati Sufi Order). When I next returned to Hyderabad in 2002, I took that book with me and the time was ripe to call Pir Rasheed.

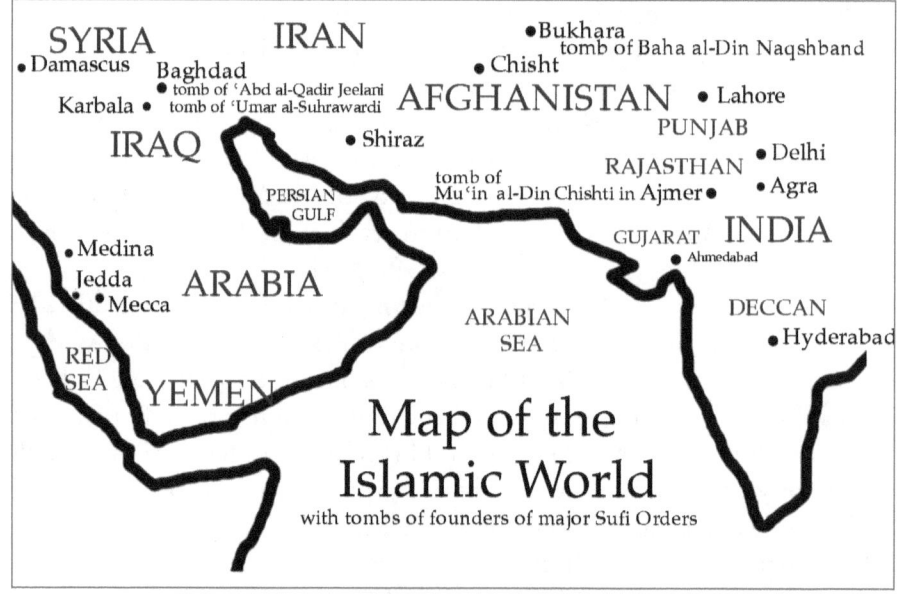

Map 2: The Islamic World

INFLUENCE

Today, I had the great pleasure and potent blessing of visiting my Pir. It had been one year since I had seen him. Pir Rasheed's countenance was radiant and he greeted me warmly as if I were of great worth to him, though in fact I had been negligent in keeping in contact and more negligent in following his example. Such is the nature of a Pir's generosity that, though he has a very high stature, he makes others feel that they deserve honor and praise and not him.

Pir Rasheed took my hand and hugged me three times—to the right and the left and then right again. He asked about my health and my state, then he turned to get a chair for me to sit. I refused the chair and said I would be happy to sit on the rug, to which he offered the one bolster in the room for me to sit against. I simply sat down away from the bolster, for there was only one bolster and I could not imagine taking that comfort instead of him. He sat down as well, facing me and ignoring the bolster as if it did not exist. He was wearing the gold embroidered cap that looks so charming upon his head, of the very same type that he had gifted to me at my initiation, which looks so completely goofy and out of place on my head.

He had not been well lately, and was recovering from a cold and fever, but was still energetic and gave me his full attention. As I approached his home, I wondered whether I should ask the questions that I had been pondering all year. But I didn't need to ask anything. He initiated the discussion by asking me what effects I had noticed within my inner self since taking initiation into the Sufi lineage, for "there is no doubt that joining this lineage will influence your spiritual life, and you

Photo 2: Pir Rasheed and Pir Zia at the dargah of Nizam al-Din Awliya

are looking at the world now through a different lens." I told him that I felt some influence, especially in feeling more intensely dissatisfied with myself in my routine life. This is true, though I stated it most generally. I have been overcome with a profound sense of disappointment, as if the way I have been living is not courageous, does not have a high enough aspiration, and is too full of compromises. I feel that this is due to my innate incapacities and weakness, my reliance upon ego and reason, and to my easily giving in to the desires of the moment.

At the same time, I have felt an increased yearning for something different, some way of life more directed and intentional, shared with a circle of friends who are spiritually inclined and share in my sensibilities. I mentioned to him, for example, how warm and wonderful it felt to be in South Africa during Ramadan with friends who practised zikr regularly. I did not tell Pir Rasheed this, but I have also felt acutely more sensitive to music, indeed to sound on the whole, but especially to music and to qawwali in particular. Changes seem to be happening deep within my personality, below the level at which I am aware. I spoke with Pir Rasheed about some of it, but that appears to be the tip of the iceberg. Much is left unsaid, like deep currents flowing underwater that only appear sporadically as ripples on the surface. Influence means a "flowing-in" as a person experiences powers and forces that are not apparent on the surface of routine experience, but which nevertheless cause real changes within. I hope that I can be open to the changes that may occur, even if their first sign is deep dissatisfaction.

CHAPTER 2
THE DOOR'S THRESHOLD

INITIATION

One morning, I walked from my rented room in Red Hills, my neighborhood in Hyderabad, to a nearby eatery for a breakfast of idli and wada, steamed rice cakes and fried lentil fritters, served with coconut chutney and sweet strong Madras coffee. Then I called the phone number I had been given for Pir Rasheed, half thinking that the number must have changed in the intervening seven years. I was amazed to find that he answered. It was a terribly awkward conversation because I really did not know what to say. How could I explain that I was seven years late and still did not really know why I was calling him? Luckily, Pir Rasheed was used to such things. He heard Pir Zia's name and chuckled with pleasure and invited me to his home that very day. The instructions he gave to reach his home made no sense to me. Finally, he just said—"Come to the Old City. Tell any autorickshaw driver to take you through Yaqutpura neighborhood to Islamia College for Girls. Get down from there. Across the street is a bakery. Tell the owner of the bakery to send someone to Pir Rasheed. I will come and get you from there." So, for the first time, I ventured to Yaqutpura along a route that would become second-nature to me.

When I first met Pir Rasheed, I have no idea what we spoke about. I kept no journal record of that conversation. It must have been insipid because I can only remember being disappointed and confused. His neighborhood was dingy, his home was impoverished, and he himself seemed like a kind but rather confused old man. He was nothing like what I imagined a Sufi teacher should be like—no dazzling display of knowledge or demonstration of charisma. Several times, I felt that Pir Zia must have mixed up the phone numbers that he gave me so many years ago. But after lunch, as I was ready to leave, Pir Rasheed said, "The day after tomorrow we will celebrate an ʿurs here at my home. There will be qawwali and dinner. If it is possible for you to make a little time free, please come in the evening after maghrib prayer at sunset." With that, I said goodbye thinking I would never come back.

I began to think that in fact I had no idea what an ʿurs would be like in a private home and how qawwali might be offered there. Years earlier, I had gone to Ajmer during the days of Khwaja Muʿin al-Din Chishti's ʿurs, the celebration of his death anniversary as a joyful occasion. The ceremonies happened at his dargah, a huge institution with vast courtyards and monumental buildings that was entirely thronged with crowds. On the third day of the ʿurs, which lasts for six days, the crowds got thicker and I started to get nervous. Crowds make me anxious. When trying to cross the courtyard before the tomb inside the dargah, suddenly there rang out the *azan*, the call for noontime prayer. People began to rush toward the mosque, eager to get a space to pray inside. They began to push, knowing that there were too many people and not enough space inside the mosque. I found myself lifted off my feet, moving toward the mosque involuntarily as the crowd surged in waves, even though I was trying to head in the other direction. There were moments when I could not breathe, yet I was thinking that I am at least one foot taller than everyone else here! What was happening to women or children in this crush? I peered over my shoulder toward the Khwaja's tomb and asked for forgiveness, because I had to flee. I got out of Ajmer as soon as I could.

That was my ʿurs experience. I had no idea how a private gathering in a home would celebrate an ʿurs. Out of curiosity, I decided to go that night to Pir Rasheed's home. It happened to be the ʿurs of Shaykh Kaleemullah, and what I witnessed there changed my heart and mind completely. Listening rapt to qawwali in the intimate setting of the mehfil-e samaʿ, Pir Rasheed appeared to be an entirely different person. He became the embodiment of grace and beauty, completely transfixed. His face glowed as he blessed those who came near him to make offerings. As the singers delivered a poem about the urge to meet the Prophet Muhammad in Medina, Pir Rasheed stood and began to walk toward them, with such lightness in his steps, as if he were floating toward them, all humility cast aside. There was an incredible energy coursing through him despite his fragile frame. It was as if a crack opened in the outer world of routine appearances, a crack through which gleamed the light of an inner world of beauty and mercy and grace, a crack that widened to reveal itself as a doorway, a doorway shaped like Pir Rasheed. I do not know if other people saw him the way I saw him. But after the music ritual was over and dinner was served, I went over to take permission to leave. When saying goodbye, I asked him if I could take initiation with him. He looked at me very kindly and said, "No."

I caught an autorickshaw and went buzzing back through the twisted alleys of the city back to my room. I was totally distraught. For years, I had been studying Sufism from books, incredible articulate books that explain how Sufism can never be learned from books. I had met so many Sufi teachers and scholars but I never felt moved to offer myself to anyone as a disciple. And now, having seen beauty and light for a moment in the form of a person, I mustered up the courage to ask for initiation, only to be gently turned down. I prayed for guidance because I was very confused.

The next day, I got a phone call from Pir Rasheed. "How are you, Mr. Scott? I hope the biriyani we served was not too hot for your palate? Your health is fine? Very good. Did you enjoy the qawwali last night? I'm sorry that the house is so small and it was crowded." The politeness and kindness poured out endlessly, until finally he asked me, "Did you ask me for something last night?" Yes, I told him. "What was it that you asked for?" I told him I had asked for him to give me

Photos 3 A, B and C: Pir Rasheed in ecstasy whilst listening to qawwali

initiation by his hand. "Oh yes, I thought so. What answer did I give?" I told him that he had said no. "Well, let me ask you this—are you a Muslim, Mr. Scott?" I answered yes. "I see, well then please come back tonight after sunset prayers." I was packing to leave the next day to return to America, but I rushed to make time to go back to the Old City.

Map 3: Hyderabad

When I got to his home, there were about ten or fifteen people there, waiting for me. Pir Rasheed performed a simple ritual and the people sat quietly to serve as witnesses. He asked me to state my intention to join the Kaleemi Sufi Order, and asked me to vow repentance from my past misdeeds and negligence, and he vowed with me to repent. He asked me to promise to follow him as spiritual guide, to honor the Prophet, and to love God. Then he took my right hand in his right hand. Those who were witnessing came closer to place their right hands on my shoulders, and those further back placed their right hands on the shoulders of those holding my shoulders, until all were connected in support of me. Taking the name of the Pir who initiated him, Sayyid Muhammad Zia al-Hasan Jeeli Kaleemi, he asked me if I would accept initiation into each of the Orders that are woven together in the Kaleemi tradition—the Chishti, Qadiri, Naqshbandi and Suhrawardi Orders, one after the other. At this point, a very tall and imposing man with a wild beard dyed bright orange with henna spoke up suddenly, saying, "And the Shattari Order!" This was Pir Rasheed's *khaleefa* who was also his son-in-law, Afsar 'Ali Osmanabadi. At this interruption, Pir Rasheed hesitated; he began to glance over his shoulder in censure but then stopped, turned back to me and with a calm demeanor continued, "Yes, and the Shattari Order… do you accept it?" I said yes. He placed a golden embroidered cap on my head and tied twenty-foot long marigold-yellow cloth around it as a turban. I did not fully understand the significance of the turban-tying ceremony (*dastar-bandan*) until much later. He laid a cloak on my back and a shawl over my shoulder, and I was ready to travel the path of *suluk*. I had no idea where I was going, but I was ready to go.

Pir Rasheed gave me a booklet, like a passport, that lists the chains of initiation in each order that he had given me from himself through his grandfather and back to the Prophet Muhammad. He signed the booklet at the end of each chain of initiation and stamped it with his seal, then asked several of the witnesses to sign also. He took me aside and taught me a very simple zikr, a phrase for meditation. Then it was done. The next day, I was on a flight back to America, a different passport in hand, one with less consequential stamps.

INSTRUCTION

Sometime after I took initiation, Pir Rasheed instructed me in the fundamental way to practice zikr in the Chishti path. When I visited him, I had wanted to request precisely this from him but had no need to ask him, may God bless him and raise high his remembrance. The way he taught me zikr was exactly the way a great Sufi from the nineteenth century, Hajji Imdadullah

Muhajir Makki, had written about it in the books I had studied in university. This gave me great joy—two joys in fact: joy that what Pir Rasheed was teaching me was in fact the deep tradition of Chishti practice and also joy that what I had read about in books was in fact a living oral tradition, which was now flowing over me and through me.[8] He showed me how to clench the *kimas* nerve in the left leg, and mentioned how keeping this tightly clasped by the toes "will generate an internal heat that will power your zikr." He said, "The best of words for zikr are *la ilaha illa 'llah*—There is no god but God." He showed me how the word *la* is raised up from the left knee, negating everything in the environment and in yourself. How the word *ilaha* is raised up to the right shoulder in aspiring toward God, and how the phrase *illa 'llah* is thrust down upon the heart. "It is directed toward Khannas, the small bit of Shaytan that is lodged in the heart, and which generated waswasa or tempting whispers of thought that swirl around the heart and distract it from God." To illustrate, he recited *a'udhu bi-rabb al-nas* from Surat al-Nas (chapter 114 from the Qur'an):

> I seek refuge with the lord of humanity
> The master of humanity
> The god of humanity
> From the harm of the creeping tempter
> That whispers in the chests of humanity
> From among jinns and humanity

When I heard this, my joy tripled, as I recalled how Hazrat Nizam al-Din Awliya taught how Khannas got inside the body of Adam, a teaching recorded in *Morals for the Heart*. He taught that Khannas, Satan's son, "ceaselessly has tried to penetrate the heart of Adam's offspring. Only when humankind is absorbed in remembering God can Khannas be deflected from his goal." To illustrate, he recited a story:

> After Adam descended from heaven into this world, Eve was one day sitting by herself. Iblis came and brought Khannas with him. To Eve he said: "This is my son. Take care of him." Then he left. When Adam returned he saw Khannas. "Who is this?" he asked Eve. "Iblis brought him," replied Eve. "He told me: 'This is my son; take care of him.'" "Why did you accept him?" rejoined Adam, "This is my enemy." Then Adam cut Khannas up into four pieces and cast him upon the mountaintops. When Adam left, Iblis came back and asked Eve, "Where is Khannas?" "Adam cut him up into four pieces and cast him on the mountaintops," she

replied. Hearing this, Iblis shouted: "O Khannas!" Khannas immediately appeared and in his original form! When Iblis departed, Adam came back. He saw Khannas standing there. "What's this?" he asked. Eve told him what had happened. Adam then killed this Khannas and, having burned him, scattered his ashes in a river. Then he left and as soon as he was gone, Iblis returned, enquiring about Khannas. Eve told him what had transpired. Iblis again shouted: "O Khannas!" and again Khannas at once reappeared. Iblis departed just as Adam was returning. Adam saw Khannas, this time in the form of a sheep. He learned from Eve what had happened, and resolved to kill Khannas yet again. This time, since he was in the form of a sheep, he cooked and ate him. Soon thereafter Iblis returned and shouted: "O Khannas!" Khannas answered from the heart of Adam, "At your service! At your service!" "Stay there!" commanded Iblis. "That was my design from the beginning."[9]

The Tempter, or Satan, is not just a spiritual being external to us, against whom God warns us to be on our guard. No, rather the Tempter is also within us, in the form of his son Khannas, as a spiritual force integral to our personalities and within our bodies. To combat the Tempter as an external enemy is only to make him stronger within us, as his laughter echoes through our conscience, "That was my design from the beginning!" Poor Adam continued to be deluded by misrecognizing his true enemy, and thinking that the external, lesser jihad was actually the greater, real, internal jihad. He has been duped once again in the lower world just as he had in the upper world of the garden. If only he had listened to Eve!

Pir Rasheed instructed me to perform this zikr in the morning, upon first waking. Then he also told me that during the day, during other activities, I should perform the *zikr-e ruhi* or zikr of the spirit. This is inhaling through the nose as if saying *Allah*, and exhaling though the mouth as if saying *hu*. This is indiscernible to others, and does not prevent one from other work, and if practised enough it will engender its own dynamic force and your spirit will be making zikr with each breath.

He also stressed the importance of *tasawwur-e shaykh* while making zikr. One should close one's eyes and imagine the image of one's own Pir as if he were present. I thought that this meant imagining him present facing me, or sitting beside me. Pir Rasheed implied that this was a natural place to begin, but could be a kind of *shirk*—associating others with God. We had been discussing the Hindu and Buddhist practice of meditating or worshipping before idols or images of a person, and so he wanted to clarify how tasawwur-e shaykh is different from this. In fact, he said, that when he practises zikr and imagines the presence of his own shaykh, Zia ul-Hasan Jeeli Kaleemi, he imagines that the shaykh is present and that he himself is not! That is, he imagines that he is not and his shaykh is, and that his shaykh is doing the zikr rather than he himself. That way, there is no duality and no threat of *shirk* or worshipping another being or image.

I was stunned to hear this. I had never heard such a thing or experienced it, though I had been imagining, at some points during the past year, that my shaykh's image was before me as I tried to make zikr or sat quietly after prayer. A Persian ghazal by Bu 'Ali Shah Qalandar of Panipat, the Chishti master and poet, expresses this experience forcefully and was sung in qawwali in former times.[10]

In the form of my Shaykh it is Muhammad that I see No, not just Muhammad— it's really God that I see	بشکلِ شیخ دیدم مصطفےٰ را ندیدم مصطفےٰ را بل خدا را
I am effaced from my ego, I witness the abiding One I see no duality—in my essence, it's God that I see	ز خود فانی شدم دیدم بقا را ندیدم غیرِ ذاتِ خود خدا را
Oh ascetic, stop your lifeless opposition! Do you Perceive the secrets of the oneness of God that I see?	مکن اے زاہدِ خشک اعتراضے چہ دانی سرِّ توحیدِ خدا را
If you accuse me, "You are worshipping idols!" I respond, "What idols are there? It is God that I see."	اگر گوئی مرا تو بت پرستے بگویم در بتاں دیدم خدا را
Am I of noble stock or of golden coin? Don't ask! The answer to "Who am I?" is a secret with God that I see	چہ گویم اشرفم یا اشرفیم مپرس ایں سرِّ پنہانِ خدا را

LOVE

Pir Rasheed told me, "The single most essential thing in Sufism is love. Without love, nothing one does is of any benefit. Love for God is the main thing, as expressed in prayer through feelings of awe and humility. Without this emotion, prayer is just movement, like exercise. Without love, it is not beneficial—in fact, it could be very harmful. Love for other people is also crucial. Just as I love you, and you have come to love me and place me in the circle of your love."

He instructed me to burn with love, like a candle. Its nature is to burn down, slowly dwindling away toward death, but giving off so much light. "Wherever it is, in whatever environment or surroundings, the candle gives off light. It may be in a mosque or temple, it may be in a party where people have gathered to celebrate, it may be in a bar where people come to drink in oblivion. Wherever it may be, the candle burns and in burning it gives others light. That is the way you must be." Hearing this made me rapt with joy, for I thought perhaps he was acknowledging that I might find myself in such unusual environments, which people don't always associate with Islam, like temples or bars. But he later said exactly the opposite, when he was stressing the importance of the *sharee'a*. I had asked him if there were conditions to whom one could give *bay'at*, especially whether they had to be Muslims at that moment. He said that if they were to take bay'at, that would be a "promise" to practise the way of meditation of the *tareeqat*, which as he had just shown me involved the *kalima tayyiba* and statement of faith. He asked me rhetorically, "How could someone who is not a Muslim take up this practice?" In a way, of course, this makes total sense. He answered my question with reference to concrete practice, not through abstract theory.

ANCESTORS IN AURANGABAD

A small group of Pir Rasheed's followers had come with him to Aurangabad, to visit our spiritual ancestors. I was fortunate to be among them. We were sitting with him in a small room at the dargah of Hazrat Nizam al-Din Aurangabadi. It was the time of his 'urs, so we had come to Aurangabad to pay our respects to this anchor in our Kaleemi lineage.

Aurangabad is a small city in Maharashtra, an overnight train journey away from Hyderabad. It used to be included in the Hyderabad State ruled by the Nizam; the first Nizam is buried near Aurangabad, in Khuldabad at the dargah of Burhan al-Din Ghareeb. The dynasty he founded, the Nizams, ruled over the former Mughal Deccan province when the Mughal empire began to crumble. But at its zenith, the Mughal Emperor Aurangzeb conquered this southern region in the mid-seventeenth century; he made Aurangabad his garrison and then his capitol, and like any proud Emperor, named the new city after himself. Under his patronage, it became a cosmopolitan city with new buildings, government offices, literary activities and music concerts. The city also attracted Sufis who settled there to teach.

One of the great Sufi masters of this era was Nizam al-Din Aurangabadi. He was the disciple and successor to Shaykh Kaleemullah, who spread the Kaleemi branch of the Chishti Order from his home base in Delhi. Their branch of the Chishti Order integrated initiations with the Qadiri, Suhrawardi and Naqshbandi Orders also. Shaykh Kaleemullah hoped this would make its teachings more universal and its followers less partisan, such that the Kaleemi Sufi Order could spread throughout India to all classes of people and bring them into a greater unity. Shaykh Nizam al-Din Aurangabadi studied Islamic sciences with Shaykh Kaleemullah, as the master ran a *madrasa* in Delhi. But he also took inner blessings from Shaykh Kaleemullah and became his most noted follower. Shaykh Kaleemullah sent him down to the Deccan as the Mughal empire spread southward. It is from Delhi and Aurangabad that the Kaleemi Sufi Order reached Hyderabad and took root there.

On his own, Shaykh Nizam al-Din Aurangabadi at first refrained from taking on disciples, because his master was still alive in Delhi. But Shaykh Kaleemullah urged him to accept disciples as his calling. With his magnetic personality, Shaykh Nizam al-Din Aurangabadi soon had disciples from all classes. "He used to treat each person with great respect by standing to greet them and praise them, such that he would treat a four-year-old child in the same way that he would treat a sixty-year-old elder!"[11] He had many contacts among Mughal nobles and officers. Common people would come to him with complaints, and he would pass their cases on to high officials to get justice done.

Soon, even Mughal nobles were joining his circle of disciples, which numbered in the thousands. Two administrative officers who were his notable disciples were Kamgar Husayni and his brother Nur al-Din. Though they came from a Naqshbandi family, they joined the Kaleemi Chishti circle of Nizam al-Din Aurangabadi and soon became his trusted followers. Nur al-Din was the Shaykh's closest follower in terms of inner spiritual values but his brother Kamgar Husayni was a special disciple in outer ways. First, he donated his manor house to the Shaykh who turned it into a Sufi *khanqah*, a hospice for teaching, prayer, devotions and music. The brothers had intimate access to their Sufi teacher, and Kamgar Husayni wrote malfuzat on the teachings of Nizam al-Din Aurangabadi. In it he writes:

One day, this lowly person arrived to enjoy the felicity of kissing the feet of the master. I came to the khanqah and saw that Hazrat Nizam al-Din had retreated to his room and was sitting alone. I stood at the threshold and said *salam* to him. The master requested me to enter the room with utmost kindness. He sat me down and asked me how I was with the greatest of concern. He told me, "The esteemed Sayyid, Mirza Muhammad Ja'far, has arrived here from Hyderabad. He has expressed the desire to meet the Qawwals who play on the rebab while singing. He wants them to be present along with himself at the next assembly (*majlis*)." I replied, "The rebab is an instrument constructed in such an ingenious way that it has a much greater impact on the listener than any other instrument." Hearing this, the master recited the following poem.[12]

Map 4: The Deccan

> I get such blessing from the empty bowl of the rebab
> Any dust mote experiencing it glows like the sun

Upon hearing this poem from his blessed lips, I experienced a tremendous shuddering and tears began to uncontrollably weep. After this, the master recited another two couplets.[13]

> Dried skin, brittle wood and strung gut
> From this how does my beloved's voice come?
>
> Not from skin, not from wood and not from gut
> From beyond these does my beloved's voice come!

After reciting these couplets [which are attributed to Maulana Rumi, who himself was a reputed rebab player], the master's own eyes flowed with tears. For some time, this humblest creature of God sat in the presence of the master. I heard him recite these poems but after that, such a state came over us that I do not remember whether he said anything more. About this state, one must realize that people who have not yet achieved a profound understanding still read Sufi books and extract colorful sayings from them and memorize them to display to others. Nowadays, in every assembly and gathering, we find such people giving speeches and trying to show off their knowledge. They don't realize that knowledge from divine intimacy (*'ilm-e laduni*) has no relation to spoken displays. Outer knowledge that is acquired through study and reading is totally separate from inner knowledge that is experienced through the heart—how could one even compare the two![14]

By teaching about this inner knowledge in Aurangabad, Nizam al-Din Aurangabadi spread the Kaleemi Order and its method of soul training throughout the Deccan. The Shaykh blessed the first Nizam of Hyderabad while he was still a common Mughal soldier, so that he might rule with justice in the Deccan and foster Sufi learning and moral virtue for all in Hyderabad, the city ruled by his family for many generations thereafter.

CONTROLLING THE SENSES

We had arrived at Aurangabad to attend the 'urs or death anniversary of Shaykh Nizam al-Din Aurangabadi. The death anniversary is not a time of sorrow but rather of great joy. It is celebrated as a wedding night, when the soul of the saint is finally united with God, like a lover being wedded to his beloved. The 'urs takes place at the dargah of Shaykh Nizam al-Din. In the center is his tomb, covered with a shrine building and lofty dome, painted bright yellow and decorated with lights and golden marigold flowers. Around it is a vast courtyard. On one side is the open hall for listening to music, and beside it is the mosque with its ancient lime-plaster arches scalloped in the strong but graceful Mughal style. Across the courtyard are several small rooms where visiting delegations of Sufis can sleep, and one of these rooms is reserved for Pir Rasheed and his followers who come every year from Hyderabad.

On this occasion, we were sitting together after the noon prayer, I and two other *mureed*s along with our Pir, in the small cramped room on thin mats. Pir Rasheed began to discuss the five senses, turning toward me as if the topic were intended for me rather than others. He said that we must understand the five senses and from where they come. We experience the world through seeing, hearing, feeling, tasting and smelling and we can do no work in the world without them—but from where did these powers come? The Qur'an says that God is One who sees (*baseer*), One who hears (*samee'*) and One who knows all things (*'aleem*). God senses like we do, but in an ultimate way. God knows not only all things we have done outwardly or thought inwardly or intended, but also knows all things we will do. Our powers of sensing, when rightly understood, we can say are granted by God. They are given to us by God, as poor reflections of God's own powers of perception and sense and knowledge.

By means of these five senses, we experience the world. We come to know things. We are enabled to think about things, not only what is happening now but what has happened in memory or could happen in our rational deliberation. God has given us thought, reason and mind in order to perform acts in the world. We have used the mind to create atom bombs, he said, or to fly to the moon. These things were imagined in the minds of men, engineered through our senses, and crafted by our hands. The ability to do these amazing things is given to us by God. We have the freedom to use our ability for good or for bad, and that choice is given to us by God as well. Just as the limbs can be used for taking us to the mosque or dargah, which is good, or to the park for a picnic, which is a bad waste of time, so also the mind can be used for projects which are good and accord with God's will or for things that are bad.

In America, he said, he saw that people lived with no restraint. Their Christian religion allows them to do what they want with themselves, their bodies, their money and their time. The government also does not impose restraints. Men and women can mix. Women can go out with men or with whomever they please, and do whatever they want. Nobody stops them. None has the right to interfere. This, he said, is a terrible situation. God imposes upon us, upon Muslims, restraints and boundaries that we must not cross. We can choose to go to any restaurant and eat any kind of food we like, but as Muslims we must pause and ask whether it is *halal* or *haram* food, for God has imposed limits. This is to force our minds to restrain, not to give in to any old path that the five senses open up for us as a possibility.

This is to preserve our nobility, he explained. The human being is the best model and image of God in this world. Our senses are reflections, though dim, of God's power of perception and our reasoning is a reflection of God's own knowledge and thought. Therefore, we must keep these reflected qualities pure, clear and full of light. We can see, but God is the One who sees. We can hear, but God is the One who hears. In this sense, we must strive to understand and acknowledge from where our powers of sense have come—they have come from God.

Pir Rasheed continued with an example. The power of electricity comes through all the wires in this room from a generator, and it powers the lights and fan here. If the generator is turned off, then it doesn't matter how many of the switches in this room we turn on or off, no power will come and none of our appliances will work. It is God's presence with us and will for us that provides us with our five senses, the knowledge that these bring, and our ability to think about experiences. We think of our senses as belonging to our body in our anatomy. Sight is in the eyes. Hearing is in the ears. Tasting is in the tongue. Smelling is in the nose. Feeling is in the skin. We think these parts and their powers belong to us, constitute us. But in fact, God is closer to us than these.

The Qur'an says that God is *closer to the human than the artery in the neck* (Surat Qaf 50:16). God is with you and in you, and that is what gives you the senses and their powers. Without acknowledging that, the five senses and the thoughts which arise from them will mislead you. That is the meaning of the Persian phrase *hame ust*—all is One. The same thoughts were expressed in a compact poetic quatrain by Shaykh Kabir Shibli.[15]

Do you know what you are and who you are? In your heart ponder if you are not or if you are.	هیچ می دانی که چیزے ہستی یا کیستی در دلت دریاب نیکو ہستی یا نیستی
If One who sees is the seer, One who hears is the hearer And One who knows is the knower, tell who you are!	اینکه می بیند بصیر است وانکه می شنود سمیع اینکه می داند علیم است پس بگو تو کیستی

INNER WORSHIP AND OUTER WORSHIP

Later, we were joined by a fellow from Aurangabad named Wajahat. He is a disciple of Pir Rasheed's khaleefa in Osmanabad, Afsar ʿAli. Wajahat made prolific excuses for not having been there at the station to meet Pir Rasheed when he arrived at 4:30 in the morning. He blamed Pir Rasheed for not calling ahead to warn him, but persisted in inviting the Pir to his family house. Pir Rasheed declined to come. Wajahat insisted, "Our house is big and our hearts are big!" The Pir laughed and said, "But the big One is in my heart, what need have I for anything else?" In the end, after the young man continued to insist, the Pir agreed to come for breakfast the next day along with his mureeds, his disciples.

The fellows from Aurangabad told how their community, *ahl-e nisbat* or folk with a Sufi connection, are now a minority among Muslims in Aurangabad's old town. The Salafi group that calls itself *ahl-e hadees* now has three or four new mosques in the neighborhood. A mob of them even accosted one Sufi fellow who was a follower of the Hanafi school, and they insisted that he was praying wrongly and should change to their way, which sees the four Sunni schools of law as heretical innovations. The man was surrounded and all the people in this mob were telling him to do this and do that and not listening to his rejoinders, so he did a clever thing. He told them that he cannot discuss these points with a mob—they should select from themselves a leader, who can express the group's complaints and with whom he can speak directly one on one. The mob then turned on themselves and began to argue about whom should be their leader. They could not agree about this at all, and fell to arguing among themselves, thus freeing the Hanafi Sufi man to escape their assault! The Pir commented that these are ill-fated fellows, *bad-qismati*. They have lost the ability to understand Islam.

Pir Rasheed turned to me and said, "Doesn't the Qurʾan tell us that God says, 'I created the jinn and human beings only to worship me?' (Surat al-Dhariyat 51:56). How is it possible for a human being to spend each moment worshipping God through ritual prayer as these ahl-e hadees people insist? If one tried that, one would shirk other duties. One would leave one's family to starve. One would fail at one's profession. One would eventually die of thirst and hunger. Worshipping God cannot mean only ritual prayer or outward actions, but these ahl-e hadees people and literalists have lost the ability to understand this. Only Sufis can give the real explanation of this verse in Qurʾan, because they know that each breath—inhaling and exhaling—can be prayer if it is done with sincerity and mindfulness. This is the only kind of prayer that one can do in every moment, while still fulfilling one's other duties in the world." The Pir breathed in and then out, showing how the inward breath was saying *Allah-* and the outward breath was saying *-hu*. It was the technique he had taught me earlier called zikr-e ruhi. "As for those who oppose this teaching and call it *bid'a* or innovation, they can go to hell," said the Pir.

Pir Rasheed was worried that Wahhabis and Salafis were running the mosques in America and Europe. He urged me to use my knowledge of Arabic and English to translate a book of sermons that are read each Friday in mosques in India. These speeches in Arabic are the standard sermons given in Hanafi mosques, and they focus on basic Islamic piety, remind listeners of holy days throughout the lunar cycle of the Islamic year, while promoting veneration for the Prophet, his family members, companions and the saints who follow them. Imams memorize the sermons and recite them from the pulpit, a specific one for each week of the year.

Most Muslims do not understand the Arabic sermons very well, if at all; I always marvel at how tranquilly Muslims in Hyderabad listen to the cascade of florid Arabic, without demanding to know the meaning of what is being read! They catch a few words that are borrowed into Urdu from Arabic, or recognize a quote from the Qur'an here and there. But by and large, they listen as an act of devotion without demanding that understanding follow listening. Indeed, simply listening every Friday at noontime respectfully counts as one cycle of prayer. In India, these sermons are considered a buffer against extremist beliefs and reformist rage. For this reason, the tradition continues despite the language barrier.

Pir Rasheed wanted Muslims in the West to likewise be protected against the sweet poison of Wahhabi thinking. "They should have proper moderate Sunni sermons to give in the mosques," he said. Why should Imams in the West have to make up sermons on the spur of the moment or succumb to shallow piety or political protest during Friday gatherings? The proper sermons were right there waiting to be translated into English. He procured an Imam's copy of these sermons in Arabic, handed it to me, and requested that I "do the needful" and complete the translation. I thought it unusual that Pir Rasheed would urge me to translate sermons into English, when he never commented that they should be translated into Urdu languages for Muslims in Hyderabad. I started the project sincerely, but Pir Rasheed must have sensed my lagging enthusiasm, and after a while he stopped asking me about the progress of the translations. I only completed half of the year's sermons until I let the project quietly drop. If outer worship is a wall of Islam like a boundary wall, and inner worship is a vast garden that this wall contains and protects, then I would rather spend my time pruning the garden than patching the wall.

ETERNAL GARDEN

The next day in Aurangabad, Wajahat invited us all to breakfast at his house. We ate a morning stew of lamb bones in broth, called khaliya, which is served with mango pickles and barley bread. He also served a strong decoction of black tea and ayurvedic herbs, because Pir Rasheed was feeling cold from sleeping on the floor at the dargah. Wajahat rented a jeep for us all to accompany Pir Rasheed to Daulatabad and Khuldabad, a place that is commonly known as *Rawzat*, the walled garden where the saints of God live. We were going to Khuldabad to visit the resting places of the *Awliya* there.

Khuldabad is a tiny town, nestled in the hills a short drive outside of the bustling modern city of Aurangabad. One drives along a deep ravine carved by the river and up into the hills. Khuldabad means "The Eternal Garden" where blessed souls live in peace. It houses more dead people than living, and the dead are certainly more eminent than those who hang on there now. It is filled with tombs and shrines for Sufi saints and poets who lived and died there. The domes and walls of their dargahs have been white-washed year after year since the twelfth century, such that their corners are rounded out and rough stones are smoothed over and their surface appears like the inside of oyster shells gleaming in the bright Deccan sunlight.

Khuldabad was sacred ground since long ago. On the other side of the hill from the Muslim settlement is previous habitation of Buddhist and Jain monks

Photo 4: The tomb of Shaykh Nizam al-Din Aurangabadi

who carved intricate monasteries and devotional halls into the cliff face, far from any threats. Later the Rashtrakuta kings of Deogir, a formidable fortress on a steep mountain nearby, patronized Hindu temples as well as Buddhist monasteries. Under their patronage, a monument to Shiva was carved from the living stone of the cliffs, turning a whole mountain into a temple writhing with sculptures and interior halls—the monumental Kailash temple of Ellora. While Hindu kings were still ruling, Muslim pioneers came and settled nearby. The first of them was a Shaykh of the Suhrawardi Sufi Order, Jalal al-Din Ganj Ravan "Dispenser of Treasure." He lived at a small abandoned shrine to Shiva and gained a reputation for warding off demons that consume children in infancy. He was buried at his home and it became a shrine with remnants of Shiva devotion in carved stones which lie about its gateway.

The Suhrawardi Sufis were soon joined by Sufis of the Chishti Order, which was spreading under the careful attention of Hazrat Nizam al-Din Awliya in Delhi. He sent his delegates to every province of India, and to Deogir he sent Muntajab al-Din Zar Zari Zar-Bakhsh "Gold Golden Giver of Gold." After his demise, his brother Burhan al-Din Ghareeb "The Stranger" was sent to take his place. Burhan al-Din was a senior disciple of Hazrat Nizam al-Din and was a great lover of music. Burhan al-Din Ghareeb chose to stay outside the capital city, at Khuldabad hills, to keep aloof from the rich and powerful. Many Sufis and scholars settled here under his patronage and that of his successor, Zain al-Din Shirazi, who was a learned scholar who at first rejected Sufi teachings but embraced them wholeheartedly when he saw the ethical example set by these Chishti masters. With them came Ameer Hasan Sijzi, who was a court poet in Delhi and wrote down the oral teachings of Hazrat Nizam al-Din Awliya; his Persian poetry shifted from secular boasting to spiritual pondering on the mysteries of love and the power of beauty; his tomb at Khuldabad is just next to that of Azad Bilgrami, a later litterateur known as the greatest Arabic poet that India ever produced. Nearby is the tomb of Shaykh Raju Qattal "The King Slayer" who took refuge here as Delhi slid into political chaos and whose son, Sayyid Muhammad Gesu Daraz "He of the Long Locks," became the patron saint of the Deccan region.

These personages are memorialized in poems and songs and Sufi manuals, some that they themselves composed and some that were written about them. Their tombs were built up into great shrines, patronized by Sultans and Emperors from every dynasty that ruled the region, from the 15th until the 18th century. After that, European colonialism and then modern nationalism shifted attention elsewhere and Khuldabad settled back into a peaceful daydream, preserving its otherworldly atmosphere. With Pir Rasheed and some fellow disciples, I visited these shrines to pay our respects to the holy personalities that they house. The place and its luminaries were memorialized in an Urdu poem by Waheeda Naseem, a Pakistani lady with a literary fervor who travelled here before me.[16]

Nestled in the lap of the hills
is this light of the world
For mystic folk, it is simply
the Sinai height of the world

پہاڑوں کی حسیں آغوش میں یہ نور کی دنیا
یہی اہلِ بصیرت کے لیے ہے طور کی دنیا

One faithful man spread incense
of intuition to the world
Here Ganj Ravan gave spiritual
erudition to the world

بسائی ایک مومن نے یہاں عرفان کی دنیا
یہاں گنجِ رواں نے بخش دی فیضان کی دنیا

The Chishti lamp burned bright
despite the winds blustery
Here Zar Zari Zar-Bakhsh
handed gold to all and sundry

چراغِ چشتیاں زد میں ہواؤں کی جلایا ہے
یہاں پر زر زری زربخش نے سونا لٹایا ہے

Here seekers of mystic knowledge
will come till judgment day
Since saints like Burhan al-Din Ghareeb
chose this place to stay

یہاں آتے رہیں گے حشر تک عرفان کے جویا
تصوّف کے لیے یہ اولیاء برہان ہیں گویا

Zain al-Din Shirazi decorated
the Chishti Order's royal audience
From his spirit blossomed
the Chishtis' garden with radiance

سجایا اس میں زین الدین نے دربار خواجہ کا
مہکتا ہے انہیں کی ذات سے گلزار خواجہ کا

How many humble beggars
were raised up in veneration here
How many royal heads with crowns
were bent low in prostration here

ادائے سرفرازی دی ہے اس کو خاکساروں نے
یہاں سجدہ کیا ہے جانے کتنے تاجداروں نے

With divine might and emotion,
the father of Gesu Daraz arrived
That precious pearl, Baha al-Din Ansari,
to stay aloof he strived

جلال و جذب لے کر والدِ گیسو دراز آئے
بہاءالدین دُرِّ بے بہا اپنے الگ لائے

That jewel which kings always
eyed with acquisitive envy
Nizam al-Din Awliya fixed in this
ring setting with equanimity

ہمیشہ رشک سے دیکھا ہے جس کو بادشاہی نے
نگینے جڑ دیے ہیں اس میں محبوبِ الٰہی نے

This realm gleams with the radiance
of the Chishti masters' method
This garden is verdant by the light
of the Prophet Muhammad

چمکتا ہے یہ خطہ خواجگانِ چشت کی ضو سے
دمکتا ہے یہ سبزہ گنبدِ خضرا کے پرتو سے

The breezes blow by here
bowing their heads in respectful care
Clouds rise from mountains
after washing scrupulously for prayer

یہاں جھونکے ہوا کے با ادب ہو کر گزرتے ہیں
وضو کرتے ہوئے کوہسار سے بادل اترتے ہیں

In this valley Ameer Hasan Sijzi
found his place of peaceful repose
Leaving his homeland, Azad Bilgrami
came, and this garden he chose

حسنِ اعلائے سنجر نے یہاں آرام فرمایا
وطن کو چھوڑ کر آزاد کو یہ گلستاں بھایا

Its tombs and domes are
to this day in the world unique
This silent village is in fact
the wine tavern of the Sufi clique

اسی خاموش بستی میں تصوّف کا ہے میخانہ
یہ گنبد آج بھی ہے گردشِ دوراں سے بیگانہ

Guardian of the Tughlaq treasuries
this valley you could reckon
still echoing with the clamor of
Khilji caravans to the Deccan

یہ وادی ہے امانتدار تغلق کے خزانوں کی
صدائیں گونجتی ہیں اس میں خلجی کاروانوں کی

With silent tears, Naseem comes too,
this simple gift offered up
With one kind glance won't you
please fill her proffered cup?

نسیمِ بے نوا اشکوں کا آئی لے کے نذرانہ
نگاہِ لطف سے بھر دیجئے اس کا بھی پیمانہ

NATURE IN THE POTTER'S HANDS

During the jeep ride to Khuldabad, I was fortunate to sit next to Pir Rasheed in the front seat, because my legs are too long for the backseat. While we bounced along, Pir Rasheed reminded me of the teaching he had given me the day before, about understanding the five senses. Only when you understand the five senses, he said, when you understand that they come from God and that they make you a reflection of God's qualities, can you truly become the khaleefa of God. The khaleefa of God is the one who takes responsibility for doing good and keeping order in the world, who acts according to the will of God. When you are no longer a slave to your five senses, then you become the khaleefa of God. Then you perceive God in everything, behind every phenomenon. I asked if this is what was meant in the poem by Hafiz-e Hindi.[17]

Unveiling of my dear one on every side I see The beauty of my beloved in each thing I see	بہر سو جلوۂ دیدار بینم بہر صورت جمالِ یار بینم
As I look within me I see that all is he All of my beauty as my beloved's do I see	چو خود را بنگرم دیدم ہمونست جمالِ خود جمالِ یار بینم
Ascetics think prayer is with arches and pulpits With nooses and gallows, a lover's prayer I see	نمازِ زاہداں محراب و منبر نمازِ عاشقاں بردار بینم
When that beauty gives Hafez one sip of wine All knowledge and reason as useless I see	چو یک جرعہ رسید از وے بحافظ ہمہ عقل و خرد بیکار بینم

Pir Rasheed smiled and said yes, and this is just like another poem. He then quoted the poem by Rumi, to which I echoed the next line to him.[18]

> He is the pot and he is potter
> > He is the clay and the drunken reveler

> Reeling up the wine-vat to buy a cup
>   He smashes it and disappears

Pir Rasheed laughed and said, "Yes, that expresses it perfectly." Perhaps because the poem by Rumi mentioned the divine as both potter and clay, the Pir's discussion turned to nature. Pir Rasheed said that God is in nature: that is the most important thing to see. Nature must be preserved and protected, as in trees and in the environment, for all these are phenomena through which God manifests in the world. They are things of beauty and we feel awe when we appreciate them and reverence when we protect them.

Pir Rasheed gestured out beyond the windscreen of the jeep, to the dry windswept landscape of Maharashtra, the bright hills, the tall trees. God is in all these things, he said, but most people do not notice. When we appreciate the beauty of these natural things, we are really in awe of God who created their beauty and is more beautiful. We have reverence for these things, like trees, he said, but we do not worship them. The Hindus misunderstood this reality, and began to worship the trees as Gods when they felt awe and reverence at their strength and beauty. But we do not worship them, though we feel the same awe. We worship only God who created them, and then protect the tree because God created it for us. We have to see in nature the manifestation of God, and worship God with increased intensity through our appreciation and protection of nature.

The Pir told me that Sufism is in its entirety good *adab*, meaning proper respect and good manners. It is how you treat people and the environment and all things around you. Sufism is not about rites and rituals, customs and ceremonies. Some people think, he said, that Sufism is about having a long beard, or wearing a cloak, or putting a certain colored cap on your head. These things are not Sufism at all. They are only customs. Sufism is an attitude of respect and benevolence toward all people and all things around you. It is adab, and it comes directly from the heart.

The person with the better adab is the better Sufi. It is in being kind and compassionate in all situations, in being forbearing and forgiving with all people, and in putting aside your own wants and needs to serve others. Everything else is a means toward this goal. He emphasized that good adab also means being good and kind to the natural environment, not just to people. I wanted to ask him whether this means that Islamic rituals and customs are not really necessary, and whether any person from other religions might not also be good Sufis, because they had kind and loving conduct toward others, but I did not ask.

THE GOLD GIVER

Our jeep bounced along the roads of Maharashtra, leaving behind the bustling little city of Aurangabad with its industrial factories and crumbling Mughal monuments. We passed by Daulatabad, with its soaring fortress on an imposing hill, and followed a small river up into the hills. Over the crest of the hill we approached the village of Khuldabad. It is really more a necropolis than a settlement and the village has more dead people than living ones, with monumental white domes of dargahs looming above the simple homes and shabby shops. The whole valley has a strange atmosphere of quiet reverence. Our jeep slowed down in front of the dargah of Muntajab al-Din Zar Zari Zar-Bakhsh, the first Chishti Sufi to settle here.

Muntajab al-Din was from Hansi, a town in Haryana between Delhi and the Punjab.[19] He was a khaleefa of Shaykh Farid al-Din Ganj-e Shakar, who sent him to be the spiritual guardian over Delhi. Later, when Shaykh Farid al-Din trained the young Nizam al-Din Awliya and made him a khaleefa at age twenty, he sent Nizam al-Din Awliya to Delhi, the capital of the realm. He was signaling that Nizam al-Din Awliya would succeed him as leader of the Chishti Order. In accord, he ordered Muntajab al-Din to move south to the Deccan at Deogir, which was the then capital city of the Yadava Kingdom that patronized Buddhism, Hinduism and Jainism. Muntajab al-Din took up this challenge, and moved south along with 700 Sufis and scholars to settle in the Deccan, and to start an experiment there of nurturing Islamic culture in a new environment. The *wilayat* of the whole Deccan was assigned to him. He chose to live outside of Deogir, with its impregnable fortress and Hindu kings, over the hills in a quiet valley that used to be the abode of Buddhist monks, who lived and worshipped in the cave chapels of Ellora. Indeed, Muntajab al-Din found a small cave on a hillock near where he and his companions settled, and he used to retire there to meditate and pray. During his lifetime, the Muslim Sultans of Delhi invaded the Deccan, defeated the Yadava kings, and incorporated this area and neighboring regions into their Islamic empire. They renamed Deogir as Daulatabad, the Abode of Fortunate Rule.

Following the teachings of the Chishti Order, Muntajab al-Din avoided cozying up to rulers and aristocrats, whether Hindu or Muslim. When Daulatabad became a thriving Islamic city, he stayed in his peaceful valley beyond the urban bustle, living with his mother and five sisters and companions. Far from his Chishti teachers in Delhi and removed from urban business, living in that settlement was hard. Yet from the unseen, wealth would come to Muntajab al-Din. Legend says that every morning and evening, a gold brocade cloak would come to him during his devotions, as a gift from the divine. As a mark of spiritual authority and world-renunciation, Sufis would wear cloaks made of simple rough material, given to them by their teacher and master. Muntajab al-Din was far from his master, so God provided the cloak; rather than rough wool or rustic cotton, he received a cloak of glimmering gold brocade. These cloaks, the legend goes, he would not wear but rather sell, and he would distribute the coins among the Sufis who followed him and those who visited them. Thus, he got the nickname Zar Zari Zar-Bakhsh or "Gold Golden Giver of Gold."

Despite the wealth flowing through his hands to support his community, Muntajab al-Din lived in poverty. It is said that he had a servant who used to work in manual labor or sell firewood to earn money to cook a little food for Muntajab al-Din. One day, he ate a little of the simple food as was his custom and then returned to his devotions. After a little while, he called over the servant and said, "Today I am not feeling the normal delight and rapture that usually accompanies my worship of God. Tell me the truth now, did you make any oversight in your legal earning to bring this food?" After a profound silence, the servant offered this reply, "Your servant made no oversight, except that today I forgot to bring salt, so I just went to the corner vegetable vendor and borrowed some salt from him promising to pay him tomorrow." Muntajab al-Din replied, "Do you or I dare to hope that we will live until tomorrow in a fit condition to work labor and earn enough to pay back a loan? Be warned, in the future never make such a mistake again!"[20]

Eventually, Muntajab al-Din died and was buried at the foot of the hill overlooked by his cave, and Muslim rulers built a domed shrine over his grave. This dargah became known as Rawzat, a walled garden resembling paradise where the saint's tomb served as a refuge and devotional center. Many other Chishti saints lived nearby, died and were buried, such that Rawzat—as the place was then called—became a holy town. Later, the Mughal Emperor Aurangzeb desired to be buried nearby, despite his suspicion against many Sufis during his lifetime, and after his tomb the locality became known as called Khuldabad, or the Eternal Garden.

Muntajab al-Din was trained as a *qazi* or religious judge. He had a vast scholarly knowledge of Islam. He followed the sharee'a scrupulously, but tempered it with a noble ethic of love and hospitality for others. Once he met his elder brother, Burhan al-Din Ghareeb, who was also a renowned Sufi and follower of Nizam al-Din Awliya in Delhi. The elder brother later recalled, "One day, Muntajab al-Din set some food before this humble person and bid me to eat. I told him, 'Today I am fasting.' That great teacher replied, 'You should break your fast and eat! You can do fasting another day.' I did not accept this advice. Later that day, I went to see Shaykh Nizam al-Din Awliya. When I sat in his presence, he commanded, 'Set some food before Shaykh Burhan al-Din so that he can eat.' I could not help but to break my fast and eat as my master ordered! By the time I finished eating and took leave, the time for the afternoon prayer had passed. I desperately wanted to pray with others [which gives greater blessing than praying alone] but everyone I met replied to me that they had already prayed the afternoon prayer. Finally, I was afraid that the proper time for the afternoon prayer was passing quickly, so I prayed all alone. With great regret, I realized my disgraceful behavior! I should have followed the wise advice of Muntajab al-Din, and instead both my fasting and my praying were spoiled."[21] Any ostentation in worship or showy display of piety was perceived as arrogance among these Chishti personalities, and the primary goal was love through the humble give and take of hospitality, care and concern.

After the death of Muntajab al-Din Zar Zari Zar-Bakhsh in 1309 CE, his brother Burhan al-Din Ghareeb was deputed to come to the Deccan to take his place. Under him, the Chishti Order flourished and spread throughout the Deccan. His circle of followers included poets and scholars, who recorded at least four different records of his oral teachings. In them, he told many stories of his pioneering brother, Muntajab al-Din. 'Abdi, a poet and chronicler of Sufis, later penned this praise for them both.[22]

Master Muntajab, Gold Golden Giver of Gold Was a very great Shaykh, as many have told	منتجب شیخ زر زری زر بخش گو شفیق کلاں بود بشمار
A disciple of Khwaja Farid Ganj-e Shakar He came to Deogir alone in a move so bold	از مریدانِ خواجہ گنج شکر کرد اول بہ دیوگیر قرار
Every dawn and dusk, each night and day From beyond, gold robes his form did enfold	در صباح و رواح و لیل و نہار خلعتِ زر زغیب می آید
Giver of Gold is the name that he earned As each robe for the good of others he sold	شد ازاں نام زر زری زر بخش مے نمودش براہ خیر نثار

Feeling poverty's sting, to heaven he'd look Complaint from others he would ever withhold	رختِ زیں تنگنائے جوں بربست بجز امید سوئے دارِ قرار
Till Khwaja Burhan came to the Deccan to keep The Prophet's teachings alive for all to behold	خواجہ برہان سوئے دکن آمد زندہ زد گشت سنت و آثار
Stay silent now, 'Abdi, stop singing their praise Their virtues will always be told and retold	شو خموش از ثنائے او عبدیؔ کہ توان کرد وصفِ او تکرار

GENEROSITY

After visiting the dargah of Muntajab al-Din Zar Zari Zar-Bakhsh, our little group with Pir Rasheed paused in our journey to drink a cup of tea. While sitting waiting for the tiny cups of powerfully sweet milky tea to arrive, Pir Rasheed pointed out to me a huge tree growing near the tea-stall. It was a wide-spreading banyan tree but it had only one rather narrow trunk. Look at that tree, he said, how wide its branches are spread and how green and full it is, even though its trunk is so narrow. Yes, I said, it is like the tomb of a holy person, which takes up such a narrow piece of earth, but spreads its shelter so wide. Pir Rasheed answered, "Yes, and how many people take shelter in its shade! How many people benefit from the life of a single person, if he has good adab."

Then I remembered my own resentment against all the people at the dargah who ask for money, especially the caretakers of the tomb who whisk visitors with a peacock-feather broom that lies on the tomb, in order to transmit to them *baraka* or blessing from the saint. I resented their request for money for this "service" and thought I would receive the blessing of the saint directly. Now while sitting with Pir Rasheed and considering that tree, I realized that all those people at the tomb are like birds nesting in the shade and branches of a huge tree. Some are crows and some are doves, but all have a place in that tree. The tree resents none of them. The doves do not fight off the crows. There is room for all.

I was wrong to judge those people, and regretted the chance to give them a little livelihood. One of our fellow mureeds would give ten rupees to each

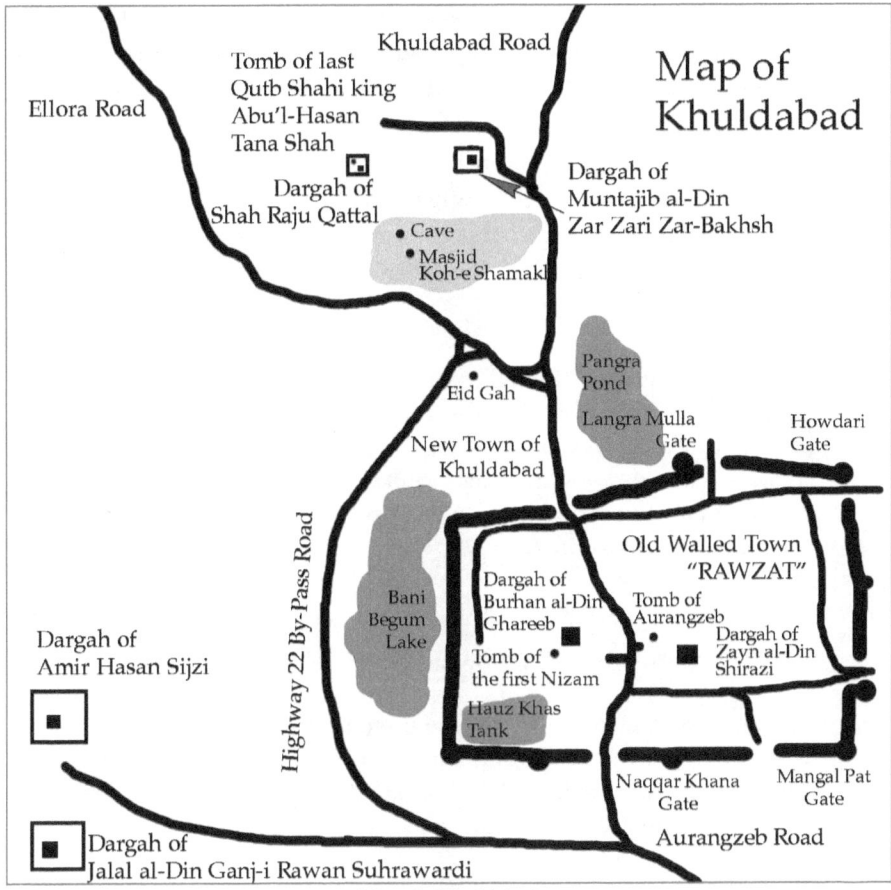

Map 5: Khuldabad

one, and he had much less money in his pocket than I did. In my heart, I asked forgiveness for this miserliness and vowed to change my perspective. For doesn't the Qur'an warn us: "Here you are, a people invited to give of what you have for the sake of God, yet among you are those who are stingy. Whoever withholds from giving in reality is stingily withholding from himself! For God is free of need but you all are deep in need, so if you turn away know that God will replace you with another people who will not be like you" (Surat Muhammad 47:38).

God gives to us continually, so why should we refuse to give to others? Generosity is the most basic virtue and the ultimate touchstone of adab, whether it is outer generosity (in giving of one's wealth, talent and attention) or inner generosity (in assuming the best of others' intentions).

Later, I found that Hazrat Gesu Daraz, the great Chishti teacher who lived here at Khuldabad when he was a boy, had written about generosity through the metaphor of a tree. The tree represents being (*wujud*). The tree generously gives through its branches, leaves, flowers and fruits. It gives because it understands from where it came, from an invisible seed, and to what it ultimately reverts, to the same invisible seed. When existing things—like the majestic tree—perceive their being as a circle and not merely a line, then being itself is love and love is essentially God. He writes the following in his Sufi epistle entitled *The Being of Lovers*.

> The start of all is love. The end of all is love. Love is love and nothing exists outside of love, which alone is eternal. Understand just this much: without love, there is no being! Being is essentially love. Without love, no being can exist. Thus, the phrase in the Qur'an that says *this One is the first and the last, the outer and the inner* refers to love (Surat al-Hadid 57:30). Love is all that is.
>
> Who is Adam and what is Eve? Love is the essence
> Even if untold thousands proceed as its consequence
>
> You know the basics of love, so now listen to the furthest perfection of love. Love is the seed from which grows a tree, through which existence is known and it is called "the body." This tree grows from five roots, which are called intellect, imagination, spirit, knowledge and life. These roots are also called "the divine reality" (*haqeeqat*). From the tree based upon these five roots grow five branches. Corresponding to the root intellect grows the branch called seeing, to the root imagination grows the branch called hearing, to the root spirit grows the branch called speaking, from the root knowledge grows the branch understanding, and from the root life grows the branch called doing. From these five branches extend five leaves. From the branch seeing extends the leaf called greed, from the branch hearing extends the leaf called hatred, from the branch speaking grows the leaf called anger, from the branch understanding grows the leaf called pride, and from the branch doing grows the leaf called jealousy. These five leaves are also called "the self" (*nafs*) and they constitute the heart, which must be trained by religion (*sharee'a*). As a wise Sufi once said:
>
> The self, spirit, intellect and heart are all as one united
> For the person with spiritual insight, can this be doubted?

You have considered this tree's roots, branches and leaves, so ponder now its flower and fruits! Through the obscuring foliage it blossoms with five flowers: worship, renunciation, recitation, contentment and generosity. These altogether are called "the spiritual path" (*tareeqat*). My dear, the fruits that ripen from these are also five: kindness, love, compassion, blessedness and aspiration. These five fruits are united in love, and in fact they are nothing but love. They are altogether called "mystical insight" (*mar'ifa*). Now listen carefully…the seed that is hidden in the center of these fruits is called "unity" (*wahdat*). This whole tree was in the beginning a seed and at the end of its perfection is the same seed. The whole circle of its being is called love (*'ishq*), and love is God, through whom all that is comes into being. In this way, you should understand that the One through whom you manifest in this phenomenal world of being and becoming is the eternal and everlasting One.[23]

How profoundly Gesu Daraz describes the inner nature of apparent Nature! In this arid landscape where trees are precious, I will never look at a tree in the same way again.

CHAPTER 3
THE DOOR'S JAMB

SUBMISSION'S KNIFE

In Hyderabad, we celebrated the ʿurs of Hazrat Qutb al-Din Bakhtiyar Kaki. He was the dear friend of Khwaja Muʿin al-Din of Ajmer and was delegated to be his successor in the Chishti Order. He is buried in Delhi but we celebrate his ʿurs here in Hyderabad, with *samaʿ* in the evening at Pir Rasheed's home, followed by a meal.

In the evening, people assemble for a large gathering at Pir Rasheed's house in the old city, the house which serves as his khanqah or Sufi gathering place. I had come early with Zaida Nassier, a visitor from Bangalore who wanted to meet Pir Rasheed and spend some time with him. I had not met her before this weekend, though Pir Rasheed had asked me to speak with her on the telephone. She is a follower of Hazrat Inayat Khan, and took initiation into his lineage in the Netherlands where members of his family had settled and still teach. Zaida's family history is a complicated portrait of the post-colonial world: they were Muslims from Bihar who moved to Suriname, a Dutch colony in South America that became independent in 1975, after which they moved to the Netherlands. Zaida had a tortured relationship with the Netherlands where she grew up and always longed to return to her Indian roots. In her thirties, she came to Bangalore to study Bharatnatyam dance, and she was anxious about how to balance her "Islamic" identity inherited from family with her devotion to Indian music and dance, which she sees as "Hindu." The custodian of the dargah of Pir Inayat Khan in Delhi had recommended that she contact Pir Rasheed, since she was living in Southern India, and Bangalore is not so far from Hyderabad. She called Pir Rasheed, who asked me to take care of her while she was visiting. As I picked her up from her guesthouse and got to know her better, I hoped that spending time with Pir Rasheed might allow her to see that this binary differentiation between "Islamic" and "Hindu" was not so simple. Certain things transcend such communal distinctions, such as mysticism and music.

Zaida and I arrived together and sat talking until other mureeds began to appear. Then Zaida went inside with the women behind the curtain, and I went downstairs to sit with the men who were coming in. It was the first time I had arrived early and so I got to experience the Qur'an recitation that precedes samaʿ. Every one of the men sat around silently reciting a different sipara of the Qur'an. I suppose that if enough people came in early, as a group we could read the entire Qur'an in the hour before the sunset prayer, but we were too few people to achieve that.

When the azan sounded for prayer, everyone put the sheaves of Qur'an back in a stack, cleared the floor, and recited our *namaz*. Then we had vocal Qur'an recitation by a few members of the group, who read together the short chapters from the Qur'an: Surat al-Fatiha, Surat al-Ikhlas, Surat al-Falaq and

Photo 5: Pir Inayat Khan and his daughter Noor

Surat al-Nas. Then *na'at* or poems in praise of the Prophet Muhammad, were recited by Zakir 'Ali. Zakir was an old Hyderabadi, of Yemeni origins. We call them Chaush and they had settled here as tough warriors who served in the Nizam's private guard, but had a reputation as thugs. For a living, Zakir drove a public bus through the narrow lanes of the old city. He usually showed up with some broken arm or bandaged leg; when I asked him how he got injured, he usually just smiled and told some story about how people crashed into his bus and had to be disciplined. In reality, he was a *majzub* with a strong and emotion-drenched voice. He recited poems until the Qawwals arrived. The singers settled down at one side of the room with their harmonium and drums and little notebooks of song lyrics scrawled in Persian, Urdu and Hindi. Facing them across the room was Pir Rasheed, wearing his pale-yellow turban and tawny aba robe with his green shawl folded over his left shoulder, seated on a shabby carpet. Next to him, facing the singers, sat his family members and honored guests, the leaders of other Sufi orders. We disciples and visitors sat in crowded rows along the sides of the room, completing a closed rectangle, a ritual frame which would soon resound with spiritual music. Ladies from the family and female followers sat in the neighboring room separated by a curtain. The musicians finished tuning the drums and sat expectantly. Pir Rasheed offered a small prayer and senior disciples recited a few verses from the Qur'an, and then the sama' began in earnest.

Because it was the death anniversary of Hazrat Qutb al-Din, I was especially eager to hear the music, expecting it to have a touch of magic. Hazrat Qutb al-Din died while listening to qawwali, after experiencing an extended rapture that kept the musicians singing one phrase over and over in variations for days in an attempt to support his spiritual struggle and emerge from his trance. But he never came back to this world. I was hoping the Qawwals would sing the verses that drove Hazrat Qutb al-Din over the edge into the most blessed type of death. If one must die—and who can avoid it?—then the best one can hope for is to die while soaring upward on the wings of melody. He passed away listening to Persian verses by Ahmad-e Jam—"Those who are slain by submission's knife…" But the singers did not choose this song and I had to restrain myself from requesting it.[24]

Love's goal is to reach for a different place	منزلِ عشق از مکانے دیگر است
People of insight leave ever a different trace	مردِ معنی را نشانے دیگر است

Those who trade in love
have at every booth
Nooses at ready
to hang a different youth

Those who are slain
by submission's knife
From beyond always
attain a different life

Those devoted to
a wise Chishti master
From top to toe
have a different character

Don't drift, Ahmad,
hone your attention span
This bell's distant peal
leads a different caravan

بر سرِ بازارِ صرّافانِ عشق
زیرِ هر دارے جوانے دیگر است

کشتگانِ خنجرِ تسلیم را
هر زماں از غیب جانے دیگر است

عاشقانِ خواجگانِ چشت را
از قدم تا سر نشانے دیگر است

احمدا تا گم نہ گردی ہوشدار
کایں جرس از کاروانے دیگر است

ALLAH ALWAYS GIVES

The following day dawned. It is the 'urs of Hazrat Sayyid Zia al-Hasan Jeeli Kaleemi, who is the grandfather of Pir Rasheed and was Pir Rasheed's own Pir. He died in 1941 and his death anniversary is one of the biggest days in our devotional calendar. It is a very emotional gathering. I met Pir Rasheed and his other disciples and followers and family members at the Astana Kaleemi, where Hazrat Zia al-Hasan's modest tomb lies beside that of his father, Sayyid Muhammad Hasan Jeeli Kaleemi (who died in 1890). We swept the room clean, then removed the grave cloth and brushed the dust off the tomb with peacock-feather brooms. While everyone recited *durud* in praise of the Prophet Muhammad, Pir Rasheed tenderly mixed rose water and attar oils into the sandalwood powder to make a fragrant paste. He rose and, with the bowl of this heady paste, he lifted the sheet over the grave just a bit to anoint its head with sandal. Everyone rushed to follow suit, jostling to get a small finger-full of the sandalpaste to quickly anoint the tomb. There is a hush over the group as the tomb is exposed and the aroma of rich rose and sacred sandalwood wafts up, from years of sedimented anointings that have dried on the tomb.

Quickly, the cloth is laid back over the tomb and everyone together covers it with the brocade grave cloths. Pink roses and white jasmine woven into a chadar or sheet, like the flower veils worn by a groom on his wedding day, are laid over the tomb with murmuring of prayers. Then fatiha is recited, and the lineage of his initiatory chain is read out, in both the Chishti and Qadiri Orders. Then more praise is raised for the Prophet by reciting the *Durud-e Taj* or "Benediction of the Crown."

> Allah, grant praise and blessings on Muhammad, our beloved guide and leader
> Master of radiant crown, heavenly ascent, lightning steed and victory banner
> Who repels disaster, affliction, scarcity, illness and suffering of every manner
> His name is written by divine pen on eternal tablet, raised as intercessor
> He is leader of the Arabs and Persians and all people beyond their boundary
> His body is sanctified, purified, perfumed and illumined in the holy sanctuary
> He is the sun at noon, the luminous moon, the chief of paradise
> He is the light of guidance, the heart of humanity, the lamp in darkness
> His example is beautiful, his intercession is bountiful, his character is generous
> Allah is his protector, Gabriel is his companion, Buraq is his spiritual steed
> Ascension is his journey, cosmic lotus is his station, nearness is what he seeks
> What he seeks is his sole aim and his aim is the essence of his own existence
> He is leader of Messengers, seal of Prophets, intercessor for sinners
> He is friend to the helpless, mercy to the cosmos, respite to the lovers
> He is the goal of those who yearn, light for those who learn,
> He is the guide for those who seek, the lamp for those who draw near,
> He is the lover of those who are poor, alienated and prone to fear
> Master in both worlds, prophet of both shrines, leader of both prayer niches
> He is our means for reaching to God in the two abodes,
> He is possessor of intimacy nearer than the length of two bows
> He is the beloved for the Lord of two easts and two wests
> He is the grandfather of Hasan and Husayn, the two martyrs
> He is our leader and the master of the two worlds
> He is Muhammad, the father of Qasim, the son of 'Abdallah
> In reality, a light from the light of Allah
> If you yearn for the light of his beauty
> Invoke blessings on him and his family
> and the followers in his company
> Wish them peace and harmony
> From now until eternity

Durud-e Taj is a poetic praise formula used since long ago in the Chishti Order and other Indian Sufi communities. Its rhyming phrases in Arabic encode a complex theology of love mysticism in which the Prophet Muhammad is the axis of the cosmos. As the prayer finishes, people pay their respects to their Sufi masters, both living and passed away, and slowly disperse.

There is nothing at the Astana to teach one who Sayyid Muhammad Zia al-Hasan is or for what principles he stands. The Astana is a bare room. Outside, it is coated with layers of lime white-wash that rounds out every hard edge of the stone building, such that it resembles the smooth texture of dried bone or the inside of an oyster shell. Arches and cusped brackets carved of stone mark this building as an old Deccani construction, and it was built in the seventeenth century as part of the mosque next to the dargah of Husayn Shah Wali. Inside, the room is paved with black and grey slabs of smooth *shabad* stone, a locally quarried slate that is a specialty of old Deccani architecture: it keeps the floors cool even in the oven-like summer. Two rickety fans swing precariously from the ceiling and tube lights dangle their wires from high up on the walls, all nailed into the lime plaster at off angles. Accoutrements of modernity do not fit easily into this space. The walls have been recently painted over in glossy enamel of sandalwood yellow and vibrant green. The walls are bare, except for some framed calligraphic signs giving the names of the Sufis buried in the two tombs that take up most of the space: Sayyid Muhammad Hasan and Sayyid Muhammad Zia al-Hasan, with the tomb of the latter's son, Sayyid Muhammad Fakhr al-Hasan, occupying a small annex built later.

The Astana gives no clue as to who Sayyid Muhammad Zia al-Hasan is or how he lived. I heard occasional stories from Pir Rasheed about Sayyid Zia al-Hasan, his grandfather. Luckily, there is also a written record consisting of

Photo 6: Astana Kaleemi

THE DOOR'S JAMB

a description of the life and qualities of Sayyid Muhammad Zia al-Hasan Jeeli Kaleemi, in the introduction to a slim book of Sayyid Zia's published poetry in Urdu and Persian. The written record is translated as follows.[25]

> As for the teachings of our master, Sayyid Muhammad Zia al-Hasan Jeeli Kaleemi, I can say this. He was born in 1287 AH [equivalent to 1870 CE]. His father [Sayyid Muhammad Hasan Jeeli Kaleemi] was a descendant of Shaykh 'Abd al-Qadir Jeelani, whose lineage reaches back to Imam Hasan [the elder grandson of the Prophet Muhammad]. His mother, Poti Begum, was the daughter of Shah Pir ibn Shah Mir 'Usmani, whose lineage comes from Shaykh Jalal al-Din Kabir al-Awliya of Panipat [the great Sabiri Chishti master and successor of Shams al-Din Turk Panipati, the successor of 'Ala al-Din Ahmad Sabir] and reaches back to the third Caliph of Islam, 'Usman Ghani.
>
> Sayyid Muhammad Zia al-Hasan Jeeli Kaleemi learned Islamic sciences from his father. He had profound insight into Islamic knowledge. He recited the Qur'an with beautiful cantillation and memorized half the Qur'an. Under the guidance of his father, he underwent continuous ascetic discipline and devotional exercises, traversing the stages of the spiritual path. He used to spend many days in isolation for worship and stayed engrossed in asceticism. He also undertook a forty-day retreat. During the blessed months of Ramadan and Shawwal, he would observe fasting, and also during the full-moon days of other months [the 13th, 14th and 15th days of the lunar month, known as *ayam-e bayza* or days of the luminous moon]. In addition, he would fast many other days. When he did eat, he would take only simple ordinary food of a minimal amount.
>
> Every day upon waking early before sunrise, he would [go to mosque and] pray the pre-dawn vigil prayer called *tahajjud*. Then after the dawn prayer he would meditate with zikr then recite the Qur'an for some time. He would pray again at morning light and at noon, then go home to take some food. Then he would turn his attention to his disciples.
>
> Each day from far afield—even from villages and rural areas outside of Hyderabad—people would come to Sayyid Muhammad Zia al-Hasan Jeeli Kaleemi to sit with a group of those who were his disciples or followers. With just one glance, by the permission of God, he would drive away evil forces and black magic that afflicted people. People would often experience healing after just one meeting with him. During the day, he would be engaged in teaching the Qur'an and the Sufi message—especially from the book entitled the *Kashkul-e Kaleemi* or *The Alms Bowl of Shaykh Kaleemullah*—yet he was always ready to serve the people who came to him with troubles. Then after the late-

afternoon prayer, he would stay engrossed in reciting Qur'an and doing zikr. At sunset, he would make the required prayer and then perform six cycles of additional prayer (*namaz-e awabeen*), two cycles for preserving the faith (*hifz al-iman*) and two cycles for purifying the heart (*tasfiyat al-qalb*). Then after doing the nighttime prayer, he would take some rest.

He was unique in his age. He was renowned for his knowledge and his practice, his worship and his devotion. The most famous Islamic scholars of his era acknowledged his simple Sufi lifestyle and his spiritual stature. Such was his virtue of contentment and reliance upon God that he lived in tight circumstances and in the grip of poverty. He spent his whole life in submission, patience and thanksgiving. Usually his household was in dire need. The servants would complain, "How can we cook anything today when the house is completely empty of provisions?" He would answer, "Be patient for a while until something turns up—Allah always gives." After some time passed, something or other of food or provisions would somehow come to his home. Then he would remind them, "Didn't I tell you that Allah always gives?"

The former chief scholar of *hadees* at Jami'a Nizamiyya [the largest Islamic university in Hyderabad] was named Maulana Mufti Muneer al-Din. He used to say, "In my lifetime I have never seen anyone like Hazrat Zia who relies upon God for provision yet treats his guests with such hospitality!" His generosity was proverbial: whatever he received of wealth or gift offerings he would spend or give away that very moment, saving nothing for the coming day. Despite this practice, he would regularly feed fifty people at his home after every Friday communal prayer.

He was so scrupulous in looking after other people's needs that he would ask the news of everyone in his neighborhood without distinction, whether that person was his disciple or not, whether Hindu or Muslim. He would inquire, "Who is going hungry? Who is feeling ill?" If he knew of someone in need, he would order help to be sent, placing grain or money on a platter, which he would carry himself to their home. Yet when there was nothing in his own home, he would rely only on God and wait patiently. He never requested help from anyone.

His ethics and love were such that each and every person was fooled into thinking that she or he was his absolute favorite. This was because Hazrat Zia had such a loving way of greeting each person—whether rich or poor, all were treated equally in his kindness. In every gathering of his—whether for listening to devotional music, dining together, or for any other reason—there was no place reserved for anyone or any special treatment. Likewise, there was no cushion or raised seat for Hazrat Zia to sit upon; he would just sit simply on the floor wherever he found an open space. At his home, rich and poor would sit at one dining cloth laid out on the floor to eat their meals together. He never gave special welcome to any visitor who was rich and he never looked with contempt upon any visitor who happened to be poor.

Hazrat Zia was without compare in the qualities of patience and forbearance, humility and self-deprecation. Once, several women from a village developed a bad opinion of him over some issue, and they started to abuse him with harsh words that escalated to foul abuse. Hazrat Zia's eyes flowed with tears and he burst out sobbing and cried out, "God keep us safe! Whatever you are saying about me, I am certainly far worse than that!" Hazrat Zia's love of the truth and his honesty were such that when his father died, he insisted that his younger brother, Sayyid Zuhur al-Hasan Jeeli Kaleemi, become their father's successor rather than himself. He refused to take that position. Yet when his brother died, then he did take on that mantle as successor (*sajjada-nasheen*) to his father.

Hazrat Zia was very passionate about listening to devotional music. He used to experience intense states of ecstasy during the music. Even after three days, he would feel its effects still and he would continuously weep. It was while listening to music that Hazrat passed away. He was also an excellent poet. His poetic verse contains excellent lessons and lofty teachings about passion and love, spiritual secrets and insights, Sufi training and refinement. With God's help, I was able to collect his poetry and publish it for the first time twenty-three years ago in 1401 Hijri [1981 CE]. I am related to him by blood. He was a maternal cousin to my paternal grandfather, Hafiz Sayyid Altaf al-Rahman, and also to my paternal grandmother, Wazeer Begum, and to my maternal grandmother, Qurayshiya Begum. In addition, the famous Sufi scholar, 'Abd al-Qadeer Siddiqi, was married to one of his cousins.

Hazrat Zia always commemorated the 14th of Rabee al-Awwal, the day when Hazrat Qutb al-Din Bakhtiyar Kaki passed away in a trance while listening to music. Every year on this 'urs day, Hazrat Zia would host a reading of the Qur'an and a concert of spiritual music, after which he would distribute specially baked biscuits called "Kak" [after which Qutb al-Din got his nickname "Lucky Biscuit"]. One year, as was the custom, on the 14th of Rabee' al-Awwal, after the late-afternoon prayer, the music session began in Hazrat Zia's house. During this session, he experienced such overwhelming ecstasy that he lost his senses. The music session ended and everyone dispersed, but Hazrat's ecstasy would not cease. Tears continuously rolled down his cheeks as he wept uncontrollably. In this very state, he passed away on the following day, on the 15th of Rabee' al-Awwal of 1360 Hijri [1941 CE], at the time of late-afternoon prayer, at the age of 82.

He was buried in a grave next to his father, in a room adjacent to the mosque [known as Husayni Masjid] that is beside the dargah of Hazrat Husayn Shah Wali. For his funeral, masses of people—commoners and Sufis alike—showed up to pay their respects. Besides scholars and nobles, relatives and disciples and followers, there were also thousands of Hindus who came. The funeral prayer was led by that sea of knowledge, 'Allama Muhammad 'Abd al-Qadeer Siddiqi [former professor of Islamic Studies at Osmania University and poet who wrote under the pen-name Hasrat].

THE KALEEMI ALMS BOWL

One week later, I came to Pir Rasheed's home for the celebration of the 'urs of Shaykh Kaleemullah. Pir Rasheed calls him "the formative leader of the Kaleemi lineage." In fact, the Kaleemi lineage took its name from Shaykh Kaleemullah. In America and Europe, I found that some people get confused by this. Many Arabs and Iranians nowadays think that "Kaleemi" refers to the Jews, because Muslims know the Prophet Moses by his praise name in Arabic, Kaleemullah or "The One who speaks with God." For this reason, some people think "Kaleemi" refers to a follower of Moses, meaning the Jews. But in our circles, Kaleemullah refers to the great Sufi master of Delhi, and the Kaleemi lineage is the order perpetuated by his followers in India and now all over the world.

Shaykh Kaleemullah is buried in the heart of Mughal Delhi, known as Shahjahanabad, near the Red Fort and the Jami' Masjid. He was born in 1650 and died in 1729 CE.[26] Shaykh Kaleemullah led a renaissance of the Chishti Order that breathed new life into the ethical principles and mystical creativity of the early Chishti masters.[27] Shaykh Kaleemullah had his primary initiation into the Chishti Order, but he also received from his spiritual guide simultaneous and equal initiation into others: the Qadiri, Naqshbandi, Suhrawardi and Shattari Orders.[28] Shaykh Kaleemullah was a Muslim intellectual and prolific author in addition to being a prominent Sufi master. Shaykh Kaleemullah's home in Delhi became a religious center: it was a madrasa where people came to study, a khanqah where they came for devotions, and it became a dargah when he was buried there. People still visit his tomb and pray there, though the original building was destroyed by the British colonial army in the war of 1857. He initiated into his Sufi Order both men and women, both Muslims and people of other faiths.

Shaykh Kaleemullah wrote many original books to explain Sufi principles and practices. One of his most ingenious compositions is *Kashkul-e*

Photo 7: Tomb of Shaykh Kaleemullah Shahjahanabadi in Delhi

Kaleemi (*The Alms Bowl of Shaykh Kaleemullah*). Pir Rasheed taught me from this book, and his grandfather used to read it along with his disciples. In *The Alms Bowl*, Shaykh Kaleemullah gives instruction on how to perform various kinds of meditation and contemplation, and he explains the principles involved and their intended effects. Each practice he compares to a morsel of nourishing food that is dropped in his alms bowl as he goes begging at the door of different Sufi guides and diverse Sufi orders. His tone of voice is much like a doctor giving prescriptions for various cures. Shaykh Kaleemullah wrote many other books. His *Muraqqa'-e Kaleemi* (*The Patch-Work Cloak of Kaleemullah*) describes different methods of praying and making invocation. His *Tasneem-e Tawhid* (*Cups from the Font of Paradise*) describes God's absolute unity and the mystical insight this gives us into the true nature of existence.[29]

Shaykh Kaleemullah's personality was memorialized by a follower of Shaykh Nizam al-Din Aurangabadi, named Kamgar Husayni. In 1720, he traveled from Aurangabad in the Deccan up north to Delhi, along with a Mughal nobleman's caravan. Political events in the capital of Delhi forced him to tarry there for three months. He took advantage of this by attending the assembly (*majlis*) of Shaykh Kaleemullah, the guide of his own spiritual guide, Nizam al-Din Aurangabadi. He wrote down what Shaykh Kaleemullah said and the questions asked by those in the assembly, to create a malfuzat record to carry back to Aurangabad and share with his brother, Nur al-Din Husayni, who was a fellow disciple. Both brothers yearned to travel to Delhi to meet Shaykh Kaleemullah, but their Shaykh only gave permission for Kamgar to go. Before Kamgar Husayni could return to Aurangabad, he received news that his brother had died. In great sorrow, he decided to take the record of Shaykh Kaleemullah's lectures and make a formal book for other disciples, in memory of his deceased brother. He arranged the record of Shaykh Kaleemullah's teachings in chapters and then interspersed them with his own observations and Persian poems. The result is a short but valuable observation of Kaleemi teachings from their source: the mouth of Shaykh Kaleemullah in the context of 18th century Mughal capital of Delhi.

> Shah Kaleemullah was speaking about the book *Fusus al-Hikam* or "*The Bezels of Wisdom*" by Shaykh Ibn Arabi. He said, "Writing a book creates an immortal memorial for the author. If the writing is good, then the good reputation of the author stays alive. Such is also the case with a spiritual guide training a disciple. If a guide gets even just one good disciple, then the glory of his spiritual order is augmented and the

guide's fame will be spread throughout the region. Such is the case also in poetry! In a ghazal, if there is just one couplet that is excellent, then that is enough to call the poem good. In the terminology of poetry, this is specified as 'the couplet that makes the poem' (*bayt al-ghazal*)."

Shah Kaleemullah explained all these things with the most beatific smile and radiant happiness on his face. This humble listener was sure that he gave these examples to really praise his best disciple, Nizam al-Din Aurangabadi, but hidden behind the veil of metaphors. This is because no disciple has shown himself more excellent than Nizam al-Din Aurangabadi; though that refuge of saintliness Shah Kaleemullah has countless disciples, no other disciple has achieved such renown throughout the land. His face was radiating such happiness and showing signs of such joy because of the intense love of Nizam al-Din Aurangabadi for him, of that I am absolutely certain.

Time and again I have carefully observed that whenever Shah Kaleemullah would mention the name of Nizam al-Din Aurangabadi, the same blissful happiness and utter contentment would show on his face. Yes indeed, when the beloved's name is mentioned, the lover's face shines with these signs. There was such love and sincerity between these two great spiritual masters, as this humble person has witnessed with his own eyes, that the pen is simply incapable of expressing in words! May Allah increase in me love for them both.[30]

It was the 'urs of Shaykh Kaleemullah, so after quietly reading the Qur'an while all the participants arrived, we moved aside to make room for the Qawwals. They assembled their drums and harmoniums by the door of the room in Pir Rasheed's house that served as the khanqah. Pir Rasheed sat on the far side of the hall on a carpet, facing the Qawwals. Beside him his family members sat along with Sufi leaders from other orders who were specially invited. On either side of the hall in rows sat his disciples and followers and admirers, packing the small hall until there was hardly room to breathe.

Pir Rasheed's disciples took turns reciting key verses from the Qur'an to bless the ritual, and then the Qawwals began with a harmonium melody in the form of a prayer. Then before they could begin their first song, Pir Rasheed made a request—no, it was so urgent that it was more like a demand! He called out *Sala Allahu 'ala Nurin* "God bless that Light"—a poem by Jami.[31] It is a na'at or song in praise of the Prophet Muhammad, in the form of a ghazal that mixed Arabic with Persian. In the very first line, Pir Rasheed was on his feet, his face radiant, his eyes misted, walking as if he were about to fall over or alight and fly away. He walked up to the Qawwals in his delicate and powerful way, half stumbling, to give them a gift and get them to repeat the line and he was in ecstasy outside himself by the time he took the five steps to get there.

May God bless that light from whom all other lights shine May sky spin with his love, in his embrace may earth recline	وصلی الله علیٰ نورٍ کزو شد نورہا پیدا زمین از حبِّ او و ساکن فلک در عشقِ او شیدا
The Creator praised him as Muhammad, Ahmad and Mahmud For existence he's the source, for things seen he's the sign	محمد احمد و محمود ویرا خالقش بستود کزو شد بود ہر موجود کزو شد دیدہ ہا بینا
If in Muhammad's name all our sins were not forgiven Could Adam've found repentance or Noah deliverance divine?	اگر نامِ محمد را نیاوردہ شفیعِ آدم نہ آدم یافتہ توبہ نہ نوح از غرقِ نجینا
His bashful eye recalls *that his gaze did not turn aside* *By night as it falls* traces his dark curls as they twine	دو چشمِ نرگسینش را کہ ما زاغ البصر خواند دو زلفِ عنبرینش را کہ واللیل اذا یغشیٰ
Jami, recite *did we not lay open* to guess his heart's secret Of *him who called for a night journey* your questions resign	زِ سرِّ سینہ اش جامی الم نشرح لک بر خوان ز معراجش چہ می پرسی کہ سبحان الذی اسریٰ

The phrases in italics in the last two couplets of this poem come from the Qur'an in Arabic. The poet Jami weaves them into his Persian poem in a very artful way. These phrases come from verses that describe the Prophet Muhammad's night journey and ascension to heaven, known as *Shab-e Mi'raj*.

The mi'raj was a miraculous journey, in which the Prophet flew up to God's throne on a winged steed called *Buraq* or "swift as lightning." In its outer form, the ascension was a miracle affirming the sincerity and efficacy of the Muhammad as the seal of the Prophets. Indeed, it was during the ascension that he learned the ritual of namaz, experienced the contemplation of God's face, and received the holy cloak of initiation. Shaykh Kaleemullah explains that the ascension also consists of an inner meaning, and this meaning can be experienced by others who are merely humble followers of the Prophet. In his book, *The Alms Bowl*, he describes a method of contemplation called "Ascension of the Sages" (*Mi'raj al-'Arifeen*).

> You imagine all existing things as a multitude of mirrors. Then all that you see in them of sensory and rational phenomena you should understand as reflections of the forms of the names and attributes of God. Then imagine them and indeed the entire cosmos as a single mirror, and gaze into it in order to see the face of God with all the divine names and attributes. Do this until you become one of the people who witness divine reality just as you started out as one of the people who receive divine inspiration. Then go further and observe that you see yourself like the whole cosmos, and know that your essence encompasses everything existing and that everything existing is formed within you. Come to realize that your essence is a mirror in which all things are reflected. Just as in the beginning you saw God reflected in all things other than yourself, now you witness God reflected within yourself.[32]

Shaykh Kaleemullah's exposition of different methods of meditation and contemplation is his most valuable book. Yet he wrote many other books on Sufism in addition to texts about medicine, astronomy and interpretation of the Qur'an.[33]

Many great Sufi leaders of the modern era trace their heritage back to Shaykh Kaleemullah. These include 20th century masters, such as Khwaja Hasan Nizami who defended Sufism in Delhi through journalism and scholarship, Hazrat Inayat Khan who left India to teach in Europe and America, or Soofie Saheb (Haji Ghulam Muhammad Sufi Siddiqi) who went to teach in Durban, South Africa. Sayyid Zia al-Hasan was among Shaykh Kaleemullah's followers in Hyderabad, who wrote poems in praise of him, like this ghazal that rhymes using his very name.[34]

I am afflicted by illness without a cure, Kaleemullah Extend to me aid now I implore, Kaleemullah	ہوا مجھے مرضِ لادوا کلیمُ اللہ مدد کرو مری للہ یا کلیمُ اللہ
How long must I stay apart from you, Kaleemullah? For God's sake, call me to your door, Kaleemullah	رہوں میں آپ سے کب تک جدا کلیمُ اللہ بلائیے مجھے بہرِ خدا کلیمُ اللہ

The tempter and my lower self have ruined me May God send you to save me as before, Kaleemullah	کیا خراب مجھے خوب نفس و شیطاں نے اب آئیے کہیں بہر خدا کلیمُ اللہ
Having wiped out my ego, I am joined to God Upon me such blessings you pour, Kaleemullah	مٹا کے اپنی خودی میں خدا سے واصل ہوں اب ایسا فضل ہو مجھ پر ترا کلیم اللہ
God forgives every fault of those clinging hopeful To your hem as it drags on the floor, Kaleemullah	خدا سے ہی بخشوالوں گا سب گناہوں کو پکڑ کے دامن اقدس ترا کلیم اللہ
Let no breath of mine go empty till my dying day God's remembrance fills my heart's store, Kaleemullah	خدا کی یاد رہے دل میں تا دم آخر نہ خالی جائے کوئی دم مرا کلیم اللہ
No illusion of worldly existence remains for Zia He remains in Oneness with no after or before, Kaleemullah!	رہے نہ ہستی موہوم کے یہ دھوکے میں فنا ہو ہستی حق میں ضیا کلیم اللہ

It seems as if Zia al-Hasan Kaleemi, for whom "no illusion of worldly existence remains," had practised Shaykh Kaleemullah's method of contemplation to achieve obliteration in God's oneness. In this way, the leaders of the Kaleemi Astana in Hyderabad serve as living examples of the teachings found in Sufi books.

THE KALEEMI ASTANA IN HYDERABAD

It was the 'urs of Sayyid Muhammad Hasan Jeeli Kaleemi. He was known also as Dehlavi because he came to Hyderabad from Delhi. He had originally come from Medina but settled first in Delhi. He was a Sayyid (a descendant of the Prophet Muhammad) from a family whose ancestor was Shaykh 'Abd al-Qadir Jeelani, the great Sufi teacher of Baghdad; that is why his name is Jeeli, meaning descended from 'Abd al-Qadir Jeelani (Jeelani is an Arabic pronunciation of the name of a person from Gilan, a Persian town, and in medieval Arabic it is often rendered as Jeeli). Sayyid Muhammad Hasan Jeeli Kaleemi moved from Medina to Delhi sometime in the second quarter of the 19th century. In Delhi, he met Sufi masters of the Kaleemi lineage who had initiations into both Chishti and Qadiri Orders (as well as the Naqshbandi and Suhrawardi Orders).

When Sayyid Muhammad Hasan Jeeli arrived in Delhi, he was especially impressed with one Kaleemi master, known as Kale Miyan or "The Black Master" (his full name was Ghulam Naseer al-Din Chishti). Though impressed with Kale Miyan, Sayyid Muhammad Hasan Jeeli was a Sufi of the Qadiri Order and also a genealogical descendant of Shaykh ʿAbd al-Qadir Jeelani, so he felt some resistance to taking initiation with a Pir in the Chishti Order. He wrestled with this for some time. Finally, he had a dream that instructed him to overcome his prejudice and take initiation into the Kaleemi tradition with Kale Miyan, in which he would be both Chishti and Qadiri without betraying his Qadiri ties.

Sayyid Muhammad Hasan Jeeli Kaleemi stayed in Delhi until 1857, when an anti-British uprising was put down in a big war, during which Kale Miyan died and Delhi was wrecked. Then Sayyid Muhammad Hasan Jeeli Kaleemi moved to Hyderabad and became the Imam of a small mosque called Masjid Husayni, which is next to the one of the big Chishti dargahs of Hyderabad, the dargah of Hazrat Husayn Shah Wali. When he died, Sayyid Muhammad Hasan Jeeli Kaleemi was buried next to the mosque, and the rooms that house his tomb are now called the "Astana Kaleemi." Next to his tomb is that of his son, Sayyid Muhammad Zia al-Hasan, who wrote a poem to commemorate his father's saintly personality.[35]

From the tongues of the eloquent this phrase is audible Enumerating Muhammad Hasan's virtues is impossible	یہی قول ہر دم ہے اہلِ سخن کا نہیں وصف ممکن محمد حسنؔ کا
Oh God, give me also a flame of that radiant blaze That which burned within Hasan's chest unquenchable	الٰہی مجھے بھی وہ دے تھوڑی آتش جلایا تھا جس نے کہ سینہ حسن کا

Now with face pale with longing,
now with sighs cold
The Shaykh of his time gave
this impression visible

Some lips open sighing,
some eyes closed praying
This is the state of those
who around him assemble

Why should I put into words
this pain of separation?
My body's blood flows
from my tears irrepressible

All the trials of this lowly world
will cease when
Your imagination turns
to your original home incredible

Oh God, let me see
the verdant dome of Medina's king
The flowers of his garden
inhabit my vision unstoppable

From his shrine wafts fragrance
of aloe wood and ambergris
Before which Tibetan musk
bows with shame commendable

Oh God, the humble request
of Zia is that you allow
The impression of Hasan
to remain in my senses tangible

Pir Rasheed told me all these stories about his ancestors. I prompted him to tell me more, for they were both family members and also spiritual guides in our tareeqat.

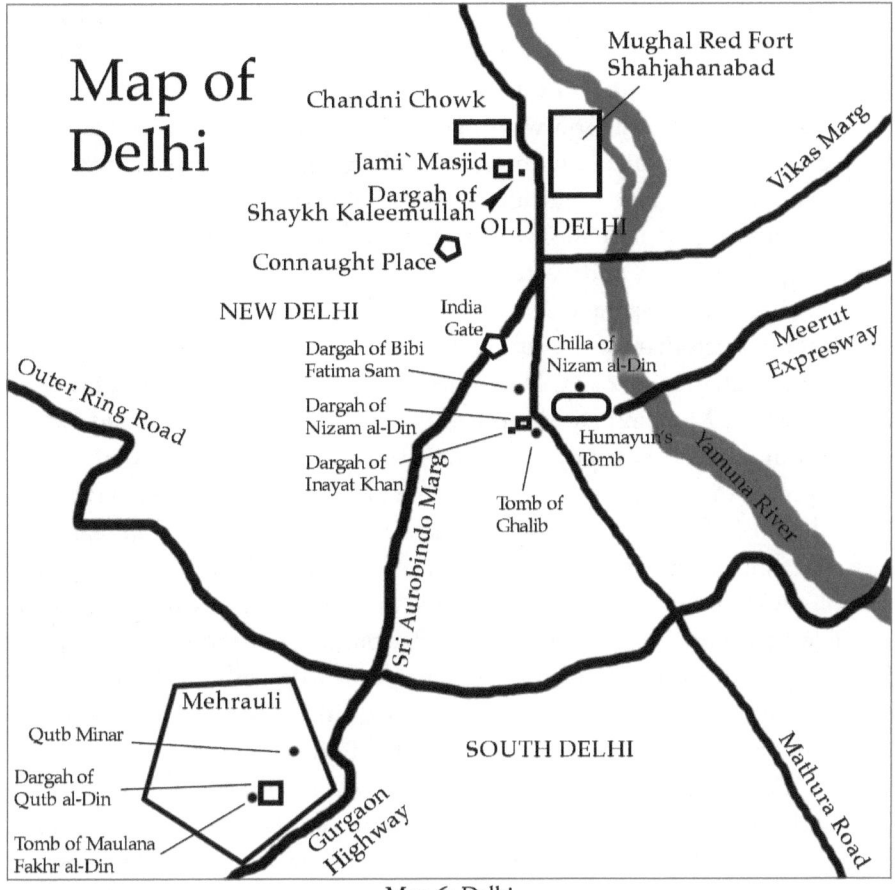

Map 6: Delhi

Pir Rasheed informed me that he took initiation directly from his grandfather, Sayyid Zia al-Hasan Jeeli Kaleemi. When he said this, he looked shy and added, "You know, actually he is not my grandfather!" I was surprised to hear this. In so many stories, Pir Rasheed had called him grandfather. "How could that be?" I asked in shock. He answered, "I was also surprised to learn this! I grew up thinking that Sayyid Zia al-Hasan was my grandfather. I learned from him and took initiation directly from him. Only later in life, I learned that he was not really the father of my father. Rather, he was the uncle of my father. My real grandfather was Sayyid Muhammad Ahsan Hasan Jeeli Kaleemi."

Then Pir Rasheed explained his whole family lineage to me, so that I would understand the order of who served as *sajjada-nasheen* of the Astana Kaleemi in Hyderabad. Sayyid Muhammad Hasan Jeeli came from Medina to Delhi, and took initiation into the Kaleemi lineage. Then he settled in Hyderabad and was granted the position of Imam at the Masjid Husayni.

His family was given a house there, and they were all buried nearby. He had three sons. The eldest was Sayyid Muhammad Ahsan Hasan, who is Pir Rasheed's real grandfather; he became the sajjada-nasheen after his father passed away. The middle son was Sayyid Muhammad Zuhur al-Hasan, and he became the next sajjada-nasheen after his elder brother passed away; but his personality was like a majzub so he was always in a state of trance and stayed away from society most of the time. After a short while, he gave up being sajjada-nasheen and passed that position on to his younger brother. The third brother was Sayyid Muhammad Zia al-Hasan, who served for a long time as custodian of the Astana Kaleemi.

Sayyid Muhammad Zia al-Hasan had no sons who survived, but his elder brother Sayyid Muhammad Ahsan had two sons. Sayyid Muhammad Zia al-Hasan took care of these boys as if they were his own. The sons were Sayyid Muhammad Ahsan II and Sayyid Fakhr al-Hasan, and they considered their uncle as their own father: that is why Pir Rasheed always calls Sayyid Muhammad Zia al-Hasan his grandfather. After Sayyid Muhammad Zia al-Hasan passed away he was buried directly next to his father in the Astana building, while his older brothers were buried outside the building in the courtyard. After him, Sayyid Muhammad Hasan II became the sajjada-nasheen. He passed the position on to his brother, Sayyid Muhammad Fakhr al-Hasan, who is buried in the Astana building next to Sayyid Zia al-Hasan.

Now Sayyid Muhammad Hasan II had a son named Sayyid Muhammad Ahsan II and Sayyid Fakhr al-Hasan had sons also, including Pir Rasheed. These sons were all cousins. The next sajjada-nasheen was Sayyid Muhammad Hameed al-Hasan, the elder son of Sayyid Fakhr al-Hasan. When he passed away, the position did not go to his younger brother Pir Rasheed, but rather went to his cousin Sayyid Muhammad Ahsan II. That cousin served as sajjada-nasheen until his death, and he left a letter in the care of Pir Rasheed with instructions to open it after he died.

That letter stayed in Pir Rasheed's care for nineteen years until his cousin passed away. When opened, the letter stated that Pir Rasheed should become the sajjada-nasheen. This caused some disturbance, because Sayyid Muhammad Ahsan II had a son but the position of sajjada-nasheen passed not to his son but rather to his cousin, Pir Rasheed. The son was dissatisfied with this decision and appealed to some powerful Sufi leaders in Hyderabad's Committee of Sufi Masha'ikh. They decided to play politics and supported the contention of the son, against the claim of Pir Rasheed. Pir Rasheed asked for a *fatwa* from Jami'a Nizamiya which ruled in his favor. Since then, the Sufis of Hyderabad consider Pir Rasheed to be the rightful sajjada-nasheen

THE DOOR'S JAMB

Photo 8: Flowers on the tomb of Muhammad Hasan Jeeli Kaleemi

of the Astana Kaleemi, who has the right to designate who will succeed him. But the disgruntled son of Sayyid Muhammad Ahsan II continues to maintain that he is the custodian of the Astana, and for some years he persisted in performing separate ceremonies on the occasion of the ʿurs of Sayyid Muhammad Hasan Jeeli Kaleemi, along with a few family members. I witnessed them myself in 2009 as they rushed to the Astana—after Pir Rasheed and his community finished anointing the tomb with sandal paste and reciting fatiha and prayers in the early morning—in order to do their own ceremony and repeat everything from scratch. It was very disturbing to see this family disagreement spill over into the rituals of the ʿurs.

The list of those who served as sajjada-nasheen, according to the story that was told to me by Pir Rasheed, is the following:

- Sayyid Muhammad Hasan
- Sayyid Muhammad Ahsan, son of Sayyid Muhammad Hasan
- Sayyid Muhammad Zahur al-Hasan, son of Sayyid Muhammad Hasan
- Sayyid Muhammad Zia al-Hasan, son of Sayyid Muhammad Hasan
- Sayyid Muhammad Hasan II, son of Sayyid Muhammad Ahsan
- Sayyid Muhammad Fakhr al-Hasan, son of Sayyid Muhammad Ahsan
- Sayyid Muhammad Hameed al-Hasan, son of Sayyid Fakhr al-Hasan

- Sayyid Muhammad Ahsan II, son of Sayyid Muhammad Hasan II
- Sayyid Muhammad Rasheed al-Hasan, son of Sayyid Fakhr al-Hasan

The last name in this list is Pir Rasheed. His family lineage is complicated; there were troublesome issues over several generations about who—among brothers and sons and nephews—should take on the mantle of being the sajjada-nasheen or custodian, the spiritual head of the Order.

Yet all agree that Sayyid Muhammad Hasan Jeeli Kaleemi was the original ancestor and teacher of this lineage. His son and successor praised him in poems, such as this one written to celebrate the day of his death anniversary, a joyful celebration of his leaving this lowly world to join the divine beloved.[36]

Come to celebrate the 'urs of your spiritual guide at his home Come weeping to spread fragrant sandalwood on his tomb	جو عرسِ پیر و مرشدِ برحق میں آئیں گے رو رو کے قبر پاک پہ صندل چڑھائیں گے
Today is the holy *sandal* ceremony for Pir Muhammad Hasan Attending will be the spirit of those related to Fatima's womb	صندل یہ آج شاہ محمد حسنؑ کا ہے ارواحِ پنجتن کے بھی تشریف لائیں گے
Our Pir comes from the lineage called Chishti and Kaleemi So Khwaja Mu'in al-Din of Ajmer will be present in the room	چشتی کلیمی سلسلہ ہے میرے پیر کا خواجہ معین دیں بھی پے شرکت آئیں گے
From paradise angels will descend bearing platters of light Over his grave they hang lamps to disperse the gloom	لائے ہیں خلد سے جو ملکِ نور کے طبق انوار کے چراغ لحد پر جلائیں گے
You will see how fresh morning breezes bring the public To spread veils of flowers and make his resting place bloom	تم دیکھ نا کہ پبلک صبا کے ذریعہ سے اہلِ چمن بھی پھولوں کی چادر چڑھائیں گے

The moment they recall to mind his character and virtue From the eyes of all present tears well up and spume	جس وقت یاد آئیں گے اخلاق آپ کے سب حاضرین رنج سے آ نسو بہائیں گے
To attend the 'urs, from far and wide people come saying Let's anoint our brows and eyes with the dust of his tomb	آتے ہیں لوگ عرس میں کہتے ہوئے یہی خاکِ مزار آ نکھوں سے ہم بھی لگائیں گے
From the raging sea of troubles God will deliver those who Carry on their heads trays bearing sandalwood perfume	اللہ دیگا بحر الم سے انھیں نجات جو لوگ سر پہ کشتیٔ صندل اٹھایٔں گے
On judgment day, Zia, why fear the blaze of the sun In his shade, your faults are pardoned on the day of doom	کیوں ڈر ہو تابشِ خورشیدِ حشر سے اس روز اے ضیا تمھیں یہ بخشوائیں گے

ADVANCING ALONG THE ROAD

I returned to Hyderabad from a trip with my father to Spain. We had strolled through the gardens of Granada and the forest of arches that is the mosque of Cordoba. It was a beautiful journey and I was happy to have spent time with my father, since I live so far from him. But my heart was burdened by sorrow. It was not his advancing age that saddened me, for his personality was also mellowing with age and that was soothing. Rather I was sad that he was not so robust in health, and was having difficulty walking. For this reason, I was happy to have taken him on a trip but I returned to Hyderabad not knowing whether another trip would be fated for the future. Doesn't the Qur'an say, "Those to whom we grant long lives we also make weak as they advance in age, so do you not ponder and understand?" (Surat Yaseen, 36:68).

Back in Hyderabad, I found that Pir Rasheed was very ill. He had been in the hospital for over a week, in the Intensive Care Unit. I rushed to New Life Hospital in Malakpet to see him. His eldest son Mukarram was there to take care of him so that was reassuring. His grandson Abrar had come back from Gulbarga to help despite his college exams. Pir Rasheed was in a delicate condition. Mureeds were saying many different things: that he had a urinary tract infection, that his lungs were filled with fluid, that his heart had become weak, that the medicines the doctors gave him enfeebled him. I stopped listening after a while, so many rumors and reasons were bandied about.

When I saw him, he was conscious but spoke with a very weak voice. An oxygen tube was up his nostrils. An intravenous tube was in his arm. A urinary catheter snaked from beneath the sheet to its hiding place under the bed. Pir Rasheed smiled when he saw me there, and laughed. "I was not resting enough at night," he said, "So God decided to give me some forced bed rest. I was brought here!" He waved at the hospital room, as robustly as the intravenous drip would allow. He lay quietly when his taciturn disciple, Babu Khan from Golconda, came in to make a special *du'a* for him. Babu knew some healing prayers. So Pir Rasheed just lay quietly while prayers were murmured over him, but he seemed impatient as if he let them go on for the sake of those praying, but didn't really require them himself.

After some days, his health improved. He moved home but had to stay hooked up to the catheter. When I visited him at home, he was restless. "For three weeks, I have not been able to go to Friday prayers because I'm stuck with this tube," he said, waving meekly at the yellowish catheter. "I can't go out of the house, and I can't keep my *wuzu'*. This is terrible. How can I go to the Astana? Maybe tomorrow." Tomorrow would be Friday again. Everyone in his family told him sternly that he could not go to the Astana the next day. He just looked up and said, "Maybe tomorrow."

When I left the room, his eldest son Mukarram complained to me that Pir Rasheed kept trying to get rid of the catheter so he could go to the Astana on Friday for prayers and to visit the tombs of his ancestors. "He begs us to take him on a motorcycle to the Astana! Can you believe that? He thinks only about going there and not about his health. Isn't that unbelievable?"

BACK TO THE PAST AND INTO THE FUTURE

Pir Rasheed used to travel every Friday from his home deep in the old city of Hyderabad to the Astana Kaleemi located on the other side of the city in Shaikhpet. This locale used to be on the outskirts of town but is now engorged by the expanding modern city of Hyderabad. The journey takes over an hour due to traffic congestion. When his family's van was broken down, which seemed to be most of the time, he would perch precariously on the back of somebody's motorcycle to be whizzed through traffic, his delicate almost 80-year-old body wafted with diesel fumes. He would do anything to get to the Astana to perform his Friday congregational prayers at the Husayni

Masjid, the mosque where his great-grandfather had been the Imam. Beside the mosque is a small building that houses the tombs of his ancestors who were leaders of the Kaleemi Sufi Order in Hyderabad. Beyond it, on the other side of the alley, is a wide graveyard where many of his family members are buried along with their followers. Just down the road was his ancestral home; this is the neighborhood where he grew up. But that home is now demolished and the ancestral property stolen by relatives. The whole neighborhood is now ringed by high-rise apartments that are growing steadily skyward, sucking up the ground water and filling in the reservoirs while shutting out views of the rocky pink hills and green toddy palms that once defined the horizon.

This neighborhood is named Shaikhpet due to the dargah of Shaykh Husayn Shah Wali. Husayn Shah Wali was a Chishti Sufi master who blessed Hyderabad for posterity even as builders and rulers are now ruining it with thoughtless development. In the sixteenth century, he served as a courtier in the Qutb Shahi dynasty of Golconda and he engineered the building of their city's main water reservoir. He was a descendant of Hazrat Gesu Daraz, the first descendant of this great Chishti saint to settle at Hyderabad. He was well-received by the king of Golconda, Ibrahim Qutb Shah, who was a Shi'i but welcomed this Sunni from the Chishti Order who was also a Sayyid, a descendant of the Prophet.

Husayn Shah Wali, like many Sufi leaders, mediated in the often-bitter contest between Shi'i and Sunni Muslims. One later chronicler of Sufis in the Deccan explains his position in this way.

> Those who were Sunni were very pleased that the king had demonstrated his attitude of reconciliation and protecting the rights of all… It was the policy of the Qutb Shahi rulers to protect reconciliation between different sects and keep their distance from those who wanted to sow dissent and strife… Husayn Shah Wali chose to get so close and intimate with the kings of his age so that by means of his influence, the common people might have their needs met and their rights protected, so that each one, whether rich or poor, can have his cares conveyed to the king. Outwardly he was a prince, but inwardly he was a Sufi.[37]

As this Sunni courtier, who was a Chishti Sufi master, oversaw building a reservoir, friction developed between him and his Shi'i patron. The king wanted to name the reservoir "Ibrahim Sagar" after himself, but the people called it "Husayn Sagar" after the builder. As royal proclamations tried to assert its proper name, a popularity contest ensued which neither side had instigated. When laborers were asked where work was to be found, others would answer that jobs were to be found at Husayn Sagar. No matter how hard the nobles and royalty tried to change the name to Ibrahim Sagar, none of their labor changed the situation.

The tongue of common people proved to be the authoritative decision of fate and Husayn Sagar remained its name. The King, Ibrahim Qutb Shah, relented and ultimately decided to build a new reservoir further from the city, which he named Ibrahim Sagar. It still exists and provides drinking water to Hyderabad, though it is now drying up due to exponentially greater demand as the city grows. But Husayn Sagar has become the center of Hyderabad and its symbol. The state administrative buildings were built next to it. Pleasure parks ring its banks. The new IMAX mega theater was built close to its shoreline, now that cinema is the major hobby of all Hyderabadis. A huge statue of Buddha was erected in the center of the reservoir, and massive plaster effigies of Ganesh are immersed in its waters every year after they are worshipped by Hindus during the riotous 10 days of Ganesh Puja.

When Husayn Shah Wali died in 1626, the kings of Golconda built him a massive dargah with a lofty dome. The neighborhood around it became known as Shaikhpet, or "Village of the Sufi Master" in the local Telugu language. That village was fed by another small water reservoir, perhaps also built by Husayn Shah Wali to nourish this parched landscape. The village that grew up around his tomb is overtaken by the growing city, and is merely a neighborhood of the vast metropolis of Hyderabad. The dargah of Husayn Shah Wali is still well known but it is almost invisible until one is just upon it, encroached as it is by new high-rise buildings along the Hyderabad-to-Bombay highway. Pir Rasheed would visit this dargah every Friday, after offering his *namaz-e jum'a* or congregation prayer. He would walk through the courtyard and stand at the door with his disciples arrayed behind him, and offer Fatiha for the soul of Husayn Shah Wali. Pir Rasheed would thank the saint for having granted his descendants a place to stay, at the mosque beside his dargah, and for having allowed a small room of this mosque to house their tombs and develop into the Astana Kaleemi. However, Pir Rasheed never entered into the dargah proper, but always offered his prayers and blessings from the doorway. He was sure to never encroach upon the space overseen by others. He would hand roses to the caretakers of the dargah, and they would enter to place these flowers on the tomb. This was a Friday ritual of commemoration and respect.

On the far side of the Shaikhpet neighborhood, beyond the small water reservoir that marks its border, rises a high barren hillock. That is where one of the earliest Sufis to come to Hyderabad is buried, long before there was a city called Hyderabad. That is Baba Fakhr al-Din Pahari and his tiny dargah with high green flags flapping in the wind still stands on the hill, a sentinel guarding the welfare of the city by looking out into the future and back into the past. When Pir Rasheed's family lived near the Astana Kaleemi, they served as caretakers of that lonely dargah on the hill; each year his family would organize the 'urs celebration at the dargah. The Astana Kaleemi, far below and closer to town, was the closest Sufi institution so Pir Rasheed's family naturally adopted these duties and kept alive the memory of this Sufi pioneer in Hyderabad.

Baba Fakhr al-Din Pahari is one of the earliest Sufis to settle in the region of Hyderabad. He is said to be one of several brothers who belonged to the Suhrawardi Order and came from Baghdad, though it is not clear if they were brothers by birth or "brothers" by initiation since they were all disciples of Shaykh Shihab al-Din Suhrawardi in Baghdad. The eldest brother, Baba Sharf al-Din Pahari, settled on a rocky hill south-east of the city along with his brother Musa Suhrawardi. From among their siblings, Baba Shihab al-Din Pahari settled on a rocky hill south-west of the city (near where the new airport of Hyderabad is at a place called Shamsabad) and Baba Fakhr al-Din Pahari settled on a hill to the west of the city.[38] Pahari means "of the hill" in Urdu. The leader of this group of Sufis was Sharf al-Din. He was born in Iraq and was a Sayyid descended from Sayyid 'Ali Naqi (the tenth Imam as recognized by the Shi'i community of Hyderabad). He was not a Shi'i Muslim but rather a Sufi of the Suhrawardi Order. That was the first community of Sufis organized into a discrete Order with rules and customs and guidebooks. The Suhrawardis were pioneers. From the capital city of the Sunni Caliphate in Baghdad, they spread out over the Islamic world to preach by word and teach by deed. In most regions of India, they were the first Sufis to settle among the local population and Hyderabad is no exception. Baba Sharf al-Din Pahari was a disciple of Shihab al-Din Suhrawardi, who ordered him to shift to India when he was 45 years old. He came by boat, sailing on the monsoon winds that blow eastward every year, which brought merchants and missionaries from Jewish, Christian and Islamic communities to India since ancient times.

Legend relates that he arrived in 1233 CE with his brothers and seventy followers. They traveled inland by caravan from the coast to the rocky hills of the Deccan.[39] In those days, the Kakatiya Dynasty was in power. Its rulers built monumental temples for Shiva and high mud-walled forts on the hills to control trade routes and diamond mines. Their glorious capital was at Warangal, whose gateways were carved with ferocious lions, majestic elephants and fearsome crocodiles, and they built a strong fort at Golconda to control the area that would later become Hyderabad.

The caravan of Suhrawardi Sufis arrived at this fort town and lived on small barren hillocks outside the settled area, about a century before the armies of the Islamic Sultanate of Delhi marched south to conquer this region. The Islam of peaceful coexistence came first and has deeper roots than the Islam of conquest and domination. The stories of these brothers from the Suhrawardi Order may be legendary but they preserve a kernel of truth. They lived in peace as Muslim guests of predominantly Hindu communities that turned to them for healing, advice and practical help. Stories are told of these Sufis finding lost buffalos and healing sick cows for their local hosts.[40] In turn, the Suhrawardi Sufis tried to wean the local population from reliance on idol worship and reinforce ethical values.

Photo 9: Pir Rasheed praying at the doorway of dargah of Husayn Shah Wali

THE DOOR'S JAMB

The dargah of Baba Sharf al-Din Pahari is a very famous place now. The sixth Nizam of Hyderabad, Mahbub 'Ali Pasha, used to make *chilla* there for weeks at a time and not come out to administer his kingdom! It was the sixth Nizam who invited Hazrat Inayat Khan to Hyderabad to perform as a court musician, leading to a transformation in that Sufi's life. The beloved sixth Nizam was a great patron of poetry, music and Sufism, though it is debated whether he was an effective ruler. In any case, he and his family members in the ruling dynasty patronized the dargah in the late 19th and early 20th century, building it up in a rich way. Today, people from Hyderabad go there for devotions and to get fresh air and sit on the terrace for picnics. Blessings, health and happiness—all the ingredients for a good life—can be found there in one place. In contrast, the dargah of Baba Fakhr al-Din Pahari is a lonely little place, one room for the tomb, one room on the side for the custodian's family, and on the other side of the rocky peak, a cave shelter where Baba Fakhr al-Din used to meditate. A dirt road goes up at a precarious angle to the top. That is the extent of it.

Baba Fakhr al-Din lived so long ago that no successors remain to care for his tomb and shrine. Nobody lived on the hill back then because there was only as much water as could be held in reservoirs that collected rainwater during the monsoon months in channels and tanks carefully carved into the living rock. There was enough water for visitors to wash for prayer or take a needed drink, but not enough for a family to live there. Now water is piped up and a little house has been constructed—a family has moved in and has taken over custodial duties. Pir Rasheed's family, who used to take care of that place, have settled in the old city closer to schools, jobs and modern amenities.

Still, from the Astana Kaleemi, one can look westward and see the hillock with the dargah barely visible at the top. Nowadays, smog and traffic fumes often obscure the view, as the highway towards Bombay snakes its way past both the Astana and the hill, carrying traffic westward. Just beyond the hillock, the new financial district and high-tech business hub are growing to the north of the highway, while the University of Hyderabad and the new airport are expanding south of the highway. High-rise buildings are coming up: one complex called Lanco Hills is stationed at the foot of Baba Fakhr al-Din's hill, threatening to block the view from the Astana to the dargah. Lanco Hills construction blasted one side of the hillock into bits, to grind up into concrete for the construction. The blasting caused a section of the dirt road up the hill to collapse, and almost destroyed the tomb of Baba Fakhr al-Din's co-traveler, Baba Burhan al-Din, who is buried on the hill's edge.

Sufi authorities of Hyderabad charged Lanco Hills Construction with violating their *waqf* endowment lands, but Lanco Hills was very connected to the ruling Congress Party politicians and everyone knows that the state government's Waqf Board (which regulates the land donated by Muslims to upkeep of mosques, madrasas, dargahs and charitable institutions) is corrupt. The construction continued while pilgrims shifted the road slightly away from the blasted side of the hillock. Then the US economy collapsed in 2008 and ripples of distress spread through international finance. Indian politicians and businessmen crowed that the Indian economy was insulated from the economic disaster. For a year it appeared to be so but Hyderabad's high-tech firms, pharmacy companies, off-shore data-processing offices and banks relied on the US economy to fund their growth. The overheated bubble of Hyderabad's new urban growth cooled, then popped. The cranes perched above the steel beams of the skeletal towers of Lanco Hills remain motionless, and their concrete skin was left unfinished with huge piles of blasted stone and sand laying at their feet.

APPEARANCES THAT DECEIVE

It is the nature of worldly power to crest and to ebb. Wealth, power and prestige flow like the tides of the ocean. They advance and recede with a rhythm of their own. Their inexorable flow carries along everything in its path, pushing and pulling with a force that nobody can control. Those intent on getting power or staying in power only deceive themselves as they destroy or damage others on all sides.

The very embodiment of ambition and worldly power is the Mughal emperor Aurangzeb. He is one of the most vibrant characters in the whole panorama of the history of the Deccan. The Mughal empire was based in North India at Delhi, Agra and Lahore, but it looked with acquisitive thirst toward the South and the riches that it harbored. As a prince, Aurangzeb built his power-base as the Viceroy of the Deccan province. When he wrested the position of Emperor from his own brothers who competed with him, he remained intent on conquering the Deccan and eliminating its Qutb Shahi kings. They were Shi'i rulers who had generously patronized many Sufis and Sayyids in their kingdom, thus creating a harmonious sectarian environment and a deep tradition of live-and-let-live. Husayn Shah Wali was the embodiment of this policy. In contrast, Aurangzeb held a more chauvinist attitude of Sunni dominance and he feared that his main enemy, the Maratha warriors who followed Shivaji, were getting support from the current Qutb Shahi ruler, Sultan Abu'l-Hasan Tana Shah. Aurangzeb swore to conquer Hyderabad, depose the

Qutb Shahi ruler, deprive the Marathas of any support, and absorb the whole Deccan region into his Mughal empire.

In 1687, Aurangzeb's army marched on Hyderabad intent on conquest. The city's ruler, Abu'l-Hasan Tana Shah, was forced to take refuge with the Qutb Shahi army in the fort of Golconda. The Mughal army ravaged Hyderabad but could not conquer its indefatigable fort. The story is told that both sides in the battle had holy men protecting their positions. As the Mughal army prolonged the siege and Qutb Shahi forces in the fort grew weary, a strange storm blew over Golconda. Dark clouds poured rain and gusty winds blew dust against the Mughal forces, ruining their cannons and forcing the soldiers to call off the assault to take shelter in their tents.

> Aurangzeb was patrolling through his army camp in the storm-raging darkness. It was his habit to do so in disguise, such that he could examine the real condition of his troops. At night, he noticed that one tent was lit up from within despite the thick darkness. He approached and noticed from a distance that within the tent, two of his soldiers with otherworldly concentration were reciting the Qur'an while oblivious to all worldly concerns. The storm winds were blowing fiercely, yet their lamp stayed calmly lit. As one poem says, "That lamp which God lights surely none can blow out."
>
> Witnessing this scene, Aurangzeb was amazed. The emperor approached the radiant tent. The two Mughal soldiers, engrossed in their recitation of God's word, did not notice him draw near, until he spoke to them saying, "What is this? Two holy men are present in my army but our siege is still unsuccessful? This is unbelievable!" The two saints raised their eyes from the Qur'an and found the emperor himself standing over them. They rose to pay him respect and replied, "How are we responsible for this matter?" The emperor replied, "Of course you are responsible! You are soldiers in the Mughal army and you know well how we have languished here for months in a long, drawn-out siege. You must certainly lend your spiritual concentration to our victory! Or are you going to simply sit there and wait for the army of Islam to suffer defeat?" They answered, "Does this war have any Islamic justification when both sides fighting are Muslims?"[41]

Aurangzeb stayed for a long time in the tent insisting on the war strategy with the two Sufis. They were Yusuf and Sharif al-Din who belonged to the Kaleemi branch of the Chishti Order in Delhi.

At last, the two Sufis saw that Aurangzeb would not leave them alone and was disturbing their recitation of the Qur'an. They said, "Very well then, bring us a piece of fired clay tile." The Emperor searched long and hard until he finally found a shard of pottery tile. He brought it to them. They wrote a message on it with a piece of charcoal. Handing it to Aurangzeb, they said, "Have this delivered to the poor shoe-maker who sits outside at Langar Hauz [outside the fortress gate that leads along the main caravan road to Hyderabad] and bring his reply." When the tile piece was handed to this unkempt cobbler sitting on the side of the road, he took it and read it. With an angry frown, he turned the tile piece over and wrote a reply on the other side and said, "Take it back!" The Emperor was befuddled but took the tile piece back to the two Sufis in his army camp, who were busy reciting the Qur'an. They paused to received the tile.

They read the reply scrawled on its backside and fell into profound silence. Then they told the emperor, "Conquering the fort will be terribly difficult. There is a great holy man protecting Abu'l-Hasan Tana Shah, the Qutb Shahi ruler, and his forces." Hearing this news, Aurangzeb said in a subdued but fiercely determined voice, "Are there no great holy men to support me and my forces? Should I not expect to depend upon the spirit of you two Sufis to lend your aid to my cause?" In the end, the Mughal emperor insisted that they try once again to write a message to the holy man protecting the fortress of Golconda. They reluctantly took up the piece of tile again and, after pondering for a long while, wrote a new message on its front side.

Aurangzeb had the tile taken again to Langar Hauz where the shoe-maker was sitting along the road that led from the fortress gate to Hyderabad city. The shoe-maker took the tile and again glared at it. His face contorted in deep perplexity while the Emperor stood quivering with impatience. After a long time, Aurangzeb hissed, "The time for dawn prayer is fast approaching and before the rise of the sun I have to get back to my own shoe-repairmen, so hurry up and say something!" The impoverished shoe-maker shook with anger as sparks of rage flew from his eyes. His hands went limp as the tile fell to the ground. He donned his worn-out leather apron and gathered into it the old pieces of shoes and tools that were scattered around him. He muttered, "Thus is the will of God! For fifty years I have sat here in isolation at the foot of the fortress ramparts. Finally, your cobblers have forced me to get up. Go and tell them—'He has moved from his place!'"

Aurangzeb returned to his army camp where the soldiers were finishing their dawn prayers. He found the two Sufis of the Kaleemi Order, Yusuf and Sharif al-Din, and now understood their true prestige despite their appearance as common soldiers. They greeted the emperor and congratulated him on the impending conquest of the fortress saying, "Tonight, the Mughal forces will enter the fortress. The one who was protecting it with unseen forces has abandoned his position. He appeared to you like a poor cobbler but in fact he was the spiritual axis (*qutb*) of this kingdom! For the past fifty years, he has been nourishing and protecting this realm and its rulers."[42]

That evening, spies sent by Aurangzeb's son, Prince Azam Shah, bribed some of the Qutb Shahi forces to betray their ruler and open a small gate from within the fortress. A brigade of Mughals snuck into the fortress at night and threw open the main gates to the Mughal army which stormed the fort. An imposing and apparently impregnable fortress could be rendered as fragile as a canvas tent. An incognito and apparently impoverished shoe-maker could be as strong as a stone wall. As the Bible says, "The stone that the builder refused will always be the head corner-stone."[43]

In the end, the last Qutb Shahi ruler, Abu'l-Hasan Tana Shah, was imprisoned in Aurangabad; when he died he was buried in the nearby sacred precinct of Khuldabad, in the courtyard of the dargah of Burhan al-Din Ghareeb. Aurangzeb conquered the whole Deccan but watched his huge empire slowly unravel; when he died he was also buried in Khuldabad in accordance with his will, in the courtyard of the dargah of Zain al-Din Shirazi, the successor of Burhan al-Din Ghareeb. During his lifetime, Aurangzeb chastised and manipulated Sufis to support his imperial ambitions, but upon his death, he consigned his mortal remains to rest in the shade of their domes in hopes of forgiveness, for he took power by deposing his father Shah Jahan and held on to power by slaying his three brothers. May God be merciful to us all and keep us from drifting in the tides of worldly power!

After Mughal armies left Hyderabad, the city was in a ruined state. Yet Yusuf and Sharif al-Din stayed on. They threw off their apparent profession as soldiers and settled into a life of service as Chishti Sufis. They are buried side by side in Nampally, near where the Mughal army headquarters had camped (a neighborhood still known as "Fateh Maidan" or Field of Victory). Their dargah is now the most active Sufi shrine in Hyderabad's modern downtown. They introduced the new community of Kaleemi Sufis into Hyderabad and laid the foundation for Pir Rasheed's family to function in the city.

The poor cobbler, who was a powerful Sufi from among the *abdal*s or hidden saints, was named Meeran Shah Husayni. He moved from the gateway of the Golconda fortress and settled in a small cave close to the dargah of Husayn Shah Wali. His grave is there in the cave formed by several great boulders leaning upon each other. The cave is now clean and whitewashed. The rocky entrance is fitted with a small wooden door painted green, through which one must stoop to enter. A small triangular opening in the back of the cave is now latticed with tile-and-plaster *jali* (lattice work) in simple Deccani style, which lets in fresh air and filtered light. It is a most beautiful and cool shelter which welcomes visitors.[44]

Pir Rasheed used to come here to offer flowers, recite prayers and sweep dust off the tomb and out of its cave. Every Friday, he would come to the Astana Kaleemi to offer Friday prayers in the Husayni mosque. He then sat in the Astana and offered Fatiha for the souls of his ancestors, the leaders of the Kaleemi Order in present-day Hyderabad. He then laid a single rose on the graves of his other family members who are buried around the Astana. Then he walked down the alley with disciples and family members to the dargah of Husayn Shah Wali, whose tomb towers over the neighborhood. He stooped to touch the stone of the entryway steps, then kiss his fingertips and run his dusty hand over his head to show his respect. He entered the dargah complex and walked up to the shrine's doorway to greet the caretakers, but he would never step inside. Gazing at the tomb from outside the shrine, he recited *Fatiha* and offered benedictions on the Prophet and his family and wished peace and blessings on those buried there. But his ancestors had promised to always keep a respectful distance from the dargah of Husayn Shah Wali when they settled in this neighborhood a century and half ago.

The Astana Kaleemi is just next door but we Kaleemi Sufis are careful never to encroach upon the dargah of Husayn Shah Wali and its custodians. The custodians offer us rose petals and incense ash from inside the tomb shrine, and we back out of the courtyard respectfully. Then we walk a few steps down the alley, through a high gateway and up a small hill to the cave of Meeran Shah Husayni. There, Pir Rasheed always recited Fatiha and blessings on him and gave thanks for his sacrifice of having resolved to move from his position. His shifting to this cave and abandoning the fort of Golconda allowed the Mughal army to conquer this region and bring the Kaleemi Order to this land.

After this ritual, Pir Rasheed was free to return to his home in the old city, to his single upstairs room that is called the khanqah. He pays his family one rupee each month as rent for the room, so that it is carefully designated as a separate entity and dedicated to the Kaleemi Order's activities. It is threadbare and simple, but there he sits. The ceiling fan slowly spins, precariously lurching to one side as if it will fly off its pivot, when the electricity is actually working. The small room is usually bustling with people who come for healing or blessings or consultations, who struggle to get up and down the narrow spiral staircase made of rickety wrought iron. The base of the stairs is piled high with worn-out shoes of leather and plastic, tossed about carelessly as people hurry to get upstairs to the khanqah room. It all looks rather shabby and unkempt, but appearances can be deceiving.

BEGGARS ABOUT TOWN

I headed to the Kaleemi Astana to meet Pir Rasheed, since he would be there for Friday prayers. I took along Zaida Nassier, who was visiting again from Bangalore. When I picked her up from her guesthouse, she presented me with a rakhi bracelet to celebrate the Indian holiday of Rakhsha-Bandhan. Women tie these bracelets on the wrists of their brothers as a token of their closeness and protective relationship. I was very moved that she would think of giving a bracelet to me, and as she tied it on my wrist, she said, "Now it is like you are my big brother—or I should say my very tall Sufi brother!"

We arrived at the Astana to find Pir Rasheed in a particularly happy mood since his daughter was visiting from Jeddah. It was good to see him smiling so radiantly, and he impressed me by inviting Zaida into the Astana room where the tombs of his ancestors are. Women are not generally permitted to enter the tomb space of a dargah, so I had hesitated with Zaida just outside the doorway, allowing her to look in but not stepping in myself. From within, Pir Rasheed called Zaida to come inside and he explained to her how his own lineage was related to that of Hazrat Inayat Khan, through the personality of Sayyid Muhammad Hasan Jeeli Kaleemi, whose tomb was just before her. Then we all went to the dargah of Husayn Shah Wali, just down the road and the cave of the majzub, Meeran Shah Husayni. Then Zaida and I went to visit the dargah of Sayyid Abu Hashim Madani. It was a fine afternoon.

Later that evening, I picked up Zaida and also Firoozeh Papan-Matin, an Iranian professor in America who studied Persian Sufi literature. She was fascinated by the writing and personality of 'Ayn al-Quzat Hamadani and authored a study of his astounding book about mystical love, the *Tamheedat* or "Fundamental Principles." She discovered that the first and best commentary on the *Tamheedat* was written by Chishti Sufis in the Deccan, and so she moved to Hyderabad to author a new study. In her personal spiritual journey, she was interested in Hindu philosophy and yoga and has a conflicted relationship with Islam, which is understandable for someone who grew up in Iran where Islam is politicized so ideologically. Firoozeh, Zaida and I went for qawwali at the Hall of Shah Khamosh (*sama'-khana*), a gathering which happens on the thirteenth day of every lunar month. They were both very impressed and had a moving experience there. Zaida said that the qawwali here was purer than in Delhi at Nizam al-Din. Firoozeh had never listened to qawwali in a ritual setting before, but reported that she went into a "meditative state" despite being distracted by all the women chatting in their separate space.

During that musical assembly, we listened to a ghazal by Jami that I had not heard before. It includes the inspiring line, "Break this duality, Jami—be of single mind and single heart!"[45] God created love in order to seduce us out of our egoistic addiction to duality.

In each moment, you show your own beauty differently You throw us in turmoil again, goad our desire differently	هر لحظه جمالِ خود نوعے دگر آرائی شورِ دگر انگیزی شوقِ دگر افزائی
What can reason grasp of you, how can intellect describe you? Thought cannot attain you and words cannot contain you	عقل از تو چہ دریا بد تا وصفِ تو اندیشد در عقل نمی گنجی در وصف نمی آرائی
Your concealment is revealed, your appearance is concealed You are concealed from all but revealed in everything	پنہائے تو پیدا پیدائے تو پنہاں ہم از ہمہ پنہائی ہم بر ہمہ پیدائی
From the shadow you cast over the dust of your appearance All beautiful creatures discover the basis of their own beauty	زاں سایہ کہ افگندی بر خاک گہہ جلوہ دارند ہمہ خوباں سرمایۂ زیبائی
You never show your face but through veils of water and dust But how can the radiant sun shine plastered over with clay?	بے پردۂ آب و گِل ما را نمائی رو خورشیدِ درخشاں را تاکے بگل اندائی
Oh you who are adored everywhere everywhere that you appear You drive mad with desire hundreds of lovers everywhere	اے گشتہ عیاں ہر جا ہر جا کہ شوی پیدا گردد ز غمت شیدا صد عاشقِ ہر جائی

> Break this duality, Jami—be
> of single mind and single heart!
> Maybe you will find your place
> of rest in the realm of unity
>
> جامی ز دوئی بگسل یکروئی شو دیکدل
> باشد که کنی منزل در عالمِ یکتائی

GOING WEST

The poet Jami urged himself to "break this duality... and find your place of rest in the realm of unity." One of the most persistent dualities that we must break is the division of the world and its people into East and West. This legacy from the colonial past continues to structure our world and create conflicts where there should be none. One of the spiritual heroes of the last century was Hazrat Inayat Khan, who broke through this duality with creative verve.

Pir Rasheed told me stories about Hazrat Inayat Khan, who achieved renown by taking Sufism to America and Europe in the early 20th century. He was a skilled musician and Sufi in the Chishti Order. Although his Sufi order took novel forms in those new environments, he belonged to the Kaleemi Order and learned his Chishti-style Sufism in Hyderabad. Those in this lineage are like cousins to those in our lineage.

Pir Rasheed told me how Hazrat Inayat Khan was born in Baroda in Gujarat but came to Hyderabad. Pir Rasheed was not present then, of course. How could he know these things about Pir Inayat Khan's visit to Hyderabad? He had heard these stories from Sayyid Muhammad Zia al-Hasan, who was alive when these events happened. Pir Rasheed told the stories so vividly, as if he had actually lived through them, or as if it were not Pir Rasheed speaking at all but rather Sayyid Muhammad Zia al-Hasan.

Inayat Khan had come to Hyderabad as a musician. Inayat Khan desired to take initiation in a Sufi Order, and indications in dreams and meditations pointed him toward the Chishti Order. In his meditations, he was shown the person who would become his Pir, and that was Abu Hashim Madani. He met several Sufi masters but did not receive a positive response from them, so he continued to search for six months, until he came South to perform in the court of the Nizam, the ruler of Hyderabad.

In Hyderabad, he met a great Sufi scholar named Khayr al-Mubeen, who is buried in Hyderabad (at a dargah called Khitta-ye Saliheen in the neighborhood of Pathargathi). He was a mureed of Sayyid Muhammad Hasan Jeeli Kaleemi, the great grandfather of Pir Rasheed. He said that at that time, Sayyid Muhammad Hasan had only two mureeds: Khayr al-Mubeen and Abu Hashim Madani. Pir Inayat Khan confided in his friend, Khayr al-Mubeen, that he desired to take initiation from a Sufi master.

In those days, Khayr al-Mubeen would organize a grand majlis or assembly on two occasions each year: one for "Gyarhween-e Shareef" on the eleventh of Rabee' al-Sani in honor of Shaykh 'Abd al-Qadir Jeelani, and the other on twelfth of Rabee' al-Awwal in honor of the Prophet Muhammad's birthday. They were so famous that the Nizam of Hyderabad would attend these assemblies. Every day from the first of the Islamic month and running continually for eleven or twelve days (depending on which celebration it was) there would be speeches on Qur'an, lectures about hadees, stories about the Prophet, and teachings about Sufi mysticism; these gatherings, called majlis, ran for two or three hours daily. Inayat Khan came to Hyderabad and attended one of these celebrations. In the majlis organized by Khayr al-Mubeen, his Pir-brother Abu Hashim Madani entered the gathering.

Inayat Khan met Abu Hashim Madani and recognized him from the image seen in his meditations. He asked to take initiation from Abu Hashim Madani then and there. He received tarbeeyat or Sufi training from him, and then Abu Hashim Madani requested him to go west. He left India, visited America and married an American woman and then settled for some time in Europe, performing music, teaching about Sufism, and giving initiation to disciples. On a visit to India in 1927, he passed away in Delhi just near the dargah of Hazrat Nizam al-Din Awliya. His tomb has become a small and serene dargah, with a fine library, educational classes, and a music school. His sons continued to teach and guide in the Sufi path in both Europe and America. His son, Pir Vilayat Khan, spread the Order widely in America, while his other children also worked in various ways to promote his teachings.

COMING EAST

While Pir Rasheed was ill in the hospital, I received by email a request from someone from the USA in the Inayati Order. He was doing some research on Pir Vilayat Khan, who had passed away in 2004 and is buried in Delhi. This fellow intended to write a biography of Pir Vilayat Khan and wanted to consult Pir Rasheed on some issues. I waited to consult with Pir Rasheed until his health improved.

The next week, I found Pir Rasheed at home in stronger health. His mureed Saleem Ghori was there with me. Pir Rasheed was lying on the bed. He asked me to sit up on the bed near him, but I didn't. Saleem and I sat on the carpet right beside his bed. Pir Rasheed insisted that I sit up on the bed, but I couldn't. Saleem and I sat on the floor and we had time for a long talk. I asked Pir Rasheed if he could listen to the account of Pir Vilayat Khan that had been sent to him, via me, from the Inayati Order in the USA. He agreed and had the strength to discuss this in great detail. I read out to him the "Autobiographical Notes of Pir Vilayat Khan," an oral account by Pir Vilayat Khan about his visit to Hyderabad, which had been penned by one of his disciples.

Pir Rasheed commented that he remembered well the visit of Pir Vilayat Khan to Hyderabad. It was in 1950 from January until April or May. He stayed for a few months and would come to Pir Rasheed's family house in the Yaqutpura neighborhood of the old city every morning. He would wear Indian clothes in the style of Hyderabad, a kurta and pajama with a sherwani coat over the top. He must have been in his late 20s at that time. He would come to the house in the morning to speak with Pir Rasheed's father, Sayyid Fakhr al-Hasan Jeeli Kaleemi. Pir Rasheed was a young man at the time, about 18 years old, working at the State Bank of Hyderabad during the day and taking college classes at night to finish his graduation. So Pir Vilayat would come to the house each morning before 9 am when Pir Rasheed had to leave for work at the bank, because Pir Rasheed served as his translator. Pir Vilayat did not speak Urdu so Pir Rasheed would translate for him while he spoke with his father, Sayyid Fakhr al-Hasan, who did not speak English.

In this record, Pir Vilayat Khan said that after his father, Hazrat Inayat Khan, had passed away: "I went to Ajmer and made a retreat there, forty days fasting. There was a *murshid* of the lineage of the Chishtis who wanted very much for me to take initiation with him and I said, 'No, I can't do that because my murshid is my father.' He respected that. That was 'Azeez Miyan (of Rai Bareli in Uttar Pradesh), a great being, with thousands of disciples. He taught me the zikr and *wazeefa* and so on. I went there from time to time. And then at a certain moment I went back to Ajmer and did another retreat. And then I heard that the son of the murshid of my father, Abu Hashim Madani, was going to die. I rushed to Hyderabad to see him before he died. And he died in the meantime." Pir Rasheed clarified that the murshid of Inayat Khan is Abu Hashim Madani who lived in Hyderabad and whose dargah is still there in the neighborhood of the old city called Rekab Gunj, near the Purana Pul Darwaza.

Pir Rasheed still visits that dargah occasionally, but very infrequently. It is not in good repair, though some mureeds of Pir Rasheed have recently renovated it and built a small domed pavilion over it and paved the gravesite with white marble. His mureed 'Abdul Rasheed did the repairs and built the dome at the dargah, while some followers of Pir Zia, like Carmen Husayn in Delhi, raised the money to pay for it. The dargah is in a graveyard known as "Takia Rang 'Ali Shah" just near the more famous dargah of Miyan Pasha, known as Miyan Paisa. That dargah is visible from the main road, but the dargah of Abu

Hashim Madani is hidden inside the graveyard beyond a wall and gate, so it is not visited much at all. Pir Rasheed did not know that Abu Hashim Madani had any other khaleefa or successors except for Pir Inayat Khan. Thus, no local followers visit the tomb and take care of the dargah.

Photo 10 A, B and C: Tomb of Abu Hashim Madani

THE DOOR'S JAMB

When Pir Vilayat came to Hyderabad, Sayyid Fakhr al-Hasan was still alive and his son, Pir Rasheed, was in college. Pir Vilayat did not come directly to Fakhr al-Hasan upon reaching Hyderabad. Fakhr al-Hasan was not so famous, his family did not live right at the dargah of his ancestors, and that dargah was not often visited in any case, so he was hard to find. Pir Rasheed remembers that Pir Vilayat had visited all the famous dargahs and well-known Sufi leaders in Hyderabad. He had gone to see Shaykh 'Abd al-Qadeer Siddiqi, who was a famous teacher and poet nicknamed "Hasrat" who is buried at the dargah called Siddiqi Gulshan. Pir Vilayat also visited Yahya Pasha Qadiri whose dargah is at Misri Gunj in the Qazipura neighborhood of Hyderabad. He also met Pasha Husayni of the dargah called Qadiri Chaman which is near Falaknuma Palace in Hyderabad. He also met 'Abdullah Shah, known as Muhaddis-e Dekkan, who was a well-known hadees teacher and Shaykh of the Naqshbandi and Qadiri Orders, whose dargah is at Misri Gunj in Hyderabad. Only after going to all these famous places and teachers did Pir Vilayat come to Sayyid Fakhr al-Hasan Jeeli Kaleemi. Maybe he learned about the Kaleemi Sufi from these other Shaykhs of Hyderabad, or maybe he knew of him by reputation before he arrived in Hyderabad but could not find him in Hyderabad until he got directions from these other masters. In any case, Pir Vilayat came to the house of Pir Rasheed's father.

The record of Pir Vilayat's mureed recalls that he continued to say: "There was the grandson of the grand murshid of my Murshid—a lovely old man." Pir Rasheed noted that this was Sayyid Fakhr al-Hasan Jeeli Kaleemi, the grandson of Sayyid Muhammad Hasan Jeeli Kaleemi who had been the Sufi master of Abu Hashim Madani. Pir Vilayat continued to write: "He was in a very mystical state. He said, 'Last night I received a message from your father that I must train you for your position as a Pir-o-Murshid. I must give you the classical training.' I said, 'Oh no, I can't do that because my murshid is my father.' And he said 'Oh yes, I'll always respect that. I'm only a mentor for you, but your lineage is directly from your father.' I made a retreat under his guidance."

At this point in the account, Sayyid Fakhr al-Hasan makes an important distinction between different kinds of spiritual relationship with a Pir. He makes the distinction that one can have a Pir who gives initiation (*bay'at*), a Pir who gives instruction in meditation (*talqeen-e zikr*), a Pir who gives ethical training (*tarbeeyat*), or a Pir who gives only blessing (*tabarruk* or *baraka*). As for a Pir who gives initiation, one can have only one such Pir in a lifetime and one's relationship with him is exclusive and special. This is what Pir Vilayat was thinking of when he shied away from any other Pir in India, because he already had initiation from his father, Pir Inayat Khan.

Sayyid Fakhr al-Hasan told him that there are other ways to have a spiritual relationship with a Pir, and that he needed to learn ways of meditating and other devotions (*talqeen*).

Pir Rasheed recounted how his father asked Pir Vilayat to make a chilla or retreat for some days (often up to forty days). He directed Pir Vilayat to go to the dargah of Baba Fakhr al-Din Pahari, which is very small and isolated, way up on a rocky hill above the city just beyond the Astana Kaleemi. Pir Rasheed's family used to sponsor the annual 'urs celebrations there, so they had a special relationship with that place. This is where Sayyid Fakhr al-Din directed Pir Vilayat to go in order to find a peaceful place with no distractions. Pir Vilayat continued to write that the spiritual teacher instructed him: "When you're doing the zikr, you should just get into his consciousness. And that's what establishes a link, you see. Don't do the zikr as though you're doing it yourself." This was the spiritual instruction of Sayyid Fakhr al-Hasan Jeeli Kaleemi. Pir Rasheed commented that this instruction was how to achieve *fana fi'l-shaykh* or obliteration into the personality of one's Pir.

Reading this account of Pir Vilayat, Pir Rasheed commented, "This is the first step of training in our lineage—to do zikr as if it were your Pir doing it." It is a basic teaching of the Kaleemi tradition, that when you do any prayer or meditation or anything important, you should hold in your imagination the image of your Pir. This is called *tasawwur-e shaykh* or "seeing the image of your Pir." This is the means by which you slowly learn to not just see the image of your Pir, but imagine that your Pir is with you, is supporting what you are doing, and finally that your Pir is actually doing it and you are not. When Pir Rasheed was commenting about this, he recited a Persian couplet with teary eyes.[46]

The caravan of mine has departed from the realm of manifestation I'm a footprint left behind—all that remains is a name and a sign	کاروانم همہ بگذشت ز میدانِ شہود ہم چوں نقشِ کفِ پا نام و نشانم باقیست

On hearing this couplet, Saleem Ghori sighed and teared up. He asked Pir Rasheed to recite it again and again. I also tried to memorize it as he said it. The couplet seemed to catch the spiritual teaching so beautifully and offer it in a lovely form.

Then Pir Vilayat continued his account to describe how he practised this teaching during his chilla retreat at the dargah of Fakhr al-Din Pahari. "That's how I was doing the zikr, 22,000 times a day. When I came back I couldn't even recognize myself. And the extraordinary thing was that he used to call me for prayer five times a day and getting into my father's consciousness, I got into the consciousness of Abu Hashim Madani and getting into the consciousness of Abu Hashim Madani, I got into the consciousness of his father and I was sitting there at the tomb of his father. He came in to call me for prayer and he said, 'Vilayat' and I thought, the name is familiar but I... Then he looked at me and he said, 'You've seen my father.' So he saw the expression of his father so it shows that it really works."

Pir Rasheed commented that in writing this, Pir Vilayat was describing the experience of *fana fi'l-shaykh*. Pir Vilayat described this with a different expression, "getting into one's Pir's consciousness." This is obliteration of the self in the personality of one's Pir. Pir Vilayat first experienced obliteration in his father Pir Inayat's image and got absorbed into Pir Inayat's consciousness. Then through this, he experienced Pir Inayat's obliteration in the image of his Pir, Abu Hashim Madani and absorption into Abu Hashim's consciousness. Then through this he experienced obliteration in the image of Abu Hashim's Pir who was Sayyid Muhammad Hasan Jeeli Kaleemi. When Pir Vilayat was recorded as saying "getting into the consciousness of Abu Hashim Madani I got into the consciousness of his father" he did not mean the father of Abu Hashim Madani. He meant that he got into the consciousness of Sayyid Muhammad Hasan Jeeli Kaleemi, the grandfather of Sayyid Fakhr al-Hasan who was guiding him at that time.

Pir Vilayat's lineage led him to Abu Hashim Madani, who was a disciple and successor of Sayyid Muhammad Hasan Jeeli Kaleemi. When he was obliterated in the personality of Abu Hashim Madani, he naturally felt that he was kneeling at the tomb of Sayyid Muhammad Hasan Jeeli Kaleemi, at the dargah called Astana Kaleemi in Hyderabad. There, obliterated in the personality of Abu Hashim Madani, he felt that he met and encountered Sayyid Muhammad Hasan Jeeli Kaleemi, who is present at his own tomb. This is why, when Sayyid Fakhr al-Hasan Jeeli Kaleemi called Pir Vilayat for the prayer-time and interrupted his zikr, Pir Vilayat did not recognize his own name or his own person. He was not himself then. He was Abu Hashim Madani becoming absorbed into Sayyid Muhammad Hasan Jeeli Kaleemi. When Sayyid Fakhr al-Hasan called him for prayer and recognized his spiritual condition, he knew that Pir Vilayat was experiencing the spiritual presence of his own grandfather, Sayyid Muhammad Hasan Jeeli Kaleemi. That is why he looked at Pir Vilayat and said, "You've seen my father."

Pir Rasheed commented about this that such experiences are the first step in Sufi training. It is fana fi'l-shaykh or obliteration in one's Pir. This is only the first step toward *fana fi'l-rasul* or obliteration in the Prophet Muhammad. This is because one's Pir who has given initiation was himself initiated, and this chain of initiations leads back to the Prophet Muhammad. So ultimately absorption into the personality of your Pir leads to absorption into the personality of the Prophet as the most realized human being. This is a step toward *fana fi'llah* or obliteration in God, because although the Prophet is a mere human being, he is in touch with God. He appears to be a person but through him one encounters God's presence. These are steps on the path toward understanding and experiencing the secret of the oneness of being. Then he recited an Urdu couplet by Iqbal:

Muhammad is the secret of oneness his hidden meaning who can know? In pious law, he's merely human his ultimate reality only God can know!	محمد سرِ وحدت ہیں کوئی رمز ان کا کیا جانے شریعت میں تو بندہ ہیں حقیقت میں خدا جانے

Pir Rasheed remembers when Pir Vilayat went into his chilla and had these experiences. He was present along with his father when Pir Vilayat finished his retreat. Pir Rasheed recalls that his father told Pir Vilayat that now he was ready to go to the West and take up his position, and that he must go back. Pir Rasheed was present when this was told to Pir Vilayat.

Pir Rasheed recalled that Pir Vilayat had told him that he met many Sufi Shaykhs in Europe and India before coming to Hyderabad. In Ajmer and in other places in North India, many of them wanted him to take initiation from them, but he was not satisfied with that until he came to Hyderabad and found that the lineage of Abu Hashim Madani was still living, in the Kaleemi Order. That is how he ended up learning from Sayyid Fakhr al-Hasan Jeeli Kaleemi and meeting Pir Rasheed when he was young.

Pir Rasheed then tuned to Saleem Ghori, my fellow disciple or pir-bhai, and asked him to pull out a briefcase from beneath the bed he was lying on—the only piece of furniture in the room. That is where all his precious items are stored, under the bed. Saleem drew out an old and battered brown case. Opening it, he rummaged through the books, files and folders that were crammed into it, to pull out a plastic bag full of old photographs. Pir Rasheed shuffled through them, sighing and smiled as he reminisced about each one, but quickly moved on to the one he sought. Finally, he came to a small black and white photo. With a triumphant smile, he passed the photo to me. There was a formal portrait of Pir Vilayat Khan as a young man, sitting next to the

Photo 11: Pir Vilayat Khan, Pir Rasheed and his father, Sayyid Fakhr al-Hasan Jeeli Kaleemi

sternly bearded Sayyid Fakhr al-Hasan and three other members of the Jeeli Kaleemi family. Pir Rasheed pointed to the young man on the far right, who could not have been more than 19 years old. "And that's me…"

After we had this conversation, in which I read the autobiographical record of Pir Vilayat out to Pir Rasheed and he commented about its contents, I apologized, "I'm very sorry to bring this task for you to do while you are recovering from your illness—you should be resting." He smiled with tears in his eyes and said, "No, you did me a great favor! You got me to remember such beautiful memories of a time long ago when Pir Vilayat came to Hyderabad and my father was still alive. You let me forget all this…" and he waved at the intravenous tube in his arm and the catheter tube for his urine.

Later he shuffled through the pile of photos again, then pulled out another one he wanted to show me. The photo was in Delhi, and pictured Pir Vilayat Khan as an older gentleman. He was there to delegate his son, Pir Zia Inayat Khan, with authority to lead the Inayati Order after he would be gone. Next to them is Pir Rasheed, who was invited to attend and help tie his turban. Earlier, when Pir Zia visited Hyderabad, he was granted khilafat by Pir Rasheed in the Kaleemi Order, augmenting the initiation that he had already received from his father, Pir Vilayat. The photo captured a moment that shows how these two parallel lines of Chishti teaching continued to converge and diverge only to converge again, generation after generation. It was one of Pir Rasheed's cherished photos, and he showed it to me many times over the years.

Photo 12: Pir Vilayat Khan with Pir Zia, Pir Rasheed, and Syed Waris Hussain

A WESTERLY BREEZE

Pir Rasheed and a few disciples were able to travel to Delhi for the ʿurs of Hazrat Inayat Khan. This unique event happens in Delhi on the fifth of February. That in itself is unusual, because the ʿurs is fixed to the date of the Western Gregorian calendar determined by the earth's movement around the sun. In contrast, the ʿurs of other Indian Sufis—like that of saints all over the Muslim world—is fixed to the date in the Islamic Hijri calendar determined by the moon's movement around the earth. The lunar calendar does not mesh perfectly with the solar calendar, such that the Islamic lunar year has about 11 days less than the Western solar year. To make it easier for admirers of Hazrat Inayat Khan from the West to remember and attend his 'urs in India, it is fixed to the Western calendar. This 'urs is also unique in drawing a very cosmopolitan congregation of lovers, from America, Europe, India and everywhere in between. It is also unique in integrating classical music—both Hindustani and sometimes Western—into the rituals, in addition to the foundational qawwali singing.

This year was a blessed gathering because Pir Zia came from the USA along with his wife and two children, Rasulan Bibi and Ravan Bakhsh. Pir Rasheed also came from Hyderabad by train, with three younger mureeds, Nazeer and Amjad and Khalid. I joined them all in Delhi; they were staying at a simple guesthouse just next to the dargah in Basti Nizamuddin while I stayed at my Auntie's house in Jangpura, just a short walk away. We were joined by Waris Hussain Chishti, one of the custodians of the great dargah at Ajmer, and it was rewarding for me to meet such a learned and light-hearted gentleman.

I arrived at the dargah while the qawwali mehfil was on-going. The hall was full and the crowd was motley, full of different colors and diverse people, from India, Europe, and America. They were dressed in all manner of clothing, Western and Indian and some hippy versions that landed somewhere in-between. It was very difficult to get into the hall as the crowd was packed in around the tomb, leaving only a small open space between the tomb and the Qawwals, Miraj Ahmed Nizami and his younger family members. I stepped gingerly over people to reach the center to offer my *nazrana*.

In the center, I found Pir Rasheed seated next to Pir Zia, with other elders from the Sufi order all around. Pir Rasheed saw me coming in, but Pir Zia had his eyes closed in rapt attention to the music; with his black robe folded neatly around him and gold cap on his head and his hair flowing long over his shoulders, he was radiating beauty. How many years had it been since I had seen him? Ten years, perhaps? I was momentarily bewildered and did not know whom to approach to make an offering, Pir Rasheed or Pir Zia. Then I recalled how it was Pir Zia who first told me about Pir Rasheed and suggested, in an offhand way, that when I go to Hyderabad I should look him up. That was in 1995, and it took many years for me to act upon Pir Zia's suggestion. Yet, it was only because of Pir Zia that I knew of him. I knelt before Pir Zia to offer nazrana, before approaching Pir Rasheed, to acknowledge my debt to him and my gratitude.

Pir Zia's eyes were still closed. It appeared that he was deep into a different world, though he was sitting in the mehfil. I inched my offering forward just a bit until it touched his hand. Then he opened his eyes and moved to accept the offering, but then he recognized me. He was startled that it was me, and instantly moved to take my hand with my offering and offer it to Pir Rasheed, seated next to him. He smiled shyly as he passed me over to Pir Rasheed, where I belonged. It was a beautiful moment that I will never forget. Then he seated me just behind him where his children and wife were sitting in the mehfil, and I joined them there. Somehow, I fit in despite the crowd.

My fellow mureeds, Nazeer and Amjad and Khalid, were also seated in the assembly. Nazeer was especially clever and sensitive to music. At a certain point, he called out to the Qawwals with a request. He wanted to hear the poem by Bedam Warsi, *Aye naseem-e bu-e Muhammad, salla Allahu alayhi wa sallim*, "A breeze arrived bearing the scent of Muhammad, may God bless and keep him in peace." He asked once very politely, but the Qawwals ignored him. They had their own agenda of songs to play, ones that the American and European Sufis knew better, like *Allahu Allahu* by Zamin ʿAli, a song to which the Western Sufis sing along and clap, in a way that is not exactly appropriate. After a song or two, again Nazeer called out a request, anything by Bedam Warsi. He called out more urgently from the back of the crowd, but the Qawwals studiously ignored him. After the mehfil, Nazeer was disappointed and angry at the Qawwals. He told me, "I didn't want that song by Bedam Warsi for myself, but rather for Pir Rasheed. That is his favorite song."[47] This is true. This song moves Pir Rasheed very deeply. In our mehfils at Pir Rasheed's house, it is usually the second or third song, and often induces Pir Rasheed to cry or slip into *hal*, a trance-like state. It can often get the whole assembly weeping as his hal is almost contagious and spreads to others.

> Gentle fragrance spread, O Bedam,
> > making fragrant the world of the heart
> When loose flowed the tresses of Muhammad
> > may God bless him and give him peace

WORSHIP THROUGH SONG

Later, at the nighttime mehfil, Pir Rasheed was too tired to join us. The chill of Delhi would get into his bones. I attended the mehfil along with my fellow mureeds. After the mehfil, when the musicians were departing, I heard a commotion. Nazeer, Amjad and Khalid were confronting the younger members of the Qawwal family, just outside the dargah. The mureeds were telling them that they did not respect the adab of the assembly. They reminded the musicians that if people in the assembly make a request it should be accepted. The Qawwals responded that it was their prerogative to sing what was appropriate, and they had a set agenda of songs for the visitors from abroad. The mureeds responded that that was a concert not qawwali; qawwali had to flow with the spiritual state of the listeners. The argument grew heated. The younger mureeds were about the same age as the younger Qawwals, and the acrid scent of testosterone filled the air. Voices rose. The younger Qawwals grew insolent, and began to cite their pedigree and say that their family had been singing qawwali at Nizam al-Din for centuries. The mureeds responded that maybe the people of Delhi have forgotten the meaning of qawwali and that if they had tried to present this kind of qawwali in Hyderabad, they would be asked to leave the dargah!

The situation grew very tense and there was some shoving. I had to step in, because I was the only one there who knew both groups. I had never pulled rank on Nazeer and the others, but this time it was necessary. I asked my fellow mureeds to keep quiet and go back into the dargah. Then I asked the Qawwals to please leave quickly. Both sides wanted to keep shouting at each other and the situation became quite shameful for all involved. The shouting in Urdu alarmed the European and American Sufis, as it seemed a fight was breaking out. As quickly as possible, I got the mureeds to go back in and the Qawwals to go home.

Outside the dargah, the Qawwals asked me, "Who are those guys?" I told them they were mureeds of Pir Rasheed. "Who do they think they are to tell us how to present qawwali?" they asked angrily. I told them that in Hyderabad, we take qawwali very seriously and it is not for show. Muttering under their breath, the singers left. I also left, ashamed that this fight had broken out and worried that the reputation of Pir Rasheed was brought into the fray. The next day, I spoke with Pir Rasheed about it and explained to him all that had happened, saying that I felt it was really bad adab for Nazeer to have shouted and argued with the Qawwals in public inside the dargah.

Pir Rasheed listened to the whole story then said, "Yes, it is not good to argue with raised voices in the dargah. But in fact, Nazeer is right! Samaʿ is not a concert. People come to a mehfil to worship and not for show. It is ʿibada. If listeners in the assembly demand to hear a particular song, then the Qawwals have a duty to perform it, to lead those listeners through a particular spiritual state. It is not up to the Qawwals to determine what is best—it is up to the listeners, if they know the songs and the tradition. Nazeer was right to remind them of this, but arguing in the dargah is not the best way to do it."

I was surprised to hear this. The anger that I felt toward Nazeer just drained away. I found a new respect for our little Sufi community in Hyderabad. Our group is small, poor and parochial, that is true. Our Qawwal singers are old, worn out and have wobbly voices, that is true. Our musical assemblies happen in a cramped and stuffy house with listeners spilling out onto the dirty alley outside, that is true. But we keep the original spirit of qawwali alive! Qawwali is not about having a fancy hall, a posh audience or an artful singer. It is about generating spiritual power in the listeners. It is about serving the needs of those gathered through music. Anything other than this might be good music, but it is not qawwali. The singers in Delhi seem to have forgotten this and nowadays approach qawwali as either empty ritual or pop stardom. I was very happy to be in Hyderabad.

Later that day, after lunch was served at the dargah of Hazrat Inayat Khan, I walked out the gateway to the alley of Basti Nizamuddin. Sitting on the wall just outside the gateway was Miraj Ahmed Nizami, the master Qawwal. I had never spoken with him, though I knew his sons and nephews, the younger members of his group. He saw me approaching and called me over to him. He was a fine gentleman, wispy now in his eighties but with a refinement about him that was very beautiful. He called me over and greeted me respectfully, and asked me pointedly, "Who were those young men with you last night?" I told him they were mureeds of Pir Rasheed from Hyderabad. He asked, "Why did they insult us by arguing like that after the mehfil?" I told him that they were disappointed that the Qawwals did not respect their request for a song by Bedam Warsi. Miraj said, "We can sing that song and twenty other songs by Bedam Warsi! We can sing in Urdu or Persian or Hindi! We are the Qawwals for Nizam al-Din Awliya and have been for many generations—how dare they question us about whether we know the qawwali tradition?" I told him that nobody can question his expertise, but that maybe the younger generation is not following it as they should. In Hyderabad, we have different expectations of qawwali, and we expect the singers to be humble enough to respond to a request, no matter who it is from, if it will serve the spiritual needs of the assembly. He grew quiet and a bit sad. "You know," he said, "my family is from Delhi originally but we stayed in Hyderabad. I lived in Hyderabad. Our tradition is the same as that in Hyderabad." Yes, I agreed, but maybe the environment here in Delhi is different now than in Hyderabad. He sighed. "The audience is not the same," he said. "And the singers want to be the stars," I said. He sighed in agreement.

He could not criticize his own sons and nephews, but he knew that they were not living up to his own example. I could see that in his eyes. He feared what might come when he was gone. In saying goodbye, Miraj said to me, "Let's not have any more fighting in the dargah." I agreed with him, but qawwali is certainly something worth fighting for. Miraj Ahmed Nizami passed away in 2015—may Allah grant him forgiveness, mercy and eternal music.

ONENESS BETWEEN FAITH AND HERESY

Pir Rasheed was beginning to attract the attention of some in the West who were looking for Sufi guidance. Pir Zia had become the head of the Inayati Order (then called the Sufi Order International) and had received khilafat from Pir Rasheed as well as his own father. Pir Zia maintained good relations with Pir Rasheed, and invited him to come to the USA as a guest teacher at the Sufi Order International's summer training camp, the Suluk Academy. Perhaps in this way his reputation grew a bit in the USA and Abdallah Lipton, an American Muslim, eventually came to Hyderabad to meet Pir Rasheed.

I had met Abdallah previously at the University of North Carolina, where he was a Ph.D. student. For his M.A., he had studied and translated the famous little book in Arabic, *al-Tasweeya*, about the oneness of being by the Chishti master, Hazrat Muhibbullah Ilahabadi. I guess he was attracted to the Chishti teachings in that way. Abdallah came for a summer to learn Persian in Hyderabad and eventually took initiation with Pir Rasheed. Abdallah later came back to visit with his wife, Latifa, who also spent time with Pir Rasheed and took initiation with him. I was grateful for Abdallah's good company in Hyderabad, because he had a very practical outlook on life. He helped Pir Rasheed to make a booklet on how to recite the *Hizb al-Bahr*, an originally Shadhili Sufi practice that was integrated into our Kaleemi lineage. Abdallah made a beautiful booklet with a fine English translation of the Arabic phrases of this *wird* or litany, which Pir Rasheed recited daily before evening prayers. Pir Rasheed was so happy to have the booklet printed, so that he could distribute it to his disciples and encourage them to take up this practice.

Abdallah also transliterated and translated the *Zanjeera,* a prayer that Pir Rasheed employed to protect people from negative energies and destructive forces. It is a wird that comes from the Rifaʻi and the Madari Orders, which are so close in the Deccan area that they seem to have fused into one. The Rifaʻi Order traces its origins to Sayyid Ahmad Kabir Rifaʻi, who is buried in Iraq. The Madari Order traces its origins back to Sayyid Badiʻ al-Din Zinda Shah Madar, the "Ever-living King" who is buried in North India. The wird calls upon both of them and their representatives in the Deccan, like ʻAli Simnani Mir and Baba Hayat Qalandar Mir (who is known as Baba Budhan, a saint who introduced coffee from Yemen to South India and started its cultivation here, transforming the region).[48] Through them, it calls upon all the saints in each of the four directions, as well as the four closest friends of the Prophet Muhammad, and through them asks for intercession of the Prophet himself to implore God's protection from negative energies and destructive forces. Pir Rasheed gave us permission to use this wird and to teach it to others who we thought capable of bearing it.

Abdallah was very American in these practical efforts. He really could not stand the chaos and clutter of India, even though he had studied Arabic in Yemen. He felt bad that Pir Rasheed stored all these precious items in suitcases under his bed. Abdallah hired carpenters to build a custom-fit cabinet in Pir Rasheed's room to store his books and papers and computer. He could do this only with the help of another mureed named Mubeen, a solid young man with an earnest face who worked in an architectural engineering firm. Even after Abdallah returned to America, Pir Rasheed would fondly call the cabinet "Abdallah's shelves."

When in Hyderabad, Abdallah brought up the question of whether Sufis should consider their spiritual master as the Prophet himself. He was worried that this thinking might violate the sharee'a. After Abdallah returned to the USA, I asked Pir Rasheed about this question. He smiled at me and said, "You know that what somebody says depends upon his state when saying it." I knew that he was talking now about *shathiyat*, ecstatic boasts. He continued, "In our Sufi path, it is obligatory for a disciple to see in his Pir the person of the Prophet. In our path, the way to develop spiritually is to embrace fana fi'l-shaykh, and through this to fana fi'l-rasul, and through this to fana fi'llah." I was thinking of Shaykh 'Abd al-Karim Jeeli, a famous Sufi from fifteenth-century Yemen. In his book, *al-Insan al-Kamil*, he states that he saw in his own Sufi teacher the image of the Prophet Muhammad. I was thinking of Dara Shikoh and how in his book *Risala-e Haqq-Numa*, he called his Pir "the *barzakh*." Pir Rasheed surprised me by saying, "My grandfather used to recite a poem about this teaching. It is not just that you must see your Pir as the Prophet! No, that is not enough. You must see your Pir as God! Yes, as God."

> One who doesn't see everything as one with God's essence
> Can you say the profession of faith's meaning he discerns?

He continued, "Of course, nothing is separate from God—that is the teaching of the oneness of being, wahdat al-wujud. But wujud doesn't mean only being, it means also finding. One finds the nearness or union with God not through just anything or everything. No, one finds it through one's Pir. It is the Pir that shows you oneness of all being and manifests to you the presence of God. You must see your Pir as God."

Pir Rasheed seemed a little uncomfortable saying this, and he was searching for words to say it, wary of sounding close to heresy. Then it came to me that the word he was searching for in English maybe didn't exist in English. I said, "Then the Pir is *mazhar-e khuda*?" Upon hearing these words from me, his face lit up. "Yes!" He exclaimed, "Yes, the Pir is the *mazhar* of God, the place where God appears, the thing through which God shines upon you." Then he smiled at me with a bewildered look and said, "That is why I love you, because such sweet and correct words come from your lips." I was touched by such a lovely compliment. Then he concluded, "So you must see your Pir as God, with the eye of insight. This is not acceptable to a person who is only following sharee'a, but it is essential for a person following tareeqat, who can keep the sharee'a in its place and follow tareeqat in its place."

I was almost flying when I left Pir Rasheed's home that day. I came home and tried to find the whole poem of his grandfather, Sayyid Muhammad Zia al-Hasan Jeeli Kaleemi. After searching through the slim book *Kalam-e Zia* I could not find it, and grew discouraged. But after looking through all the ghazals, I found at the end of the book his *qaseeda*, called "Secrets and Gnosis of the Oneness of Being, Union, Intimacy, Passion and Love."[49]

When I turn from the Ka'ba to Medina, my gut burns Each fiber shivers, toward the beloved my spirit yearns	طوافِ کعبہ سے سوئے بطحیٰ جو سوزاں نکلے روح بھی نس سے تڑپ کر سوئے جاناں نکلے
At my last breath, when a sinner like me sees The Prophet coming, a glimmer of hope returns	مجھ گنہگار کی آنکھوں میں بوقتِ نزع لائیں تشریف جو سرکار تو ارماں نکلے
My only hope is this, this is my heart's only goal That the Prophet's satisfaction my love for him earns	یہی ارمان ہے اور ہے یہی مقصدِ دل کا سرورِ دیں کی محبت میں مری جاں نکلے

THE MERCIFUL DOOR

Searing sighs, if they would
ever escape my breast,
The sun in heaven would
admire such bright lanterns

Any wonder that on Judgment Day
there's a great tumult?
With hot cries the chest of one
who loves Muhammad churns

He who doesn't see everything
as one with God's essence
Can you say the profession of
faith's meaning he discerns?

Zia, recite from the pages
of Muhammad's illumined face
You may begin with heresy,
but into Qur'an it always turns

آہِ سوزاں میرے سینے سے اگر آئے نکل
پھر فلک پر نہ کہیں مہر درخشاں نکلے

کیا عجب ہے کہ بپا حشر میں ہو شور اتنا
عاشقِ زارِ محمد کا جو گرماں نکلے

سب جگہ ذاتِ خدا کو نہ اگر دیکھے ایک
معنیٔ کلمۂ توحید نہ اے جاں نکلے

مصحفِ رویٔ محمد کی تلاوت میں ضیاؔ
شرک جاتا رہا جب پڑھ کے یہ قرآں نکلے

CHAPTER 4
THE DOOR'S LEAF

PLAY

It had always been on my mind to speak with Pir Rasheed about sex and sexuality but, honestly, it was hard to find the opportunity. Seldom were conversations private and he was constantly interrupted by people coming to his room for prayers, cures and advice. When the rare opportunities did come, often my courage lagged behind. Years passed. I had grown accustomed to people assuming and understanding that I am gay without my having to say so. I began to wonder whether Pir Rasheed also understood this, or whether it was something I needed to articulate. Would it matter if I were gay or not on this spiritual path? Pir Rasheed would break through my reticence in a most unexpected way.

I adopted Islam when I was living in Morocco, knowing fully that I am gay. I joined this Kaleemi Order in the same state of mind. Honestly, I did not think much about sexuality when making both decisions. After the attack of Sept. 11, debates about Islam, Islamic identity and human rights became increasingly heated. In the USA, my friend Omid Safi was publishing a book, entitled *Progressive Muslims: on Gender, Justice and Pluralism*, and he insisted that I write a chapter viewing homosexuality from a progressive Islamic viewpoint. After some hesitation, I did so, amid a chorus of friends saying, "What? Are you fishing for a fatwa? Do you want to be killed?" That was published in 2003 and I'm still very much alive.

Responses to that chapter sparked me to study the issue deeper, and the more I researched, the more confident I became that homosexuality and Islam were not incompatible, despite the shrill homophobia of the jurists and classical scholars who shaped the tradition. In addition, there are examples of homosexual Sufis from the past, and their personalities gave me some confidence. A good historian from Delhi, Saleem Kidwai, invited me to contribute to a book he was editing, called *Same-Sex Love in India*, since he wanted to document Sufi personas who were homosexual. That invitation led me to research about Shah Husayn, a Sufi from Lahore in the sixteenth century.

Shah Husayn began as an ascetic Sufi in the Qadiri Order, studying the Qur'an by day and doing strenuous zikr at night under the guidance of his murshid. However, beneath this conventional veneer, he harbored feelings of same-sex love. This came out when he studied the verse of the Qur'an that declares, "The life of this world is nothing but play and sport, while surely the next abode is better for those who stay conscious—so don't you understand?" (Surat al-An'am 6:32). Shah Husayn took this verse literally, and it suddenly appeared to him that this world is nothing serious at all. Life in this world is nothing but play. Social order, dignity and respect, piety and merit, marriage and children, money and trade were all distractions. The best way to renounce it is to approach it as play. He began to play music in public, flirt with disrepute, and do whatever he could to play with the expectations of others. His murshid argued that the verse criticized those who see the world only as sport and play, but Shah Husayn countered that the verse commended people who take the world lightly and disregard the expectations of worldly people who harbor ambition and care for reputation. After some time, his Pir saw that his sincerity lay in following this path of courting public blame, and blessed him.

Later, Shah Husayn fell deeply in love with a young man, a Hindu from a Brahmin family. Despite family opposition, they lived together, never married women, and earned respect of rulers like the Mughal Emperor Akbar, who asked for his blessing. Shah Husayn and his lover are buried side-by-side at his dargah in Lahore. Shah Husayn became known by the name of his same-sex lover, Madho. Even today people call him "Madho Lal Husayn." Bards recite his ardent and ecstatic Punjabi poetry. I found a long Persian poem written as his biography, from which I translated key passages.[50] Shah Husayn's story reveals that Sufism could offer a place to gay people, and his understanding of that key Qur'anic verse resounded with me. Why not throw aside social expectations for the sake of love, especially a love which society cannot recognize, misunderstands or actively despises?

One evening, I came to Pir Rasheed's house for the 'urs of Sayyid Muhammad Zia al-Hasan Jeeli Kaleemi. I arrived just at the end of the silent Qur'an reading which precedes the qawwali and dinner. About ten people who had come earlier were sitting quietly reciting the Qur'an, which had been divided into thirty slim folios, each called a si-para, so that a community could read the whole scripture at once. I sat down next to Pir Rasheed, who had been reading one folio along with the others. I moved to pick up a folio of the Qur'an from the wooden rack placed in the center of the room, so that I could read along with the others. But instead, Pir Rasheed handed me the folio he had been reading and pointed out to me exactly where he had left off so that I should pick up from that place and leave not a word unrecited. I was surprised by this. I had never before seen him interrupt his own reading to hand his folio to a newcomer.

I wondered why he had given his folio to me to continue where he had left off. My ego took delight in this, thinking it was some special gift to me, like when Pir Rasheed serves you food with his own hand; only here, he was serving me Qur'an. I was stunned to turn to the phrase where he pointed, and began to read. *The life of this world is nothing but play and sport, while surely the next abode is better for those who stay conscious—so don't you understand?* Just as I finished reading these phrases numbly, the call for sunset prayers rang out and everyone stopped reading, placed the sheaves back in their stack and sat quietly until the call to prayer was finished.

I sat horrified. *Wa ma al-hayat al-dunya illa la 'b wa lahw.* Did Pir Rasheed choose to hand me the Qur'an at exactly that phrase? Did he know the significance of those words to me? He didn't look at me again or give any indication, but just waited quietly for the azan to finish so that he could lead the sunset prayer. We sat there while the bottom fell out of my world. How did he know my admiration for Shah Husayn and how he interpreted this phrase? Was this a message about my sexual orientation? Or rather, was this a message about my spiritual negligence, that I have been treating religion as a plaything, a sport, a mere pastime? I barely had time to think before prayer began, then na'at was recited in praise of the Prophet, then qawwali was sung, then dinner was served, I ate in a daze and then I was driving back home, acting outwardly as if nothing had happened.

One week later, I returned reluctantly to the khanqah at his home for the celebration of the 'urs of Shaykh Kaleemullah. I thought with regret that I should have gone before this, to ask Pir Rasheed about what happened with the Qur'an last week. All week, I had been living in fear and trembling, spending all my time writing in a disturbed mental state. Was Pir Rasheed sending me a message or was God sending me a message, and how was I to understand it properly? I felt like a small child who had done something wrong, and was sure his parents had found out, but they gave no clue that they knew and so I kept examining and reexamining their features for a sign that they knew and were about to punish me. I felt jittery and spiritually ill at ease. I decided that this time at the khanqah, Pir Rasheed would give me some sign that there was significance to this event, or else I would take it to be a coincidence.

I arrived at the khanqah while the men were gathering, sitting in a circle reading Qur'an silently. I entered without greeting anyone, and nobody greeted me. I sat down and Pir Rasheed just continued reading. He did not hand me the folio he was holding. I took up a folio of the Qur'an, whichever one was on the top of the stack. I opened it and began to read. This folio began at the end of Surat al-Ma'ida, the fifth chapter called "The Table." It tells about Jesus being tested by his followers, performing miracles with the permission of God such as bringing a table laden with good food down from the heavens to feed the hungry, and being asked whether he taught his followers that he was God. I read along, happily, enjoying the images of Jesus making a bird shaped of clay and breathing into it until, with God's permission, it alighted and flew away.

I kept reading my folio. After Surat al-Ma'ida began Surat al-An'am, the sixth chapter called "The Livestock." In the name of God, the compassionate One, the One who cares… and suddenly there it was again. "The life of this world is nothing but play and sport, while surely the next abode is better for those who stay conscious—so don't you understand?" (Surat al-An'am 6:32). I kept reading silently, but was not paying any attention. My mind was reeling and my heart recoiling. I could not look up at Pir Rasheed. I just kept reading. It was the exact same phrase. *Wa ma al-hayat al-dunya illa la'b wa lahw.* Similar phrasing occurs four times when these words—*the life of this world is play and sport*—are used. But no, this was not a similar wording; it was the exact same phrase from the same verse. Nobody had handed it to me and nobody had pointed it out this time. I had picked it up myself, randomly and by coincidence—although I was now sure that no such event we call coincidence is ever random. There is no coincidence here. There is no coincidence anywhere, if that implies meaningless events and ignorable details. I am sure, now, that God wanted me to reexamine this verse. But why? To reexamine my relationship to it, as a way to reexamine myself?

Soon mehfil-e sama' began and the music throbbed and I was reeling in a panic. I could not look at Pir Rasheed, for I was feeling sorely ashamed. Was I feeling ashamed of my actions or my negligence? Of my sexual orientation or of not having a true love? Of my separating pleasure from love and not having a committed lover of my own? My heart kept turning from one thing to the next in a long spiral of shame, like an airplane shot down from the sky that spirals down, as if in slow motion though we all know where it's going, spewing dark smoke of shame out behind it in tighter and tighter circles as it spins out of control.

That is the state I was in as the qawwali started. In the very first song, the poem by Jami, *Wa salla Allahu ala nurin*—"May God bless that light," Pir Rasheed rose up in ecstasy. Radiance beamed from his face and the light of longing glowed in his eyes as the song spoke about the cosmic beauty of the Prophet Muhammad. When Pir Rasheed had returned to himself and settled back into his place on the carpet, I knew that my time to approach him had come. At first, I felt that I could not rise to give him an offering or nazrana; I could not even stand to approach him. But someone came to me—I think it was my fellow mureed, Zakir 'Ali—and requested silently that I go up with him. I stood and put a coin on his coin as he in turn placed both of the coins in my hand so that I would be the one to give nazrana, and together we went up to Pir Rasheed. He took the offering just as he always did, with his soft hands, with no fuss, with an absent-minded blessing, as if he were pure compassion and full mercy, with no blame anywhere in his visage or his touch. I went back again and again to give him nazrana, eager for that touch of acknowledgement. I sat in the sama', still restless and anxious about what this message to me, now written in neon after the events of the evening, could really mean.

MARRIAGE

After finishing work, I intended to visit Pir Rasheed. I called ahead to make sure he was home. On the phone, he said he had been expecting me to come and that it had been a long time. I tried to explain that in the three weeks since I had seen him, I had visitors come from Europe to stay as my guests and I had to care for them. When I arrived at his house, Pir Rasheed was with some women who had come with lemons for him to bless and use in healing rituals for them. I waited outside while he finished with them, then he came out and took me upstairs, "So we can sit in complete privacy," he said. But on the way up the stairs before we arrived at his upper room, he said, "So, you've been enjoying like anything these days!" and I was filled with dread.

We sat down on the tattered carpet of Pir Rasheed's room, and he said to me directly, "Isn't it time you got married?" I was quiet. He told me, "You are a young man in good health, so you must be having lust—thus you should get married to keep away from sinful activities." I deferred saying, "I am not concerned about getting married." Then Pir Rasheed changed the topic to complain about my elder pir-bhai, 'Abdul Rasheed. He was the retired engineer who had fixed up the dargah where the Sufi guide of Hazrat Inayat Khan is buried. Pir Rasheed noted that he had not been coming to visit much at all, and had not brought him the copy of a key to Sayyid Abu Hashim Madani's dargah. ʿAbdul Rasheed's wife passed away two years earlier, and Pir Rasheed explained that now he desires to get married to a new wife. But his only child, his daughter, is against her father getting married again! Pir Rasheed said that this daughter was happily settled with her husband and was raising her children, such that ʿAbdul Rasheed was living alone here in Hyderabad with no family member to look after him. Pir Rasheed explained, "So naturally, he wants to get married again, but is hesitating because his daughter disagrees. I told him, just go and get married. That is your right. I will go with you and stand by you if you decide to marry again. That is the *sunna* of the Prophet and you are acting in accord with the *shareeʿa*, so what shame is there in it?"

This was Pir Rasheed's lovely indirect way of sending me a message. Marriage is the sunna of the Prophet. If you want to act in accord with the shareeʿa, then one should get married. Even an older man who is a retired widower is thinking about this, so why shouldn't a younger man like me who has never married? Pir Rasheed said, "It is clear what ʿAbdul Rasheed should do, but he was being foolish and was hampered by his fickle mind. He is running around town looking for a new wife, but he can't make up his mind to get married," he said with a frown. I remained silent.

So Pir Rasheed turned to me directly, "If ʿAbdul Rasheed, at age sixty, is thinking of getting married again, then what are you doing not married at your young age? Who knows, death could come at any time without any warning. One moment you are healthy and happy, the next moment you might be dead!" He recited an Urdu couplet: *Zindagi ki ek karwat hai mawt / zindagi badal jati hai* "Life is a single turn away from death, life keeps making new turns." I replied that this poem is just like a verse from Qurʾan that says, "Every soul is tasting death and you will get your full recompense on the day of resurrection. Those drawn away from the fire and admitted into the garden have attained a great reward, and the life of this world is nothing but enjoyment of delusion" (Surat Al-iʿImran 3:185). Yes, he said, every soul tastes death. Pir Rasheed related that the word *nafs* or soul, is also close to the word *nafas* or breath. "With each breath in and out, the soul tastes death for a moment. Death is as close to each person as the space between one breath and next. How easy it is to turn over while sleeping—just like that, death is a small turn away from life. After breathing out, what guarantee is there that you will once again breathe in? That is why one has to do zikr," Pir Rasheed said, referring to the silent zikr-e ruhi that he had taught me long ago and encouraged me to always perform. "One has to make each breath a prayer, so that each breath goes in remembering God's presence and each breath goes out praising God. That way, one understands the five senses, as I told you before. Seeing, hearing, tasting, smelling... and touching." He said this last of the five senses directly to me, as a challenge.

"Why are you here?" he asked. "Why are you alive? You are a human being and the sign of a human being who is alive is the motion of breathing in and out. If you are not breathing, then you are dead. But all other animals also breathe in and out, so what is the difference? Cows, dogs, pigs, birds, snakes—they all breathe in and out. Without breathing, they are also dead. So how is your life any different from the life of an animal?" He waited, as with terror I recalled the verse from Qur'an—"They have hearts with which they do not understand, and eyes with which they do not see, and ears with which they do not hear—they are just like dumb cattle, no they are more astray" (Surat al-Aʿraf 7:179). I didn't say anything, and Pir Rasheed continued, "How is your life different from an animal's life? You have the five senses and you have the ability to understand them, to recognize the sensations but not get caught up in them which leads to craving. Consider the sense of sight. I might see a beautiful woman or a handsome man, just the same as a lowly man sees. What is the difference between Rasheed's seeing this beauty and the lowly man's seeing? There is a great difference. Because Rasheed has understanding and the lowly man is ignorant and understands nothing—he feels no restraint and does whatever he likes. He sees a beautiful woman and he reaches out to touch her body—then he fucks her."

Pir Rasheed used these words brutally. I had never heard him use a word remotely close to "fuck." I recoiled at the thought that he was using words that were in my mind and personality, not in his own. It was also strange that he was speaking of himself in the third person, as "Rasheed," which I had never heard him do before. It was as if he were not speaking from himself but rather speaking words, thoughts and feelings from my own personality, reflected and clarified by the mirror of his speaking them aloud. I was stunned to hear this, not knowing how to react at all, as if being bombarded by his words.

"Yes, he sees and enjoys, then touches her and fucks her, because he has no restraint and does not understand the five senses. He is terribly misled. He is ignorant. But Rasheed sees the same beautiful woman, sees the same vision, and remembers God who created her beauty. Rasheed says, 'Mashallah! Subhanallah! Glory be to God, what goodness God creates!' Rasheed experiences the same sensation through the five senses, but he understands them and is restrained. He sees her the same way he sees this carpet—a pattern of red and blue and black and nothing more. There is a saying of the Prophet—*Allahu jameel wa yuhibbu al-jamal,* meaning God is beautiful and loves beauty. Rasheed sees a beautiful woman and thinks of how God created such beauty, for God is the ultimate beauty. Beauty is to be praised, not touched."

I sat quietly with my eyes down-cast, feeling censured and hurt, but not wanting to say anything that might be seen as disrespectful or argumentative. Pir Rasheed paused, and seemed to come back to himself. He was quiet for a while, and then said, "I'm sorry for talking on and on for so long, please forgive me. Forgive me for anything I've said that is wrong. See, I have not even offered you tea! I'm so very sorry." I said, "I have not come for tea. I came for advice. You are giving me the advice that you feel is right. For that, I am grateful." I asked permission to leave, so he shook my hand and I walked out with a dread deep in my gut. I was amazed—how can one be angry or upset at someone who apologizes for saying the words that jab you in the gut and leave you lying flat and breathless?

That evening, driving back to town, I phoned Firoozeh and we went for dinner. She spoke about her research into Hazrat Gesu Daraz and his writings. In one of his many books, he had written:[51]

> You look at the beautiful one and see figure and stature
> I see nothing but the beauty and the art of the creator

Firoozeh was especially interested in Gesu Daraz's relationship to 'Ayn al-Quzat Hamadani, an earlier Sufi from Iran who was a brilliant writer. She had just finished writing a book about 'Ayn al-Quzat and told me, "His personality and writings have saved me from despair and probably saved my life! His mode of expression was so deep, so audacious and so insightful."

This conversation, of course, turned to Ahmad Ghazali, the teacher of 'Ayn al-Quzat. He was a great Sufi and a masterful poet in Persian, and was the younger brother of Imam Abu Hamid Ghazali. Imam Ghazali was more famous in the Arab world and the West, as an Islamic thinker equivalent to Saint Thomas Aquinas in medieval Europe. But his younger brother, Ahmad Ghazali, was more prized among the Chishtis for his love of music, his love poetry, and his ecstatic personality. As Firoozeh was speaking of his love poetry in *Sawanih,* she blithely said, "Ahmad Ghazali was gay, of course." She told the stories about his *shahid-bazi* or his practice of contemplating a beautiful young man as a kind of meditation on God's beauty. She exclaimed, "What a genius he was! What a gift it is to know these people, to have their writings and their poems and their thoughts!"[52]

Firoozeh had also published a modern edition of Ruzbihan Baqli's spiritual autobiography, *Kashf al-Asrar*. Ruzbihan was an Iranian Sufi from Shiraz who wrote: "When the soul is educated by human love and has become firm-footed in the innermost secret of love, and the heart is polished by the fire of love from the satanic and base insinuations, then the soul which commands to evil becomes peaceful beneath the strokes of the violent wrath of love."[53] The translator writes of these Sufi masters of the path of love (*mazhab-e 'ishq*) that "the treasure of beauty—for 'God is beautiful and loves beauty'—reveals itself in order to kindle love in the human heart... Beauty has not full meaning without admiration and love, and the beloved needs the lover for his own perfection. The story of Mahmud and Ayaz is a typical expression of this kind of love... Ayaz is the symbol of the loving soul."[54] The names Mahmud and Ayaz are famous to all who know Persian literature. Sultan Mahmud Ghazni was the ruler of Afghanistan who first invaded India, nurtured Persian poetry, and encouraged Sufis and scholars to settle in these lands. Ayaz was his slave, who was elevated to be his cup-bearer, advisor, minister and lover. Stories about the love between Mahmud and Ayaz were told by all the great Persian Sufi authors, from Attar to Rumi to Ahmad Ghazali to 'Ayn al-Quzat—the Sufis who were Persian poets from India also wrote of their loyal love, like Fakhr al-Din 'Iraqi and Ameer Khusro.[55] I dropped Firoozeh back to her house after dinner, and drove home thinking that the issue was about love or its lack rather than about touch or its restraint. Maybe Pir Rasheed's blunt warnings about seeing and touching were meant to point out how little I actually love. I should be having one beloved and make myself into a true lover, so that erotic love can be an "education" and can lead me to more sublime understanding of what it means to love God.

This is hard to reconcile with Pir Rasheed's actual words, which seemed to warn more directly about getting caught up in the world of sensory images, and rather to reject the world of sensory delight entirely. It is not possible for me to obey sharee'a rules about getting married. It is not possible for me to marry a woman—that would be against my own innate nature and would put a woman in an unjust and unfulfilling situation. Maybe it is possible for me to truly and deeply love a man and reject the "fickle mind" of getting involved with others. If I could love one like that, would Pir Rasheed allow me to be "married" to him? Would that give the same spiritual training and the same tempering of lust as getting married in a conventional heterosexual way? I decided that this was in my power to do, and I must try what is in my power, for God would not insist on burdening a soul beyond its capacity to bear. *La yukallifu allahu nafsan illa was'aha* (Surat al-Baqara 2:286). God does not impart a burden on any soul more than it can bear. It benefits by the good that it earns and it is penalized for the harm that it does.

CONFESSION

The next time I visited Pir Rasheed, he greeted me warmly. Fortunately, we had some private time together with no interruptions. I confessed to him that I was perplexed by what he told me about marriage and sex. Finally, I just came out with it and said, "This is because I am gay." He looked at me bewildered: the word gay did not register with him. I switched to Urdu and tried to explain, "You see, I do not want to get married to a woman. That would be impossible for me." He smiled, "Oh yes, I see. You do not want to marry. That is fine, for there were many great teachers in our Chishti lineage who remained bachelors for their whole lives. Hazrat Nizam al-Din Awliya never married and Burhan al-Din Ghareeb never married! There were so many, but that is a very hard path to take." I observed that we were having a misunderstanding. "No, Pir Sahib, I don't mean that I want to remain a bachelor and stay chaste. I mean that my nature does not incline toward loving women. When I fall in love, it is with a man. Can you understand this? If I get married, I will marry with a man." Pir Rasheed stayed quiet for a while, then said, "Yes, I suppose that such people exist. But the sunna of the Prophet is that a man should marry a woman." I replied, "Yes, I understand that is the sunna, but is it obligatory on everyone without exception? It is my nature, my *fitra*, from the time I was young and I've always known that I will not marry a woman. Surely, God must lead people closer to the divine through their own nature and not against their own nature?" I was recollecting the verse from the Qur'an that uses this term fitra or nature: "Set your face to the moral challenge in a pure way, according to the original nature of God upon which [God] based humanity, for there is no changing the creation of God" (Surat al-Rum 30:30).

Pir Rasheed reflected for a time. Then he said, "My son, I cannot tell you what to do. In the sharee'a of our Prophet Muhammad, it is clear that a man should marry a woman. This matter is between you and God. What can I say about it? You have come to me for many years and you see me praying namaz, so you know that namaz is part of my teaching. The sharee'a tells that you must pray namaz five times each day and explains how and when to do it. Now, when you come to see me, I never ask you whether you have prayed your namaz today or yesterday. No, that is a matter between you and God. If you ask me whether it is required in sharee'a to pray I will tell you that it is so, but what you do in your life is between you and God. I am not here to judge that. I am not a *faqeeh* or jurist. You know what sharee'a says and then you act according to your understanding and your conscience. It is the same with marriage. If you ask me about what the sharee'a says, I can tell you. The rest is between you and God."

At first, I was upset by Pir Rasheed's words. I wanted him to acknowledge that people were created differently, with diverse natures and varied dispositions. I wanted him to say that the Prophet gave the sharee'a for general guidance, but that everyone needs to adjust it to their own nature and path. He didn't say this. He didn't acknowledge directly that he accepted what being gay meant for me. Yet, as I drove home through insane traffic and chaotic crowds, I slowly digested what he did say rather than dwell upon what he did not. He called me his son, for the first time. He said the matter was between me and God—that it was a matter of conscience and not coercion or social control. Most importantly, he affirmed that he would not judge me or ask me to leave the Kaleemi Order. As I reflected upon the generosity of his restraint, I saw that it embodied the Qur'an when it commands us: "Say, All act according to their own disposition, yet your lord knows best who is on the most guided path." (Surat al-Isra 17:84). I urgently wanted affirmation from him but I did not get it. Yet he gave me something more valuable. He affirmed that I had choice and agency, conscience and insight. He affirmed that God alone could judge the inner heart of a person, even if their outer actions seem ambiguous or questionable.

From that day onward, I scrutinized Pir Rasheed's words and actions for any sign of disapproval or censure. I never encountered any. Once, I came to see him and found him sitting with a visitor whom I had never met. He was a man younger than me, whom Pir Rasheed introduced as the son of one of his disciples who had moved to Dubai. The son was back in India visiting family. We were talking leisurely when, at a certain point, Pir Rasheed left the room to ask for lunch to be prepared for us. When he was gone, the visitor began to ask me about my wife and family. I told him that I am not married. He was surprised and asked my age, in a routine that I am very familiar with in India. "Somebody so old and you are not married? You do not have children yet? You should get married and settle down. In Islam, you must marry. Don't worry! Pir Rasheed can help you find a good wife—just ask him."

At this point, Pir Rasheed came back to sit with us. The visitor said, "Pir Sahib, your disciple is not married! Why don't you find a good wife for him here in Hyderabad?" Pir Rasheed smiled at him and said, "Yes, I know all about that. He doesn't need to be married." The visitor was too excited by the prospect of being involved in arranging a marriage and didn't really listen to what was said. Pir Rasheed repeated to him, "This one does not need to be married. Leave it now," and he changed the topic of conversation. Many times, Pir Rasheed protected me from the misplaced goodwill of others who tried to impose their expectations on me. For that sly silence, I am very grateful.

Back in America, I felt increasingly moved to follow up on my research into the relations between homosexuality and Islam, especially to explore whether they could be reconciled in a theological framework. I applied for a fellowship at the Institute for the Study of Islam in the Modern World in the Netherlands to do a major study such as had never been done before. A few months later, I received a letter that the Institute had accepted my proposal and would fund me for two years of full time research, but I would have to move to the Netherlands. Swarthmore College, where I was teaching at the time, would not accept giving me leave of absence to complete this study. I was torn, uncertain whether to stick with a good and rewarding job headed toward tenure, or to resign and leap into the unknown. As the deadline to make a decision came nearer, one night I fell down on the floor weeping—I prayed two cycles of *namaz-e istikhara* in hope of getting insight into a hard decision. While in prostration, I saw the face of Pir Rasheed, smiling at me.

I don't know how long I wept while prostrating. My carpet was soaked when I sat up. I sat for a long time, asking for guidance. Finally, exhausted, I got up and went to bed. The next day I filed a letter with Swarthmore College explaining that I would resign. I packed my belongings in storage and moved to the Netherlands, where the Institute turned out to be a very supportive and congenial place to conduct research. Everything around me supported my efforts. The libraries at the University of Leiden and University of Amsterdam had amazing collections of Islamic books. The Institute attracted world-renowned scholars whom I was able to consult on my research, amazing minds like those of Fatima Mernissi from Morocco, Muhammad Khalid Masud from Pakistan, Asef Bayat from Iran and Abdel Kader Tayyob from South Africa. The fellowship was modest but allowed me to live simply and freely, and gave me the liberty to travel for research to South Africa and the U.K. Eventually, I was able to write two books based on this research project, *Homosexuality in Islam* and *Living Out Islam: Voices of Lesbian, Gay and Transgender Muslims*. I was also blessed to have the freedom to spend more time in Hyderabad with Pir Rasheed.

GENDER

Pir Rasheed does not challenge the gender norms of Hyderabad, which are still very patriarchal. Rather, he largely conforms to them. He sees himself as a spiritual guide and healer, not as a social reformer. He upholds the standard rules for *parda* and gender segregation in his household, but he also has many female disciples who come to visit him in his room at the front of the house, which he designates as the khanqah. Women come for advice, healing, protection for children, help in marital problems, aid in arranging the marriages that dominate their family lives. They come upstairs in full *burqa*, and once inside with Pir Rasheed, they relax and remove their face veils in familiar surroundings with a trusted advisor.

Pir Rasheed happily received women visitors even if they were not wearing the burqa or traditional covering. He invited women who were not from Hyderabad to sit and talk and eat with him and other men of his family. I took many women from abroad to visit him in this way, and he treated everyone with equal access regardless of gender. Those were interactions in his home; when interactions involved the public, then segregation by gender was the norm. At qawwali gatherings in his home on blessed days, only the men would sit with him and the musicians in the large hall. Women from his family and their female guests would sit in the neighboring room, with a curtain screening the open door from view while letting the music pour through. Often the curtain would be lifted by the little hands of his granddaughters, who boldly peered beyond it into the men's space to watch as well as listen.

In India, it is customary for women to not enter the inner space of a dargah, where the tombs of male Sufi leaders are housed. Women often visit dargahs and enjoy proximity in the courtyard around the tomb, but do not generally go into the confined space of the tomb shrine itself. At the dargah of Nizam al-Din Awliya in Delhi, women are prominent among visitors and sit in the courtyard to listen to qawwali along with the men without any screen or separation. At other dargahs, such as at Yusufayn in Hyderabad, the courtyard is screened off so that women sit slightly separated from the men. When women want to offer nazrana or offerings to the musician, they throw rupee notes over the screen. During a good song, it would be raining wadded up rupee notes and men would dutifully gather up the notes from the courtyard floor and present them to the musicians on the women's behalf. Sometimes I could hear, from beyond the screen just behind me, women go into ecstasy or call out uncontrollably, just as did the men. The separate space did not necessarily mean a separate experience of the music.

At the Astana Kaleemi, the dargah of our Order, local women would sometimes come with their menfolk, but the women would stay in the courtyard and not enter the chamber where the tombs were housed. However, when women who were not from Hyderabad came, Pir Rasheed would invite them to enter the inner chamber. I was surprised when once I came to the Astana with Zaida, and I had delicately informed her about these gender expectations so that she would not feel confused or hurt. When we arrived at the Astana and found Pir Rasheed sitting inside, he invited us both in to sit with him and make du'a.

I would often meet Pir Rasheed on Fridays at the Astana, where we would pray namaz-e jum'a at the neighboring Husayni Mosque. In most of India, women are not allowed to enter mosques at all, in conformity with decision made by the Hanafi legal school in India, Pakistan and Bangladesh. Perhaps this accounts for why women so rarely come to the Astana Kaleemi, for it is attached to a mosque. Many women go to the dargah of Husayn Shah Wali just next door, where there is a sheltered place for them in the cool, covered courtyard. Even there, women do not go into the inner shrine housing the tomb, but they often make namaz in the courtyard, where there is a women-only space.

Once, Pir Rasheed and I were walking together in the alley leading to the Kaleemi Astana on a Friday when we were going to pray. I asked him why women were not allowed in mosques. He said, "There is permission for women to pray at home, so they don't need to come to the mosque." I said, "But men can also pray at home, yet they are encouraged to come to the mosque." He replied, "There is great merit in making prayers in congregation with other Muslims, so men are encouraged to come to the mosque." I said, "But surely the same merit would come to women if they prayed in congregation with other women at a mosque?" He replied, "Women would get great merit by obeying their husbands more than they would by praying in congregation. Women cannot leave their homes to go to the mosque without their husbands' permission." I said, "What if her husband permits her to go to the mosque, hoping that she will get great merit by praying in congregation with other women?" Pir Rasheed was getting frustrated with me but he kept cool and countered, "If the men are in the mosque, where will the women pray?" I asked, "Why can't there be mosques only for women? Or spaces in the mosque segregated for women only? Other countries have this custom, so why not India? We have that in railway cars in India, so why not in the mosque?" He said, "Women would still have to go outside their home to get to a mosque, and that is dangerous for them. There are all kinds of bad people on the roads who would tease them or trouble them. So, women stay at home to pray and there is permission for them to do that." The conversation ended right back where it began. We arrived at the mosque, which was filled to overflowing with men, so many men that the rows spilled over into the courtyard and men even stood between the graves in the Astana itself. Even if a woman were allowed to come into this mosque, where is there a sheltered space for her to place her forehead on the ground?

For Pir Rasheed, certain gender rules were absolute and others were contextual and customary. When he was around people from Hyderabad, he observed more rigid gender segregation. When he was a guest in other places, he tried to accommodate the local norms. When we attended the 'urs of Hazrat Inayat Khan in Delhi, many people from the USA and Europe attended in addition to people from all over India. Many of those who come from abroad are women. In the dargah of Hazrat Inayat Khan, there is no gender segregation. Even during qawwali, men and women sit together, though even then the women from India tend to cluster together to make an informal section for women only. Pir Rasheed participated fully in the qawwali and other activities, without objecting to the lack of gender segregation even though at his own khanqah in Hyderabad, such gender mixing would not be allowed.

After being invited for many years to the 'urs in Delhi, Pir Rasheed was invited in 2009 to visit the Inayati Order's members in the USA. He also attended the Mendocino Camp organized by the Sufi Ruhaniyat Order, who claim inspiration from Hazrat Inayat Khan but do not belong to the Inayati Order as led by Pir Zia. About that camp he later informed me, "When I was in America, I experienced things that disturbed me. One night they held a zikr of saying 'Allah-hu' in a gathering of mixed gender. At a certain point, everyone rose to form a standing circle and locked arms to sway with the rhythm of the chanting. I was also doing this zikr with them and I also rose to join arms with them, but the group was mixed with both women and men. I instructed the women to form a separate circle but the people there ignored me. I insisted that those nearby me be only men, and for a few links in the circle to either side of me there were only men locking arms with other men. Beyond that, women and men were mixed. What would happen if I were linked arm-in-arm with a woman? I might touch her breast with my hand like this..." He reached over and touched my chest. "What would happen then? My zikr would be ruined. My remembrance of God would be distracted, even if for a moment. All my worship would be in vain. I don't know why in America they do this, mixing men and women together. For centuries, it has been this way and people there have gotten accustomed to it, so they don't realize anymore how wrong it is."

I was listening quietly but grew agitated. I could not just sit by and sulk while listening to his critique of American gender norms. I understood his point of view, but I had to explain that in America, men and women mix freely at work, home, school, and places of worship, but that doesn't mean that they are all sexually aroused or involved with each other. We just do not have the custom of segregating men from women. Certainly, modest dress and behavior are important when strangers meet, but sometimes its standards are more flexible between friends and close associates in the same community. Pir Rasheed did not register my protest for cultural relativism.

In the Chishti Order, there are many stories about how friends overcome the boundary of gender modesty as they interact on the Sufi path. Hazrat

Photo 13: Hazrat Nizam al-Din's dargah

THE DOOR'S LEAF

Nizam al-Din Awliya recollected the special friendship of a woman named Bibi Fatima Sam, who lived in Indraprasta (the oldest part of Delhi). He told his followers about her.

> Before this time, he observed, there lived in the locale of Indraprasta a virtuous elderly woman named Bibi Fatima Sam. I had seen her. She was a fine woman. She had memorized many verses pertaining to every circumstance of life. I especially remember these lines from her:
>
> > For love you search, while still for life you strain
> > For both you search, but both you can't attain
>
> Shaykh Najib al-Din Mutawakkil—may God have mercy on him—was very fond of this Bibi Fatima, remarked the master, in the way that brothers are fond of their sisters.[56]

Nizam al-Din Awliya lived next door to Shaykh Najib al-Din Mutawakkil, when he came to Delhi as a young man to study Islamic law. Najib al-Din was the younger brother of Baba Farid al-Din Ganj-e Shakar, the leading Chishti Sufi master of that era. Seeing patience and love in this younger brother, the young Nizam al-Din found himself longing to meet Baba Farid. Eventually, a Qawwal from Delhi was going out to the Punjab where Baba Farid lived, and persuaded Nizam al-Din to join him on the journey. After taking initiation with him, Nizam al-Din heard Baba Farid also praise this wonderful woman, Bibi Fatima Sam.

> When evening came—it was a Friday evening—a woman presented herself to the master [Nizam al-Din Awliya] and professed allegiance to him. He then began to comment on the numerous benefits that accrue from the virtues of women. He called to mind a woman from Indraprasta named Fatima. She had been such a model of chastity and virtue that Shaykh al-Islam Farid al-Din—may God sanctify his lofty secret—used to say repeatedly of her: "That woman is a man whom the Creator has sent to earth in the bodily form of a woman!" The master then declared that dervishes who ask saintly women and saintly men to intercede on their behalf invoke saintly women first because they are so rare. "When a wild lion comes into an inhabited area from the forest," he explained, "no one asks is it male or female!"[57]

When people are spiritually powerful, their gender becomes irrelevant. Conventional distinctions fall away. This is why Baba Farid and Najib al-Din

Mutawakkil considered Bibi Fatima Sam to be their sister, and interacted with her in a way that was intimate and familial. They were not related by blood or marriage, yet they were friends through bonds of spiritual striving; thus, conventions of modesty and segregation fell away. One can still visit the dargah of Bibi Fatima Sam in Delhi (in Kakanagar neighborhood, not far from Basti Nizamuddin). A government school has been built up around it, but it is spacious and quiet. Her enormous grave is always covered in roses. A few men go there, but mostly women visit, and they find a quiet sanctuary there where they can be near the actual grave, unlike in many other dargahs. But women are still not allowed in the mosque that adjoins her dargah!

After Nizam al-Din Awliya, other Chishti authors also consider gender from an unconventional point of view. Zia Nakhshabi was born in Badaun, the hometown of Nizam al-Din Awliya, about twenty-five years after the latter had died. Nakhshabi was one of the most elegant prose writers from the Chishti Order. In his book *Silk al-Suluk* or "Stages of the Path," he champions the piety of women.

> Oh you who have stepped onto the path with the tread of men! If you had heard about women who have boldly trod this path before with the steps of manliness, you would duck with shame behind the veil of bashfulness… Listen up now! Once a virtuous woman asked a sinful man, "In what way has reason been apportioned to men and to women?" The man replied, "The power of reason has been divided into ten parts, then one part was given to womankind and nine parts were granted to mankind. In the same way, the power of lust was divided into ten parts, then one part was given to mankind while nine parts was granted to womankind." The woman replied, "Oh you sinful man! That one part of reason given to me has overpowered the nine parts of lust that I have, while the nine parts of reason granted to you is overwhelmed by the mere one part of lust that you have!"[58]

Perhaps Zia Nakhshabi was quoting Bibi Fatima Sam in this story of an anonymous woman who puts an arrogant man in his place!

In qawwali, many songs are sung in old Hindi in which the speaker is a woman. The heroine of these songs is a young woman from the village, who yearns for her beloved with a simple and powerful sincerity. Only women's persona could convey the power of this yearning. Even if the qawwali singers are all men, the words they sing are in the voices of women.

Thumri is another genre of song that became popular in the nineteenth and early twentieth centuries, especially in the brothels and pleasure palaces where women singers entertained. This kind of song, also in women's voices but often sung by women themselves, speaks about love that could be secular or sacred. Sufis from the Chishti Order adopted the thumri and turned it toward spiritual expression. Even Pir Rasheed's own grandfather and spiritual guide, Sayyid Muhammad Zia al-Hasan Jeeli Kaleemi, wrote thumri lyrics in the voice of a love-struck girl.[59]

Hasan's beauty drives me mad beyond care I stay in the desert wastes to bare	حسنُ حسنَ کی ہوں میں دوانی صحرا صحرا گھوم رہی
I cling to the hem of dear Nizam's robe I am the slave girl of Ganj-e Shakar	نظام پیا کا دامن پکڑی ہوں گنج شکر کی میں چیری
Zia has come to your doorstep in love So dye him in the color of Ajmer	لایا ہے ضیاؔ کو عشق ترے در رنگ اپنا جما دے اجمیری

I BECAME YOU AND YOU BECAME ME

Many days have passed since I have written in this chronicle. Many events have transpired to make me a different person than I was when I last wrote here. I intended to record all important events related to Pir Rasheed, so that looking back I could make sense to myself and to others of my encounters with him. Many experiences I had that I did not record, which is a failure of intention. When one does not do this immediately and within the glow of that experience, then an authentic record of it is lost. That can never be reconstructed from memory, which always betrays. Enough of regrets!

Today I ate breakfast and read the newspaper as is my routine. Then I felt a strange drowsiness and decided to lie down again. At first, I berated myself for feeling sleepy at mid-morning and for being so lazy as to succumb. I had been recovering from bronchitis and had spent many days resting, so now that my energy level was coming back up, I felt ashamed to be feeling tired again. But then I realized that this was no ordinary sleepiness. It was more like a sense that the world was fading or receding. The logical response was to lie down, rest my eyes and let it recede. I would not call the state I entered sleep. But neither was it wakefulness. It was, I think, a matter of stepping into the ʻalam-e misal, that intermediate world of imaginary forms.

As I lay there, I recalled some experiences I had while I had been traveling last month in Tamil Nadu. I had been reading Shaykh Kaleemullah's *Kashkul*, and on a hot, loud and bumpy bus-ride from Salem to Thiruchirapalli, I began to silently practise the *zikr-e seh-paya* or Meditation of the Three Supports. Or rather, I should say that the zikr began to practise me. I did not have an *ijaza*, or permission, to do this zikr, though I had read about it in books by Hajji Imdadullah and Shaykh Kaleemullah.[60] This zikr involves three of the immanent qualities of God from the most beautiful divine names. One says that God is samee', baseer, and ʻaleem—the One who hears, the One who sees, the One who knows. One says this while inhaling, suspending the breath in the body and then exhaling, in a complex mental motion of ascending and descending. At that time, I didn't know how to do this zikr correctly, and Pir Rasheed had never taught me. Yet suddenly, the zikr was welling up inside me and filling my every breath. It was as if the zikr were constantly being repeated from infinity toward infinity, in the voices of a whole line of people who made time appear irrelevant. I happened to step into that line for a moment and was filled with this zikr that sprang directly from the voices of the ancient masters of Chishti lineage.

As I lay there, I recalled how that experience led me to listen for the eternal resonance, the *sawt-e sarmadi*. Shaykh Kaleemullah describes this as a buzzing, humming or roaring sound; he likens it to the sound of a continuously falling sheet of water, especially one that is falling from directly overhead.[61] It is the resonant sound of original creation and re-creation, an echo of *kun fa-yakun*, "Be and it is" (Surat Yaseen 36:82). I had just finished teaching at the Henry Martyn Institute's summer seminar, held that year in Krishnagiri, a town in Tamil Nadu. After our group zikr at the summer seminar, one of the Protestant seminarians, Lourence Das from Chatisgarh, remarked to me that he had felt a strange vibration during the meditation. He heard it as a sound emanating from within him. I told him that was the eternal resonance, and that if he could feel this, then he was doing zikr the right way. Lourence reminded me of this fact, as I had forgotten to listen for the eternal resonance, or rather I was distracted by having to lead the group and was worried about whether they were getting it. Thank God for Lourence—what a sweet man he was! He reminded me of this resonance. Later, I heard it while traveling on that bus.

As I lay down in my rented house in Hyderabad, I heard this resonance again. This time, it came through my consciousness without any zikr to carry it along. I suppose I could hear the buzz of the fan of the cooler outside the window of the next room, but the resonance was quite distinct from that mechanical sound. It came today like the sound of gently falling water, like a sheet of water gliding over a large smooth stone and falling into a pool of water, folding back into itself to gurgle and churn up bubbles and set ripples dancing and currents flowing far beyond itself. Images came to mind of hearing the gentle sound of water falling over stones, from wilderness waterfalls I had seen in my childhood and youth, after long hikes into the mountains to places of immense serenity and dynamic tranquility. Those images came up and passed away. The resonance called up these images, because of the similarity of sound, but the sound was not attached to these images and so they faded away in my mind.

I occasionally thought to myself, "Leave those thoughts and hear only that resonance." Focus on the resonance would come and go in intensity. I realized that I was a bubble floating on the surface of this water, a bubble generated by the falling of this water into itself, which throws up bubble after bubble, wave within wave, ripple upon ripple and current against countercurrent. When water falls into water, a tiny bubble dances nearby, sometimes drifting away across the surface of the water, clinging to the place where the water pours down and sometimes going under the surface completely, to the point that it is no longer a bubble. I realized that, when thoughts came to me and made me feel independent, then the bubble had drifted away from its source and was skirting along the surface of the water. I realized that, when recollection of that eternal resonance sound was present, the bubble was clinging to the fall of water itself, quivering with the motion of it and yearning to return to its origins in that stream. I realized that the bubble might get completely submerged and disappear into the water itself. A fear welled up within me that I might dissolve and then the fear dissolved. I saw for a moment my body lying there as it melted into a puddle of liquid, as it putrefied and spread soaking into the dirt, leaving an oily dark stain with only the bones lying across the surface of that stain and ribs poking upwards until they, too, began to fall away into fragments, shards and dust. They settled in a fine powder over the dark stain and they too sank into the soil. Then a wind began to blow, a warm and moist breeze that I knew was the creative breath of the merciful One. I watched as the dust became wet, the breeze blew it into ripples, the ripples rose up like a foam and the foam began to congeal into a body, just as it had been, infused with life and crackling with energy given to it by the blowing of the spirit. Then fear of death and obliteration faded away from within me. I began to take joy in the idea of disappearing like this, trusting that I would reappear.

Occasionally, the name of God—*ya 'Atee*, o Giver—would call out. Giver of gifts. Giver of breaths. Giver of life. Giver of giving. Once or twice the name of God—*ya Mani'*, o Withholder—also echoed out, but it did not impact my consciousness at all. It echoed and faded away. I was not aware of lacking anything. It was a stream of pure giving that I experienced, as it fell down gently and tumbled me along in that stream of sound that I was hearing. Occasionally the name of God—*ya Samee'*, o One who hears—swelled up as it did during the zikr of Three Supports. This eternal resonance, which I was hearing as a sound, has its origins in God who is the One who hears, and longs to be heard and gives the gift of hearing. Once I recall the name of God—*ya Musabbib al-asbab*, o One who causes all causes—rang out, and that seemed to obliterate any notion that the sound I was hearing had any origin in the phenomenal world in which I had laid down to rest.

Several times, something happened in the phenomenal world that caused me to get up. The doorbell rang, as my housekeeper Moshem had gone up to the terrace to hang up wet laundry and locked himself out. I rose and let him in from the doorway at the top of the stairs. Another time, I think I had to use the toilet. Each time I would do what needed to be done then lay down again, and in a moment the experience would continue as if it had never been interrupted.

Occasionally I saw Pir Rasheed in this 'alam-e misal. Sometimes it was only his face that I saw. Sometimes it was only the outline of his head, as if seen in silhouette with a strong light from behind. Once I saw him as a complete person. Then I greeted him and asked for his blessings and fell down holding his two feet with my hands. He leaned down to raise me up by the shoulders, as he does with people who greet him at his feet. Yet when I rose up, I found that I did not rise up on my own feet. I rose up on Pir Rasheed's feet. This is difficult to describe: his feet were my feet, such that I was rising up within the place where Pir Rasheed was standing. Then as he raised me up further, I found that his legs were my legs, his spine was my spine and his hands were my hands. It was as if I were rising up to fill the space within his body, until I was not and he was. For a moment, I was surprised by this and frightened, but his relaxed smile became my smile and that fear faded away. He has a certain smile that says, "Yes, I told you so." It was that smile.

Then I knew the reality of the different levels of being. I knew that *mulk* was the phenomenal world of sensing cause and effect that makes people greedy and craven. I knew that *nasut* is the realm of human consciousness, through which we know ourselves and each other and learn ethics and imagine a better life and are tested. I knew that *malakut* is the realm of angelic forces through which God's message comes into the world. I knew that *jabarut* is the realm of

God's qualities which radiate actively through the cosmos and call the world into being, shaping it, causing it, sustaining it, judging it, re-creating it. I knew that beyond this is *lahut*, the realm of God's essence that is beyond all names and qualities and forms and effects. It is untouched by being but is the font of all being, creating what is other while being beyond all otherness. Beyond that is unnamable, that is *hu*, that is a breath exhaled. And that is all. I cannot say that I traveled through these realms, or that I ascended into them, or that I left this phenomenal world of mulk to go elsewhere and to return again. I cannot say that I was there at all. But I came to know of these things with an immediate knowledge that was not conditioned by traveling or seeing or learning. I cannot say that I was there.

In this state of being Pir Rasheed, I saw a large old man all robed in green. He was stooped but also massive, with a body like a billowing cloud. He did not smile or say anything but he took from his head a tall cap that was green and gold and he placed this over my head. Then he lowered the cap onto my head and down through my head until the cap was in my chest. Then he lowered it down more and the cap of green and gold came to rest over my heart and sat there fitting snugly and feeling very heavy but full of light. It glittered as if studded with emerald and it shimmered as if woven with gold. I knew that this was Shaykh 'Abd al-Qadir Jeelani. Before he had appeared to me, I also saw two other figures who were like him. The first was enrobed in red. Later, I saw the second enrobed in black. I do not know who they were. Only later did I see 'Abd al-Qadir Jeelani.

Then I opened my eyes and slowly felt the circulation stir in my hands and limbs. I rose up to sit on my bed. I stood up and walked out of the room and into my house to continue my work for the day. The next time I visited Pir Rasheed at his home, he asked me to sit down cross-legged. "I want to teach you a different way of doing zikr," he announced. "This is a very ancient method in the Chishti Order and it is not for everyone. Maybe you read about it in some books…" He smiled with a twinkle in his eye, "…it is called Seh-Paya, the zikr of the Three Supports." He proceeded to instruct me in this zikr, in exactly the way I found in books from centuries ago. Shaykh Kaleemullah described it in this way:

> This is how to perform the Meditation of the Three Supports. Its form is imagined to be like an old-fashioned Grecian ewer that is a ceramic bowl which stands on three legs. Like this ewer, this meditation rests on three things and if one of them is missing the whole thing cannot stand firmly. This meditation depends on three conditions: first, the essential divine name Allah; second, the three generative attributes of God—which are

the One who knows (*'aleem*), the One who hears (*samee'*), and the One who sees (*baseer*)—and; thirdly, the medium... which refers to the form or face of one's spiritual guide.... The "a" of Allah is drawn with force from below the navel and the full breath is drawn up into the chest and there the breath is held compressed. Then one pronounces Allah with the heart coupled with samee' while imagining its meaning "God hears". Then one pronounces Allah coupled with baseer while imagining its meaning "God sees." Then one pronounces Allah coupled with 'aleem while imagining its meaning "God knows"....

The secret of the zikr lies in the fact that the sphere of hearing is less than that of seeing, and the sphere of seeing is less than that of knowing. The seeker begins in a state of reasoning about what is sensed, the narrowest of all spiritual states. As the seeker moves beyond the attribute samee' or "hears," he progresses spiritually to a more comprehensive state of understanding what is beyond sensation. As the seeker moves beyond the attribute baseer or "sees," he progresses spiritually to a more comprehensive state of understanding beyond the beyond. As the seeker moves through the attribute 'aleem or "knows," he comprehends this most expansive spiritual state... While reciting this with the heart, the breath must be suspended... Doing this generates internal heat that will burn away the greasy fat that congeals around the heart and allows Khannas, the whispering tempter, to cling to it. When the heart is cleansed of this, tempting thoughts melt away and one is overpowered by blissful oblivion.[62]

THE UNSTRUCK SOUND

Once I went to the hall of Shah Khamosh to listen to qawwali, an event that happens on the thirteenth of each Islamic month. Zaida was in Hyderabad this weekend, so we went together. It was a beautiful occasion, and the Sabiri Chishti community of Shah Khamosh always hosts a quiet, dignified and delicate sama'. Even the children are well-behaved, reflecting the persistence of Shah Khamosh's spirit in this place. Shah Khamosh was one of the most beloved Sufis of Hyderabad.

> He won over the hearts of the people of the Deccan. His ethical bearing was most upstanding. From head to toe, he was the embodiment of virtue and was beyond compare in his compassion and humility toward all, whether lowly or mighty. He was always seeking out ways to help those in need. Those who met him or served him suddenly found that their problems got solved or their needs were fulfilled! The rulers of Hyderabad were firm believers in his saintliness. When the

fourth Nizam, Afzal al-Dawla Bahadur, ascended the throne [in 1829] someone mentioned to him the good nature of Shah Khamosh. That very moment, the king called for Shah Khamosh to come to him, praised him and lauded him and showered him with gifts of gold coins and precious jewels. Shah Khamosh had the heart of a generous king in the body of an impoverished renunciant. He accepted the gifts and immediately disbursed all the valuables among his disciples and followers and admirers, keeping not a cent for himself… He never bothered anyone with his own concerns; rather, he remained steadfastly content with God's will since his very will was obliterated in God's being. Through his mediation, thousands of people got their needs fulfilled and many poor people became enriched! Strangers and beggars always found shelter in his khanqah. If anyone came to Hyderabad from another land and knew nobody, they would head straight for the khanqah of Shah Khamosh to receive hospitality, and there they would get food and drink and find respite and repose.[63]

Indeed, even after his death in 1872, Shah Khamosh's khanqah continued to harbor strangers. Even travelers like me found a welcome there. The khanqah where he lived for decades is now a special hall dedicated to qawwali music. It is located directly behind Mecca Masjid, the largest mosque of the city and the music there is often interrupted by the call to prayer.

The interplay between speech and silence is the very spirit of this place. In order to restrain his desires and quieten his ego, Shah Khamosh lived in silence. He refused to speak to anyone and if he needed anything, he would only gesture simply. In this way, he earned his name "Silent King" as explained by Hazrat Inayat Khan who spoke of him in his teachings:

> In Hyderabad, there was a mystic called Shah Khamosh. He was called so because of his silence. In his youth, he was a very clever and energetic young man. One day, he went to his spiritual master and, as usual, he had some question to ask as is natural in a pupil. The master was sitting in ecstasy and, as he did not wish to speak, he said, "Be quiet." The boy was much struck. He had never before heard such words from his master, who was always so kind, patient and willing to answer his questions. But it was a lesson which was enough for his whole life… For many years Shah Khamosh never spoke and his psychic power became so great that it was enough to look at him to be inspired.[64]

Shah Khamosh's family belonged to the Nizami branch of the Chishti Order and they were related to the family of Shah Raju Qattal and Gesu Daraz, whose descendants had settled in Bidar. As a child, he was once out playing with his young friends when a majzub strolled by. The Sufi asked, "What is a lion like you doing playing with wolves like these?" The Sufi gave the boy a sweet to eat and after that, the boy's personality steadily changed until he found solace only in zikr and remembering Allah in solitude. As a youth, he left the Deccan to go to Ajmer, where he experienced a vision of Khwaja Muʿin al-Din Chishti who told him to go to Manakpur in Punjab. There, he met his Sufi teacher and was inducted into the Sabiri branch of the Chishti Order that goes back to ʿAla al-Din ʿAli Ahmad Sabir.[65]

Shah Khamosh returned to Hyderabad much later in life and was thronged with followers. Perhaps his rule of silence was a way of living among the people without getting caught up in their demands. He kept complete silence for about fourteen years until once he was in the company of a *Qalandar*, a Sufi so rapt with intoxication that he disregarded the five daily prayers and other pious observances. The Qalandar asked him, "Why don't you speak with me?" Shah Khamosh gestured to him, asking why don't you pray with me? The latter challenged him, "I'll say my prayers if you drop this pretension of silence!" He answered out loud, "You begin praying immediately and I'll begin speaking again." The Qalandar took water and began to wash, then they stood side by side facing toward Mecca and began to pray namaz. Thereafter, Shah Khamosh honored his promise and began to speak with the people though he always spoke seldom; he never married and avoided looking people in the eye, often covering his face with a cloth. Despite his silence during his mature years, Shah Khamosh composed many Urdu poems in which he expresses mystical insights and longing.[66]

In this gathering at the Hall of Shah Khamosh, various Qawwals sang many familiar songs. Many were the ghazals of Shah Khamosh himself. One of them was new to me: in its final couplet, the ghazal mentioned the *sawt-e sarmadi*, "the unstruck sound" or the "voice of eternity." Hearing that phrase flicker through the song threw me into a deep and introspective mood.[67]

The lover who sees an arched brow Sees that brow as the arch of the shrine	جو عاشق کہ ابرو کا خم دیکھتے ہیں اسی خم کو طاقِ حرم دیکھتے ہیں
Our own understanding is something else We perceive no idol when an idol we see	سمجھ بوجھ اپنی تو کچھ اور ہی ہے صنم کو نہیں ہم صنم دیکھتے ہیں

Why should he look to stroll
in royal gardens
Who once sees
his beloved's rosy cheeks?

I have seen the rare vision
of nature's creator
O friend, how can I
describe what I see?

With eyes closed
what wonders I behold
When I open them
I see such little of worth

He is excluded
from enjoying the taste of faith
Whoever sees
this world's pride and delight

Khamosh hears
the unstruck sound each moment
As he keeps silent,
observing his passing breath

وہ کب سیرِ باغِ ارم دیکھتے ہیں
نظارہ ہے دیدارِ دلبر کا جن کو

تماشا نظر آیا قدرت کا نادر
کہیں کیا اے یارو جو ہم دیکھتے ہیں

میچی آنکھ جب تھی بہت سیر دیکھی
کھلی چشم اب ہے تو کم دیکھتے ہیں

سمجھ لو ہیں محروم لذاتِ دیں سے
جو دنیا کے ناز و نغم دیکھتے ہیں

صدا صوتِ سرمد کی سنتے ہیں ہر دم
جو خاموش بن سوئے دم دیکھتے ہیں

Shah Khamosh composed poetry that excels in capturing rapture in moments of union when there is nothing and no one for whom to search, as in one of his most beloved ghazals that is often sung in qawwali.[68]

Bewildered am I
in endless searching for you
You are like a mirror
and I'm a reflection of you

When the eyes sought you out
there you were to behold
You are hidden within me
and I am only found in you

تحیر مجھے ہے تیری جستجو ہے
تو آئینہ ساخود میرے روبرو ہے

تجھے جب کے ڈھونڈھا نظر آپ آیا
عیاں ہوں میں تجھ میں نہاں مجھ میں تو ہے

Just as a rose's aroma is found
in each petal's every vein
So every color is found
in the invisible essence of you

رگ و ریشۂ گل میں جس طرح بو ہے
بسا ہے وہ بے رنگ ہر رنگ میں یوں

How could I recoil from death
if it comes by your hand?
This neck belongs to who
if that blade belongs to you?

کرے قتل گر ہم کو انکار ہے کب
وہ تلوار کس کی یہ کس کا گلو ہے

Now just fulfill, o my master,
what I am requesting
Whether it's good or bad,
my heart longs only for you

بھلا دے تو اب مجھ سے اے میرے صاحب
بھلی یا بری دل میں جو آرزو ہے

Have no one as your enemy,
see none as your rival
Who do you fear if your lord
is the protector over you

خدا اپنا حافظ ہے پھر خوف کس کا
نہ دشمن ہے کوئی نہ کوئی عدو ہے

Since all that is in truth is
only God, be silent Khamosh!
To utter "I am the Truth"—
like Hallaj—is silly for you

جو سب حق ہی حق ہے تو خاموش ہو جا
انا الحق کی تیری عبث گفتگو ہے

SONG OF ENDURANCE

Shah Khamosh brought the Sabiri branch of the Chishti Order to Hyderabad, where it flourished in modern times. At his music hall, the Qawwals sing not only poems by Shah Khamosh but also poems attributed to 'Ala al-Din 'Ali Ahmad Sabir, the founder of the Sabiri community. Listening to them gives me a strange sense of aloofness for worldly concerns and a courage to endure any trials that come my way.[69]

Tonight, the king of kings
has come as a guest of mine
Gabriel and angels stand
to guard this door of mine

امروز شاہِ شاہاں مہمان شدہ است مارا
جبریل با ملائک درباں شدہ است مارا

> How can multiplicity enter
> the royal court of oneness?
> The 18,000 existing worlds
> are one in this vision of mine
>
> I have wandered through
> the idol-house of this world
> Worshipping my own mirror has
> become the faith of mine
>
> For lovers, o Ahmad,
> both heaven and hell are haram
> Making my lover content
> is the constant desire of mine

Hazrat Sabir called himself "Ahmad" in his poems. His given name was ʿAli Ahmad. His honorific name was ʿAla al-Din or "Loftiness of the Religion" and his nickname was "Sabir." He was the nephew and son-in-law of Baba Farid Ganj-e Shakar, and was also his earliest disciple and thus much beloved. Late in his life, Baba Farid named the young Nizam al-Din Awliya as his apparent successor sent to the capital city of Delhi as his representative. In contrast, ʿAla al-Din ʿAli Ahmad Sabir spent many more years in the company of Baba Farid, who made him a hidden successor sent to the wilderness. Baba Farid said, "Nizam al-Din Awliya is saturated by the knowledge from my whole chest and ʿAli Ahmad Sabir is permeated by the knowledge from my very heart!"[70] For this reason, perhaps, Nizam al-Din Awliya on his deathbed stated that he had only one regret in life—that it would be so much better to die while listening to qawwali. Yet ʿAli Ahmad Sabir did give up his soul while listening to music! He got his nickname Sabir because of his inner strength to endure any hardship:

> In his youth, ʿAla al-Din ʿAli Ahmad took on the responsibility of serving food every day for twelve years from the free kitchen at Baba Farid's khanqah to the renunciants and visitors. During these twelve years, he himself would keep fasting even while surrounded by food and people eating. By the light of his sainthood, Baba Farid came to know of this and asked him, "Baba ʿAla al-Din, why is it that all this time you are serving food to others from the kitchen but are not yourself partaking of the food?" He answered, "How could I swallow even one grain of this food without permission from you, my Pir?" Hearing this

reply, Baba Farid praised him saying, "Our 'Ala al-Din 'Ali Ahmad is really sabir," meaning one who patiently endures hardships. From that day, he was known fondly as Sabir.[71]

'Ali Ahmad Sabir's nickname means one with endurance but also implies one with patience. However, patience was not of his virtues. His personality was too full of *jalali* characteristics of might, power and wrath which came to him from his austere asceticism and aloofness from the world. "From the beginning of his Sufi training, he performed hard austerities and renounced worldly involvement and stayed away from social intercourse to such an extent that can hardly be described. He developed an incisive personality, meaning that anything he pronounced would cut through routine reality and immediately take place to irrevocable effect."[72] For better or worse, Hazrat Sabir could not patiently bear the foolishness of worldly ways.

As long as Sabir stayed near his Pir, Baba Farid, out in the Punjabi wilderness of Ajodhan, he lived in harmony. The empty wilderness suited his temperament and serving his Pir kept his adamant willpower in check. Yet at a certain point, Baba Farid gave him a certificate of khilafat in recognition of his spiritual maturity. This made Sabir an authoritative Sufi master in his own right. Baba Farid's custom was to send his successors away to other regions to spread the Chishti teachings. Sabir was so dear to his master that instead of ordering him to go to a specific place, Baba Farid gave him a choice.

> Baba Farid said, "Wherever you desire you can go." Sabir replied, "I propose to go to Delhi and stay there in the capital." As Baba Farid handed him the succession document, he said, "As you go there, stop to show this to Shaykh Jamal al-Din Hansvi [another senior disciple deputed to the town of Hansi that lay on the road toward Delhi] and only then head to Delhi." Arriving in Hansi, Sabir handed his succession document to Shaykh Jamal al-Din for him to read, and Sabir urged, "Finish this work quickly so that I can get underway to Delhi!" He answered, "Why this impatient rush? The guardian saint of capital (*sahib-e wilayat*) should stay cool and unflustered, but you can't even patiently wait here a moment! How will you fulfill this duty?" Sabir was overcome by his aloofness from worldly considerations and gave an immediate and fearless reply. Despite his beautiful virtues and lovely personality, Shaykh Jamal al-Din reacted strongly to this, for we are all prone to human weakness. The reins of patience slipped from Shaykh Jamal al-Din's grasp. Right there and then he tore up Sabir's document of succession.

Now Hazrat Sabir was the very embodiment of might and wrath. He could not tolerate this reaction. Immediately he proclaimed, "I sever your chain of initiations! No spiritual masters will come from your lineage!" In the end, this happened and Shaykh Jamal al-Din had no spiritual successor… From Hansi, Hazrat Sabir returned to his Pir, Baba Farid al-Din Ganj-e Shakar, and related what had happened. Baba Farid was upset by the insulting treatment meted out to Sabir and looked upon him with a gaze of affection. "That document which Shaykh Jamal al-Din tore to pieces cannot be restored, but I will write out for you an even better successorship. Take heart and do not be anxious." After a few days, Baba Farid presented a new document written in his own hand which delegated Sabir to move to Kaliyar, a town in the foothills of the Himalayas north of Delhi where the climate is cool and the water is fresh. He appointed Sabir to the guardian saint of that region and his successor took leave and moved there.[73]

Upon settling in Kaliyar, Sabir had to endure many more hardships, but he remained happy because he could fulfill his master's choice for him rather than making his own choice. Eventually, the Muslim leaders and scholars in Kaliyar got jealous of Sabir's popular following. They criticized his aloof attitude and his Qalandar-like carefree style of living. Eventually they conspired to drive him out. Sabir again lost his patience. He said, "You desire to drive me out of the region that was given to me? In turn, I will not let anyone live here!" This came to pass. The town's mosque collapsed, killing many of the scholars and leaders while they were at prayer. The town's Muslims thronged to Sabir, begging his pardon. He asked them to leave him in peace but they continued to press around him. Soon a plague struck the town, driving its inhabitants away. Hazrat Sabir lived on happily with a few disciples as wilderness encroached upon the ruins of the town.

These events reveal the hidden wisdom of Baba Farid, diverting Hazrat Sabir from settling in Delhi, where his jalali personality would have brought the capital to the ground. Instead, Baba Farid later sent his younger disciple Nizam al-Din to settle in Delhi where his jamali personality full of compassion, appreciative of beauty, and bending to care for the weak and sinful transformed the capital and its inhabitants, eventually spreading to every corner of the expanding empire of the Delhi Sultans.

Meanwhile, Hazrat Sabir passed away in Kaliyar. His disciples buried him there and scattered. The Sultans of Delhi tried to resettle the town but they could not manage to get Muslims to stay. Some Hindus struggled to live there and built a small temple near his tomb. Soon, they too abandoned the place and the temple fell into ruins. Hazrat Sabir's disciples thrived elsewhere in India; centuries later, one of them returned to Kaliyar and found only wild animals and birds living in harmony at a lonely spot. He experienced a vision of Hazrat Sabir who showed him where the tomb's fragments barely remained to be seen. That disciple rebuilt the tomb and Chishtis of the Sabiri branch began to make pilgrimage there, slowly building a grand shrine and reviving the place in the name of their long-deceased master whose presence still governs the place.

It is still hard to get to Kaliyar. I was lucky to have the chance to go along with some friends who are custodians of the dargah of Nizam al-Din Awliya. We drove up from Delhi in a jeep to attend the 'urs of Hazrat Sabir. While we were racing along the highway entering the region of Kaliyar, a village boy threw a rock; the front window of our jeep cracked in a violent spiderweb—if the fragments had not stayed in place we would all have been blinded by shards of glass. Hazrat Sabir is the only one allowed to be impatient in this place! We could barely see through the window to drive meekly into the town that grew up around his tomb.

From such an unlikely source, a vibrant Sufi community grew and the Sabiri branch of the Chishti Order made great contributions to music and scholarship. Many classical Indian musicians are devoted to Hazrat Sabir and take his name. In the nineteenth century, jurists belonging to the Sabiri Chishti Order established the influential Islamic academy at Deoband in 1864 after the British officially took over most of India. In Hyderabad, where the Nizams still ruled as kings while the British were merely their protectors, a branch of the Deoband Academy was started. It was called the Jami'a Nizamiya and it was founded by jurists who were disciples in the Sabiri Order. To this day, the spiritual head of this Islamic academy comes from the family of custodians of the dargah of Shah Khamosh. To this academy and its scholars, the Muslims of Hyderabad turn to resolve their religious differences.

Pir Rasheed had great respect for the scholars of Jami'a Nizamiya. He never studied there, and thus he always called himself "an uneducated man." He was the first one in his family to learn English and graduate from college, after which he worked as a clerk in the State Bank of Hyderabad and an officer in Saudi Airlines. Yet, Pir Rasheed still insisted that he was "uneducated" because he had not studied the Islamic sciences—Qur'an, hadees and law—at Jami'a Nizamiya. When problems arose, he naturally turned to the scholars of that academy for authoritative decisions.

In Pir Rasheed's life-story there were squabbles about authority and seniority and spiritual mastery, just like in the life-story of Hazrat Sabir. Hazrat Sabir had to endure a difficult trial, as his desire to be the spiritual master of Delhi was thwarted by a fellow disciple from the same community. In a similar way, Pir Rasheed's succession to be leader of the Kaleemi Sufi Order in Hyderabad was contested and he, too, had to endure trials.

A FRIEND MOST RARE

Hazrat Sabir's reputation lives on among his followers in Hyderabad. Even in dargahs associated with the Nizami branch of the Chishti Order, Hazrat Sabir is held in high esteem. There might have been conflicts between Hazrat Sabir and his fellow disciples, Jamal al-Din Hansvi and Nizam al-Din Awliya, over who was best suited to be the patron saint of Delhi. Now these are long forgotten as all family squabbles should be. Even in Hyderabad's biggest Chishti dargah associated with the Nizami branch, called Yusufayn Dargah, the memory of Hazrat Sabir is cherished. The Qawwals there sing poems by him and present songs that praise him as "a friend most rare." Although my initiation with Pir Rasheed in the Kaleemi Order consists of the Nizami branch of the Chishti lineage and not the Sabiri branch, I feel a special love for Hazrat Sabir.

I often remember how he settled in Kaliyar as a complete stranger, known by nobody and loved by none. It was not his choice of destination and he must often have wondered whether it was a kind of banishment to be brought to a place where few could appreciate him. Like Hazrat Sabir, I often felt like a stranger in Hyderabad. I had not come of my own choice and could explain to nobody back in the USA from among my friends and family why I kept coming back. There were fleeting moments when Hyderabad felt like home, and there were persisting moments of deep alienation.

As I sit in the mehfil at Yusufayn Dargah in the middle of a very cramped and dirty bazaar, I sometimes wonder what exactly I am doing here: everyone looks at me like a stranger. It is disconcerting to feel so much like I belong to this place and yet have everyone always react to me like I just stepped off a Boeing 747 from Chicago. It is tiring. People are happy to see a visitor and try their best to be welcoming, but I don't really need to be welcomed like this anymore. So it was really lovely when, late in the mehfil, the qawwali group called the Warsi Brothers showed up. They always come last, after midnight, and they know me, so I get a little nod of acknowledgement that makes all the difference.

In Hyderabad, the Warsi Brothers are one of the most popular and prolific groups. The contemporary Warsi Brothers group consists of two brothers (Nazeer and Naseer Warsi who sing and play harmonium) in addition to their other relatives who support on percussion and vocals. These are two of the four sons of Zaheer Ahmed Khan Warsi, who was the eldest son of Aziz Ahmad Khan Warsi. He in turn was a grandson of Muhammad Siddiq Khan, who brought this singing tradition from Delhi to Hyderabad. He was a Qawwal attached to the dargah of Nizam al-Din Awliya in Delhi, but he found patronage in Hyderabad as the court singer of the sixth Nizam. Many musicians, poets and scholars fled Delhi after the British conquest of 1857 and the subsequent fall of the Mughal court. The Nizams of Hyderabad ruled as Mughal-style kings. Their patronage helped Islamic arts in music, literature, painting and dance.

Muhammad Siddiq Khan descended from the great singer Miyan Tanras Khan who was the court singer of Bahadur Shah Zafar, the last Mughal emperor. He was a great exponent of the Delhi Gharana of singing which included qawwali and khayal styles. Tanras Khan composed many lyrics that found their way into qawwali songs, such as the lyrics of "Mustard Flowers are Filling the Fields" (*Sakal-Ban Phul Rahe Sarson*) in Raga Bahar, in which his lyrics follow a couplet attributed to Ameer Khusro.[74] Tanras Khan also composed lyrics for khayal that are dedicated to Chishti Sufi guides in more austere classical style of the court; an example is "Take my Boat Across the Waters, Master Nizam" (*Ab Mori Naiya Par Karo Re, Hazrat Nizam al-Din Awliya*) in Raga Todi.[75] Despite their ritual attachment to the dargah of Nizam al-Din Awliya, these Qawwals, like many Indian musicians, cultivate a deep reverence for Hazrat Sabir.

The Warsi family became famous in 20th century Hyderabad for singing qawwali at dargahs, but their roots go back to the royal courts of Hyderabad and before that to Delhi. There they cultivated both styles of singing: khayal in the courts of kings (darbar) and qawwali at the court of saints (dargah). In Delhi, this dualism was represented by the court of the Mughal ruler (sultan) and the tomb-shrine of Nizam al-Din Awliya (sultan-e masha'ikh). Patronage changed in the twentieth century as royal power was abolished, but patronage at Sufi dargahs continues. There, in ritual gatherings presided over by a spiritual authority and with an experienced audience, the music is performed as a means of empowering the listeners' spiritual awareness. The aesthetic qualities of the singing are totally directed to heightening this effect.

As the Warsi Brothers fiddled with the harmoniums and tuned the tablas, I wanted to request them to sing Ameer Khusro's *Lagi ri mein to charan tehari*—"I lay my head down at your feet." The song is so sweet it will melt a stone! I had been listening to recordings of it rather obsessively for the last few weeks. I dearly wanted to hear it. I wanted to request it, but nobody had made any requests in the mehfil and I was feeling already out of place, so I just sat there thinking of the song. So the Warsi brothers were fiddling around, the way Qawwals do when they start, as if confused and stringing together a few notes, until they started to sing... *Lagi ri mein to charan tehari.*

> In Muʿin al-Din's garden is a flowerbed called Qutb al-Din
> It blossoms as Farid al-Din, so Sabir's face glows crimson
> ...I lay down my head at your feet

That is when I felt as if my friend Seemi Ghazi had joined me at the mehfil. Even though she was teaching Arabic in Canada, I felt that she was sitting just beside me, listening to the music. She was a dear friend from my graduate studies, who was like my sister—a sister I never had. Her family had moved from Deoband in India to America and she married a Canadian doctor. Now she serves there as the muqaddam or representative of the Rifaʿi Maʿrufi Order in Vancouver. For many generations, her family produced Islamic scholars with links to the Sabiri branch of the Chishti Order. I felt her presence right then at the first mention of Sabir—Shaykh ʿAla al-Din ʿAli Ahmad Sabir.

> I lay down my head at your feet, o Sabir
> I lay down my head at your feet, ʿAli Ahmad Sabir
> my head, my head, at your feet is my head
> I lay down my head at your feet
> Lovely Sabir has come to Kaliyar
> I lay down my head at your feet
>
> Just as ʿAli was dear to our Prophet
> You are the darling of Baba Farid, o Sabir
> I lay down my head at your feet
> With just one look at you
> All my sorrow turns to joy, o Sabir
> I lay down my head at your feet
>
> ʿAla al-Din, my protector, a friend most rare
> di dom di dom taranana rana nananana!
> your feet my head, my head your feet
> I lay down my head at your feet

The singers were invoking Hazrat Sabir, who has been watching over Seemi's family for generations at Deoband. With the repeated mention of Sabir's name, she joined me at the mehfil. It felt as if Seemi were there. Those ancient ties are still there, and I asked Hazrat Sabir to look after her in all her trials, to be her friend in times of need—a friend most rare, *'Ala al-Din Awliya nadir dost nadir dost*!

Such was my state while this song was coursing along. My *silsila* doesn't go back to 'Ali Ahmad Sabir, so I felt shy to ask all this. But I had been to Kaliyar last year for his 'urs, so perhaps he remembered me. At Kaliyar, I was almost crushed in the crowd as people shoved and yelled to get through the gateway and into the courtyard where there was no single space to even put one's foot on the ground as it seethed with humanity. Anyway, both he and Nizam al-Din Awliya were dear to Baba Farid, each in their own, very different ways—Nizam al-Din with all his ochre gentleness and Sabir with all his scarlet might. That is why poor Sabir was sent off to the forested hills of Kaliyar, so that he would not burn too many people up with his passion, while Nizam al-Din was deputed to stay in Delhi's cosmopolis to be in the middle of the crowds.

That was my state while this song was flowing along, so sweetly, like a *dhamar* song for the spring time that makes the buds burst into bloom. How can one be shy at a time like that? I asked the Qawwals to keep singing the song, but with the original words that Ameer Khusro had set to music, and they obliged.

> Every group has a faith and a direction to pray
> I turn my face towards the one with his cap awry
> ...I lay down my head at your feet

They say that once Nizam al-Din was sitting in his *chilla-khana* overlooking the river Jamuna. Khusro was sitting with him then. Nizam al-Din gazed out over the riverbank in the early morning and watched Hindus wading into the river to pray facing toward the rising sun. He said to Khusro, "Every community has a right faith and direction to pray" translating into Persian that verse from the Qur'an (Surat al-Hajj 22:67). Khusro heard him say this, and looked at him sitting there with his cap awry on his head, as was his style. Khusro heard it as the first line of a couplet, to which he devised a fitting reply—"Every group has a right faith and a direction to pray / I turn my face towards the one with his cap awry!"

The Qawwals still sing this, set in a composition, whose rhyme and meter in Persian matches perfectly with the old Hindi of "I lay down my head at your feet."[76]

> In this world all things pray, each one worships something
> Some take the Banaras way, others toward Mecca go searching

THE DOOR'S LEAF

> Girlfriends, what do you say? I take lover's feet beseeching
> Every group has a faith and a direction to pray
> I turn my face towards the one with his cap awry
> ...I lay down my head at your feet

It was so lovely the way they sang, weaving between Persian and Hindi, singing these words of a female heroine in their blaring male voices, drawing together 'Ali Ahmad Sabir and Nizam al-Din Awliya into one song. From two to one, from two to one, from two to one to one only one!

Then something strange happened. The Qawwals asked me for my request, even after they had just sung what I really wanted. I asked them to sing another poem by Ameer Khusro—*Gul ba chaman shakl-e bashar amada dar jahan dil-ruba*, "From the garden, a rose in human form entered the world to steal our hearts." It is very old fashioned and not in much demand anymore, and it is hard to play with a beat cycle of 14, with deep emphasis on beats 1 then 9, 11 and 13 before coming down heavy on 1 again. It gives a very soul-searing feeling of awe as it builds up to 8 and then a frightening suspense as it wavers on 9 to 14 before falling back into place on 1 again. It will drive you out of your mind.

My ego jumped into the scene then when I asked for that song. The singers were uncertain at first but then settled into it, shifting their drummers around because I don't think the routine drummer knew the song. They did their best, but flubbed it up as the dhol player kept coming in on the wrong beat. They had to stop and start over again, and it all ended badly. I was sorry I had made that request. The singers looked embarrassed and everyone was out of sorts. This was a lesson to me that one should never make requests of the Qawwals, but let them sense what song the assembly needs. They are the experts at this, and requests just let the ego into the gathering where it does not belong.

Then another in attendance made a request for a modern Urdu song. They heard him and looked to me; I was not about to request anything, so I asked them to play whatever the other guy wanted. They promptly set into something completely different, not for me or for him. It was just for Seemi: a ghazal by Maulana Rumi.[77]

I'm not lost as through the lanes and markets I wander I've a taste for love so chasing my dear one I wander	نہ من بیہودہ گردِ کوچہ و بازار می گردم مذاقِ عاشقی دارم پےَ دیدار می گردم

Mercy, O Lord, mercy!
I'm wandering full of woes
I've lost all, I've done wrong—
wailing, weeping, I wander

I've drunk passion's wine
and circle my friend
I babble like a fool but
in ways of wisdom I wander

A thousand times, I plunge
into this endless sea
Searching for pearls of meaning,
its depths I wander

One time I smile, another I cry;
one time I fall, another I rise
O savior, appear now in my heart
for still so ill I wander

Come, my love, show
Maulana Rumi a little kindness
I am the slave of Shams,
so like a vagabond I wander

I came home at 2:30 am on a still and quiet night, and there is not much stillness or quietness here in Hyderabad! I called my friend Seemi on the phone, and it was a great blessing to hear her voice from afar. She had been keeping me company there in the dargah of Yusufayn in Hyderabad, though in body, she was in Vancouver. As Pir Rasheed taught me, "In relationships of the spirit, distance and time have no effect."

SKIN, STRING AND WOOD

I had spent two years in the Netherlands pursuing an intense research project on Islam, gender and sexuality. This allowed me to spend time in Hyderabad on and off. But by the end of 2006, my fellowship in the Netherlands was finished and I was facing hard choices again. Should I stay in Europe, return to America, or move to India? I always loved going to India, even before meeting

Pir Rasheed, but I never found it easy to live there permanently. Returning to America was not attractive, with George W. Bush still President and waging war in Afghanistan and Iraq. I searched for teaching or research jobs in the Netherlands, but the climate there was growing more hostile to Muslims as well. Shortly after I moved to Amsterdam, a young Moroccan man assassinated a well-known Dutch film-maker, Theo van Gogh, who had been making a documentary film about misogyny among Muslims. He stabbed the film-maker on the road outside his home, in broad daylight and left a fatwa pinned to his body. This was just a short bike ride away from where I lived in De Pijp, a vibrant and very mixed neighborhood where Moroccans, Dutch, Turks and Caribbeans rubbed shoulders daily around the Sarphati Park and the Albert Coup street market. Rightwing anti-immigrant and Islamophobic voices rang louder and louder in this formerly liberal country.

India it was to be. I applied for a Fulbright grant to do a new research project in India. As soon as the official acceptance letter came, I packed my bags and shifted to Hyderabad. God was again kind to make my research interests and abilities lead me where I needed to go. With some prudence and simple living, a Fulbright grant for one year could be stretched to two or more. I was ready to try anything to stay close to Pir Rasheed. At first, I was apprehensive about staying in Hyderabad permanently. Would I grow weary of the daily grind and the difficulty of getting practical things accomplished? I got an Indian driver's license and bought a used jeep that was rough enough to handle bumps in the traffic. I rented the upstairs of a bungalow with a terrace surrounded by tall Ashoka trees and flowering vines. I collected antique furniture made of teak and rosewood, some from the roadside markets to be renovated and some from far flung towns in the Andhra countryside. When the American economy collapsed in 2008, there was little reason to think of going back. I got along just fine in Hyderabad by doing research projects, writing books and articles, teaching courses and giving occasional lectures at Indian universities.

During this time, I visited Pir Rasheed in the holy month of Ramadan to ask his permission to study music. He immediately replied by reciting a Persian poem by Maulana Rumi.[78]

> Dried skin, brittle wood and strung gut
>   From this how does my beloved's voice come?
>
> Not from skin, not from wood and not from gut
>   From beyond these does my beloved's voice come!

He told me, "Not only should you study music but you must learn music! Music is the backbone of our tareeqat. It is the very foundation of the Chishti Order. Without music, there would be no energy and no light in the Chishti path. The better one understands music, the better one can progress in the Chishti Order."

I went away convinced that I must start to learn music as fast as humanly possible. For years, I had harbored the secret desire to learn Indian classical music, after listening deeply to it on recordings and in live performance whenever the rare occasion presented itself. In my first year of college in the USA, there was a young woman from Delhi who lived on the same floor of my dorm, and whenever she was playing cassettes of Indian music I used to sit in the hallway outside her room pretending to read while listening to the melodies that leaked out from under her door. Once she discovered me there and, rather than being angry, she made copies of her cassettes for me. The best of them was a recording of *bansuri* bamboo flute by Pandit Hariprasad Chaurasia accompanied by Ustad Zakir Husayn on tabla. Later when I was finishing college, the sitar maestro Ravi Shankar came on a performance tour, and ten of us piled into my friend's tiny Toyota to drive to University of Pennsylvania to hear him; the excitement of hearing a master perform on stage with deep improvisation was utterly thrilling. Little did I know that Indian classical music was first introduced in the USA by a Sufi musician, namely Hazrat Inayat Khan, who belonged to the Kaleemi Sufi Order that I, too, would later join! Only in hindsight do events make sense.

Despite listening to sitar and bamboo flute and tabla, the instrument whose voice held the greatest allure for me was the *sarangi*. For years I listened for its soulful and resonant voice in recordings and film songs, without ever knowing what it was called. It is a bowed instrument with gut strings that sounds like the human voice in its pathos, expressing extremes of exquisite sweetness and profound sorrow. After taking initiation with Pir Rasheed, I began to attend the Tansen Festival of classical Indian music, held each year in Gwalior beside the dargah of Shaykh Muhammad Ghaus. There I heard fine artists, such as Dhruba Ghosh and Sarwar Husayn Khan, play the sarangi as both solo and accompanying instrument, and my fascination only deepened. I never dreamed that I could learn to play it, but the sarangi followed me around, appearing in the most unlikely of places.

At the festival in Gwalior, I happened to meet a French ethnomusicologist and since we were both professors we kept in touch. Years later she happened to be in Amsterdam when I was working there. It just happened that she was staying in Amsterdam in the apartment of a friend of hers. When I arrived at the apartment to meet her for tea, I discovered the apartment was full of antique sarangis. There were at least twenty instruments in all shapes and sizes, beautiful personalities of carved wood and inlayed ivory, scattered throughout the apartment in glass cases. My French colleague caught me staring at them in wonder, and informed me that this apartment happened to belong to Joep Bor, an accomplished sarangi player and music professor in the Netherlands, one of the pioneers in teaching Indian classical music in Europe. Overcome by the beauty of these instruments, I admitted to her that "I always loved the sound of the sarangi and want to learn to play it." Surprised, she replied, "You must believe in reincarnation!" I didn't understand her point and looked at her befuddled. She clarified, "You must believe in reincarnation, because it would take you at least three lifetimes to learn to play it!" Yes, the art was handed down in families and sarangi players started learning in childhood; she certainly knew Indian music far better than I, so I trusted her assessment. Her reply dashed all hopes that I had secretly entertained. I let that dream fade. For many years, I banished the thought of learning to play Indian music because of the caustic corrosion of that one off-hand remark.

Back in Hyderabad many years later, my Urdu teacher decided to demolish the villa in which she lived with her husband, a villa surrounded by mango trees and protective geese in which I had spent many rainy seasons studying Urdu poetry. Time stands still for no one: the villa had grown dilapidated and the city was expanding rapidly, such that nobody had use for villas when land could be better used for a high-rise. My Urdu teacher decided to tear down the villa and build an apartment building. When it was completed, I rented an apartment there and my Urdu teacher also became my landlady. She decided to celebrate the new building by hosting a musical soirée in her new apartment, inviting an old acquaintance of hers who sang ghazals. I was in the audience when the singer arrived with his accompanists, a tabla player and a sarangi accompanist.

The singer warmed up on the harmonium and his exploration of the *raga* went on much too long while he kept his mouth shut. When he finally began to sing, he could barely hold a note. His voice was completely hoarse. After destroying one or two ghazals and indulging in fits of coughing and throat-clearing, he finally admitted to the audience that he had been singing in weddings for five nights continuously and thus his voice was "not as strong as it usually is." After razing another song and leaving the audience squirming in their seats, he finally had the grace to stop singing. Thank God, his accompanists were both accomplished musicians. The sarangi player graciously took over the show, weaving melodies around the beat of the tabla like flowering vines growing up a garden trellis. He was later introduced as Saeed ur-Rahman Khan, the only sarangi player in Hyderabad—nay, in the whole of the Deccan—and he kept the audience enthralled all night, transforming the worst vocal performance imaginable into a magical instrumental exploration of the heart.

After the performance, I introduced myself to the sarangi player, who is fondly known as Ustad Jigar. I asked him, "Do you ever train students?" He answered, "Yes, sometimes, if any worthy student presents himself." I asked again, "Have you ever had a foreign student?" He looked surprised, "Nothing is impossible…Why? Do you know someone who is interested?" I smiled and replied, "Perhaps that would be me." He was quiet for a moment and then asked abruptly, "Show me your hand." I held out my right hand for him to see. "No, no…not that hand," he muttered, "the other one." I meekly extended my left hand for him as if he were about to read the lines of my palm. "Not that side!" he said angrily, amazed at my stupidity. I turned my hand over palm down, and he took my fingers in his hand and raised them close to his eyes, examining the cuticles as if he were a jeweler polishing diamonds. Of course, I realized, sarangi players press into the strings with the middle three fingers of their left hand just above the cuticle, and slide them along the fretless strings to produce remarkable glides and subtle semitones. Ustad Jigar was studying my three fingers, so I also began to study them as if I had never seen them before. What was he looking for? Was I failing some test?

After a moment that seemed like an eternity, he dropped my hand. "Yes, you can learn," he pronounced matter-of-factly. "I can?" I asked in disbelief. "Yes, just come to my home later this week—here's my card. Oh, and don't forget to bring everything you'll need for an initiation ceremony." I inquired, "Initiation?" His reply was curt, "Yes, you'll bring one kilo of sweets, palm-sugar, roasted chickpeas, a box of incense sticks, two flower garlands, cash to gift to twenty witnesses, and saris for each of my two wives. I'll provide the red thread to tie around your wrist." That was it. The date was fixed. I needed to go shopping. I didn't even own a sarangi—I actually had never touched one before.

Ustad Jigar was quite a character. He talked non-stop. His torrent of speech seemed like an odd trait for a musician. He drank tea the same way other people breathed air—constantly and without thinking about it at all. That only seemed to fuel his talking, which only accelerated as he aged. At around sixty, he had a cozy if modest career playing sarangi on *Akashwani*—All India Radio. He had learned music from his father, Ghulam Muʻin al-Din, who was a medical doctor as well as a musician, and from his grandfather Ghulam Sabir, who had played sarangi in the court of the Nizam. He was named Ghulam Sabir, meaning "Servant of Sabir," because this family of musicians like so many other classical instrumentalists and qawwali singers, focused their devotion on Hazrat ʿAli Ahmad Sabir and through him traced their connection to Khwaja Muʿin al-Din Chishti. Pictures of all these ancestors were hung high on the wall of the sitting room of his ramshackle house in an impoverished neighborhood called Hakimpet. There was even a picture of the last Nizam himself, deposed in 1948 but still deeply revered by some. They all stared down at me in disbelief as I sat there, handing over my gifts of sugar, chickpeas and saris to Ustad Jigar, followed by an envelope filled with 101 rupees for each of the witnesses he had called from his extended clan of tabla players, singers and motorcycle repairmen.[79]

Ustad Jigar fed me a sugar cube with his own hands, and then I fed him one. He poured a handful of chickpeas into my mouth, and I fed him one. He draped a flower garland of roses and jasmine over my shoulders and I laid one on him. Then he tied a red thread around my right wrist as the witnesses murmured verses of the Qurʾan. He then handed me a sarangi, corrected my posture as I sat with the instrument upright in my lap, and straightened the instrument in my grip. He directed me to pick up the bow with my right hand—"not that way, this way!" He placed the cuticle of my left index finger along the gut strings. "Now press against the string," which I did. "Now move the bow along the string," which I did. No sound came forth. "Not that way—this way!" I tried again, but no sound came. "Press harder—till it really hurts!" I tried again, and managed to emit a frail high screech. I winced. The witnesses watched closely. "Press harder!" Ustad Jigar grabbed the fingers of my left hand and rammed them into the sharp tautness of the string. Teeth clenched in pain, I pulled the bow in desperation, and a sustained and resonant tone sounded. All the witnesses clapped merrily. My first lesson was over. It seemed like an inauspicious start, but there was no time to dwell on it for lunch was served.

Ustad Jigar's family belonged to the Kirana Gharana and thus, so did I. His family had migrated from Meerut near Delhi down to the Deccan, following patronage. They kept up the tradition of sarangi playing even as the world changed rapidly around them, shifting from sarangis to harmoniums to pianos to synthesizers. I purchased a sarangi from my teacher, which had just arrived from Meerut where they are still manufactured from jackfruit wood and baby goat skin and camel bone. Ustad Jigar taught me the basics, beginning with Raga Yaman, a musical mode that had been invented by Ameer Khusro, the greatest musician of the Chishti Order. That encouraged me, but my teacher was more interested in newspapers, cigarettes and tea than he was in teaching. I dutifully went to his home twice a week, and he set me to playing the seven notes of Raga Yaman in ascending and descending order, over and over again, while he read the news, yelled toward the kitchen for more tea, stepped outside for a smoke and gossip with the neighbors, or disciplined his many children. "If you can't play the seven notes of Raga Yaman in tune, how can you play a melody?" he would ask. That was true. Playing in tune is no mean feat when there are no frets to guide your fingers and when the gut strings tighten with humidity or loosen in the heat.

Luckily, Ustad Jigar lost interest in me. His eldest son, Aslam Khan, picked up the pieces. After my fifth lesson, the son said to me, "It is hard for you to learn in my family's house with all the children and the neighborhood noise. Learning at your house would be easier, right? But my father can't come to your house to teach you, right? I can. So maybe it would be better if I come to your house and teach you in place of my father—he taught me after all, so I will teach you exactly as if it were him teaching, except that I understand how you want to learn. You don't want to spend two years playing the seven notes of Raga Yaman in ascending and descending order, do you?" I shook my head. "No! You want to learn quickly, right?" I nodded. "Yes! I understand that this is the modern world now, there is no time to play the same notes for years on end. Let me teach you at your house, and then you can come play before Ustad Jigar once a month and let him correct you. Whatever salary you give to me I will give to him—after all, he is my teacher as well as my father."

As it turned out, Aslam Khan was a marvelous teacher at only 23 years old. Later I learned that he was not really the eldest son of Ustad Jigar and Ustad Jigar was not really his teacher. He was adopted from a distant relative when Ustad Jigar's first wife could not bear children. When he learned the basics of sarangi and showed aptitude, Ustad Jigar sent him to Delhi to learn with Ustad Sabri Khan Sahib, the great maestro. Ustad Sabri Khan was skeptical but allowed Aslam to join for one year on a trial basis while living in the garage of his home, without being a formal shagird or pupil. Then with his teacher's help, Aslam got a government scholarship of 2500 rupees per month. With this support, he asked to become a formal shagird, but that meant a huge expense of ritual, giving gifts and nazrana to family members, and clothes and food and sweets for his Ustad. He saved up his monthly scholarship and spent 15,000 rupees on the ritual. He explained, "Becoming a real shagird creates this influence and relationship between student and teacher. Without that, one cannot really learn music or succeed. For the first year, when I was learning while living in the teacher's garage, I didn't know what I was doing. I was practicing hard every night but it just didn't make sense in my heart. It didn't stick deeply. After becoming a shagird with the ritual, then everything began to make sense.

It is the teacher's prayers on your behalf and his gaze upon you that influences the heart." Musical training and Sufi training use the same method.

After a few years of intense training, Aslam left Delhi and returned to Hyderabad. He gave his first performance before Faisal Baba, the custodian of the Yusufayn Dargah, who belongs to our Kaleemi Order. Faisal Baba is not just a hereditary Sufi leader, but also a connoisseur of classical music, and is himself a singer. Every Friday he invites the musicians of Hyderabad to his home inside the dargah compound to play music, and guest artists come to him from all over India—whoever is coming to Hyderabad for some big program comes first to Faisal Baba to play for him and seek his blessings. Aslam was supposed to play for 15 minutes, but ended up playing for almost an hour. He told the story, saying:

> I was so nervous and I thought I would make mistakes and play off key, because it was my first time playing in front of a real audience. But by God's grace, the music just flowed out of me. My hand was right on key, the melodies just came pouring out. As I played, I found more and more music just welling up in my heart: from where it was coming, I don't know! My father, Ustad Jigar, was sitting there with tears rolling down his cheeks, so relieved that one of his children would succeed him when he was dead and gone. Faisal Baba was pleased and blessed me. I was so happy. I immediately called my Ustad in Delhi and informed him about the performance. "How did it go?" he asked. "Very well," I said. "Huh?" the teacher retorted, "Very well, you say? You have the guts to tell me on the phone that you played very well? You didn't play in front of me and you declare that it went very well? You don't know anything! How would you know if it was good or bad, without your teacher telling you? Never talk to me again!"
>
> I was shocked and dismayed. I had only meant to tell my teacher in my happiness that everyone who heard it was pleased. Then Sohail, my fellow pupil who lived in Delhi, explained to me, "You can't talk to the Ustad like that. You have to tell him that the performance, thanks to his blessings and his teacher, went alright. Explain that you wish you could have presented the music to him first, but you are living so far away." So I called Ustad Sabri Khan again and spoke with this kind of modesty, thanking him for his blessings and his teaching that preserved my respect on stage in front of an audience. The Ustad replied, "By God's grace may you always find success." The relationship between music master and student is very delicate; it is very complex. The great Ustads of former times were very strict and demanding, but the influence of their stern gaze makes all the difference for those with the discipline to handle it. It makes musicians out of students.

The students of a music teacher or Ustad are in a delicate position. They must work hard, perfecting a difficult art with long hours of practice. Yet they must attribute any success to their Ustad and his blessings, rather than to their own hard work. Without the hard work, there is no blessing. But without the blessing, hard work amounts to nothing.

The disciples of a Sufi master are in a similar delicate position. Students of music are called shagird, while disciples in Sufism are called mureed. But the process of learning is very similar. In Sufism, all that happens to a mureed that seems bad must be attributed to the mureed's own base nature; all that happens that seems good must be attributed to God's grace, channeled through the presence of one's Pir. It is a delicate position that demands great endurance and relinquishing one's ego-centric sense of justice, that one should get what one deserves. This is collapsed by the wise insight that one really deserves nothing because one is nothing, and whatever good that comes is by the grace and kindness of the other. Whether it is music or spirituality, the dynamic is the same.

FORGIVING AND FORGETTING

Today is *Shab-e Barat* or the Night of Forgiveness. I had arranged with Mubeen to meet him at night to attend the *namaz-e tasbeeh* together, as we had in past years, at the dargah of 'Abdullah Shah in the old city, but I could not find his phone number to arrange where to meet him. I called Pir Rasheed and asked for the number. He gave it to me, then said that we must all avail ourselves of the opportunity to stay awake this night and ask for pardon for ourselves, our family, our ancestors and for all of humanity. I told him I hoped to attend a late-night namaz-e tasbeeh. He said I should do that, but there was no need to go out of the house. "You do not need to do that in congregational jama'at" he said, "In my family we usually stay at home to do that. You can do the same."

I did not move out of the house that night. I did the namaz-e tasbeeh at home by myself. I tried to keep count of the times to repeat, "Glory be to God and praise be for God and there is no god but God and God is greatest—*Subhanallahi wa'l-hamdu lillahi wa la ilaha illa 'llahu wa allahu akbar.*" One has to repeat this praise of God under one's breath at least three hundred times during one cycle of prayer, begging for forgiveness and blessing. I kept losing track, but I think that is the point. There was such a sweetness in forgetting. I don't know how long it took me to finish one cycle of prayer in this way.

BEGGING

I had the blessing of going to Gulbarga today to attend the sama' that happens there every night on the 15th of the lunar month. I was late in leaving Hyderabad because my music teacher, Aslam Khan, came over to finish dressing my new sarangi.

I had been learning music from him for over a year. Learning was slow but steady. My calluses developed, permanently warping the skin above the fingernails of my left hand. That was a scar of pride. I began to learn ghamak when one slides calloused fingers quickly along the string in vigorous glides. When one played really hard and forgot the world, the string would cut one's fingers. Aslam assured me, "The sarangi is a very jealous instrument. It doesn't sound good until it drinks blood. You need to bleed before you can play it well." Now I needed a better instrument and on a recent trip to Delhi, he visited Meerut where they are made. He brought a new one back for me and saved money by getting it directly from the instrument makers. But the new instrument needed to be dressed, with its 35 thin, metal sympathetic strings and three gut playing strings carefully strung through its camel bone bridge poised over the taut skin resonator, which need to be tuned over and over until the tension between wood, skin, bone, gut and wire is perfectly balanced. It took a long time, and is called "dressing" the instrument in a new garment.

It was three in the afternoon by the time Aslam left, and my trip to Gulbarga was badly delayed. But just as he was leaving, the monsoon rains came down so hard that a mere block away, his scooter got water up the tailpipe and stalled out. Aslam came back to my house soaking wet, just as I was packing to leave. I drove him home to Hakimpet, and took the old Bombay highway route out of Hyderabad toward Gulbarga. On the way, I stopped at the Astana in Shaikhpet to offer the fatiha prayer at the tombs of Pir Rasheed's ancestors. I did not get there on Shab-e Barat, as I should have. That is the time to visit the tombs of loved ones and beg God to forgive them and preserve them, and to forgive you, too. Better late than never, as a ghazal says:[80]

> You're late in coming, but thank God at least you've come anyway
>   I never let my heart cling to hope so that despair might keep away
>
> Twilight, moonbeams, dusky clouds, stars and songs, bolts and buds
>   What all he has up his sleeve, if only his hand would come my way
>
> How could I ever explain what all in life has happened to me
>   Sparks might bloom into flower, if desire would flare up some day

> The past is full of lies that keep coming back to haunt me
> I accept it, but let my dream of youth return and for a while stay

The rain was hard and the road was long. It takes about four hours to drive from Hyderabad to Gulbarga, the ancient capital of this Deccan region.

Hazrat Gesu Daraz was a great Sufi master in the Chishti Order, and gave new life to the order here in the Deccan where he died in 1422. His given name was Sayyid Muhammad Husayni, but he is better known now by the honorific title Banda Nawaz, "He who is Kind to the People" and the endearment Gesu Daraz, "He of the Long Locks." He was descended from the family of Imam Husayn through twenty generations. His ancestor moved from Iran to India during the initial Islamic conquest of Delhi, but he was killed in a battle. Nevertheless, the family stayed on in Delhi. When Gesu Daraz was four years old, his father moved to Khuldabad, when the Sultan of Delhi forced much of the population to immigrate to the Deccan. There he educated the young Gesu Daraz in both religious and philosophical subjects, until he was sixteen and his father sent him back to Delhi. He became a disciple of Naseer al-Din Mahmud Chiragh-e Delli, "The Lamp of Delhi," who was the successor to Nizam al-Din Awliya and the central axis of the Chishti Order.

Shaykh Naseer al-Din combined scholarly acumen and ascetic rigor in his own personality, though he still loved music and poetry. He instilled this set of virtues into the young Gesu Daraz. He set Gesu Daraz to hard tasks in worship and study, but the teenager excelled. It is said that the Prophet Muhammad used to let his hair grow long so that it hung over his shoulders, so Gesu Daraz decided to let his hair also grow until it was down to his waist. For him, that was a sign that he renounced the world and was striving to live up to the Prophet's virtuous example. Once, a prince came to Shaykh Naseer al-Din to ask for initiation. This put the Shaykh in a precarious position. He struggled hard to maintain distance from kings, who connived to get the Chishti leaders to grant them legitimacy and blessings even as they were jealous of Chishti popularity. Shaykh Naseer al-Din gave the prince initiation, but said to him, "O son of a ruler, it will not be possible for you to meet me after today. Neither will you be able to speak to me or hear me speak. Rather, choose anyone from among my companions to be your teacher." The prince was quiet for a while, then indicated Gesu Daraz. Shaykh Naseer al-Din called out to him, "O Sayyid with the Long Locks, come over here!" and he entrusted the new disciple to his care.[81]

From that day, people began to call him Gesu Daraz, "He with the Long Locks." And from that day, Gesu Daraz became a Sufi master in his own right at a very young age. He took the disciple, 'Ala al-Din, under his guidance and taught him everything that his Pir had taught, such that the aristocratic disciple did not feel any loss or neglect. Gesu Daraz was so completely obliterated in the personality of his own Shaykh that those who spent time with him felt they were seeing and hearing Shaykh Naseer al-Din. They fast became friends, and when Gesu Daraz moved from Delhi to the Deccan, the prince accompanied him everywhere. Even in death, the two have stayed close. He is buried in a hauntingly isolated dargah at Aland, a few miles outside of Gulbarga, where Gesu Daraz has his own massive dargah in the center of the city which was once the capital of the whole Deccan.

When Gesu Daraz was still a young man, he once helped to carry the palanquin in which Shaykh Naseer al-Din Chiragh-e Delli was riding. His long locks got caught in the beam through which the bearers carried the palanquin on their shoulders. As they processed through the city, his hair was pulled out of his head and his scalp was bleeding, but Gesu Daraz did not notice or stop. Such was the power of his concentration and his absorption in the love of his Pir. Shaykh Naseer al-Din made a poetic couplet about him.[82]

Those who, under that Sayyid of Long Locks, as disciples take cover By God, is it any wonder that each of them becomes a true lover?	ہر کہ مرید سیدِ گیسو دراز شد واللہ خلاف نیست کہ او عشق باز شد

When Shaykh Naseer al-Din fell ill in his old age, he conferred khilafat upon the young Gesu Daraz and made him his successor. After mourning for thirty days, Gesu Daraz took his seat in the position of his preceptor, and began to take initiations in earnest. He was a major Chishti leader in Delhi until the threat of Ameer Timur or Tamerlane loomed. That Central Asian conqueror was eyeing the prize of Delhi and India. The kings of Delhi turned to Gesu Daraz to bless their rule as they prepared for battle, but Gesu Daraz repudiated them. He left Delhi and predicted the downfall of its kings. At eighty years of age, he returned to the Deccan where he had grown up as a child. He stopped at villages and towns along the way, to Gujarat and then Khuldabad, and left a trail of Chishti initiations and teachers in his wake.

The king of the Deccan at that time was Firoz Shah Bahmani. He invited Gesu Daraz to settle at this capital at Gulbarga, and Gesu Daraz accepted. He built a khanqah for Gesu Daraz just outside the fort which housed the royal palace. The king was fascinated by philosophy and rational discourse, but soon found that Gesu Daraz, despite his erudition, was dismissive of mere philosophy. His teachings at the core were about mystical love. Gradually, the king grew suspicious of the Chishti master. He watched with growing jealousy as people flocked to the khanqah and gave deep respect to the Sufi. The king began to complain of the crowds blocking the way to and from the palace, and ordered the khanqah to stop playing music. Hazrat Gesu Daraz happily gave the khanqah back to the king and moved deeper into the city, far removed from the fort, court and palace. There a far grander khanqah was quickly built without depending upon the king.

Firoz Shah Bahmani built his own spangled palace complex far from the city, called Firozabad, and it was once the wonder of the age. The king hosted intellectual debates and feasted the philosophers and scientists of his age with golden vessels and choice foods. On my trip to Gulbarga, I drove out with some friends to visit that palace. It was hard to find. Nothing is left but a ring of high walls, a few broken arches, and echoes. Farmers plow the palace for their fields and goats clamor over the walls like sentinels. There is nothing left. But the khanqah of Gesu Daraz still thrives. After his death, it became his tomb and the dargah complex is huge. Its massive whitewashed walls house thousands of pilgrims and visitors. It is the palace of the poor and shines with the splendor of the simple folk. Food is still served there for free and people come hoping to find solace. And music still resounds there on special days. I arrived for the monthly *majlis-e sama'* that happens on the night of the fifteenth of each lunar month, commemorating the day of the month on which Gesu Daraz passed away from this embodied existence.

But at Gulbarga, the qawwali singing was marvelous. One singer, Muhammad Qasim, was really lovely. He looked like a Mulla but sang like an angel. He sang one of Khusro's ghazals that is a favorite of mine and how sweetly he sang it and with such spiritual verve; its very first words send me headlong into a state.[83]

Every night I lay down near the abode of you Until daybreak I sigh and cry for the sake of you	ہر شب منم فتادہ بگرد سرائے تو ہر روز آہ و نالہ کنم از برائے تو
My dear, just come, come see this broken heart of mine I've spent my whole life, my idol, seeking the nearness of you	جاناں بایں شکستہ دلے بے وفا مشو عمرے گذشت تا شدہ ام آشنائے تو

On the day when my bones
are scattered as dust
Still my wounded heart
will bear the love of you

روزے کہ ذرّہ ذرّہ شود استخوانِ من
باشد ہنوز در دل ریشم ہوائے تو

The day never comes that brings
a night in your embrace
Woe and woe again be to him
who is enamored of you

یک دم شبِ وصال میسر نشد مرا
اے وائے بر کسے کہ شود مبتلائے تو

Just look at my pitiful state
for once, from mere kindness
You are the king of beauty
and Khusro is begging of you

بر حالِ زارِ ما نظرے کن ز راہِ لطف
تو پادشاہِ حسن و خسرو گدائے تو

When they sang the phrase, "You are the king of beauty," the image of Pir Rasheed came to my heart. With each repetition, it grew more and more intense. Khusro came as a beggar to meet his spiritual teacher, just as I came as a wayfaring stranger to Hyderabad. Khusro's poetry excels in longing and yearning to close the gap of separation, expressing feelings I know so well.

On the drive from Gulbarga to Hyderabad on National Highway number 9, my brakes failed. I could barely stop. I drove through Zahirabad at a crawl and found a mechanic. It turns out the brake fluid pipe had broken and lay dangling under the engine. In about three hours, the ingenious mechanic had procured a new pipe and fitted it into the brake system. I made it home somehow. When I told him, Pir Rasheed said, "God saved you for some purpose. Let's find out what it is."

CHAPTER 5

THE DOOR'S HANDLE

ECHOES OF A DISTANT MELODY

Hazrat Gesu Daraz holds a special place in the Chishti Order. He committed the Order's teachings to writing in a systematic effort, using every ounce of his acute intelligence and deep wisdom. He wrote in Arabic about the Qur'an and hadees. He wrote in Persian about Sufi teachings and Islamic ethics, including the first explanation of ʿAyn al-Quzat Hamadani's masterpiece of Sufi philosophy and love mysticism, the *Tamheedat* or "Fundamental Principles."[84] He also recorded his own visions in psychedelic Persian prose that bewilders his readers even while luring them into his world of dreams. Freud would be stunned into silence had he read that book. It is possible that Hazrat Gesu Daraz also wrote in Urdu—a book entitled *The Ascension of Lovers* is attributed to him. This would make him the first author to use this newly developed language in prose.[85] His contribution to Sufi ethics and literature is immense and his status in the Chishti Order is very lofty.

Perhaps more valuable than his written compositions are his oral teachings, because they emerged spontaneously from his reservoir of wisdom, the way a melody soars in improvised grace to suspend the tyranny of time. In telling stories and answering questions, his words were not limited by the pen. His oral teachings were lovingly recorded in a malfuzat text by his eldest son, in a collection entitled "The Most Comprehensive Speech" or *Jawamiʿ al-Kalim,* which reveals the importance that all Chishti teachers gave to music.

> As the sun rose toward noon, someone began playing the sarangi before the doorway [to the khanqah of Hazrat Gesu Daraz]. Everyone turned their attention toward listening to the melody of the sarangi.

THE MERCIFUL DOOR

Photo 14: Dargah of Hazrat Gesu Daraz in Gulbarga

> After a little while of listening, Hazrat Gesu Daraz told his audience, "One day, Maulana Burhan al-Din Ghareeb was listening to music—may God have compassion on him. Someone brought a sarangi to play in his presence. Burhan al-Din Ghareeb was well acquainted with the voice of this instrument. When the musician approached, Burhan al-Din Ghareeb hugged the sarangi to his chest and said to him, "Now, play for me!" The man started to play and Burhan al-Din Ghareeb was engrossed in listening.[86]

Hazrat Gesu Daraz told this story to his followers, while they were listening to a distant melody echo through their khanqah in 1399. This was at noontime on the twentieth of Ramadan that year, in the midst of the month-long fast, when Muslims leave aside food and drink during the daylight hours, avoid sensual pleasures, and devote themselves to worship.

Listening to music was considered to be neither carnal delight nor sensual distraction. It was rather a skillful means that God had given humanity to approach the divine presence directly, beyond the temptations of hypocrisy and the limitation of the ego. Hazrat Gesu Daraz told his followers the story of Burhan al-Din Ghareeb, who had died half a century earlier and who had first brought Chishti teachings and Sufi music to the Deccan.

When I played the sarangi for Pir Rasheed, he sat very still listening, his eyes closed gently to better concentrate on the sound, occasionally sighing or murmuring *subhanallah*. I was only a beginner. I was making many egregious mistakes. But he was listening to a sound beyond the voice of my instrument. He was following a movement within the clumsy sawing of my bow across the strings. His attention was fixed upon a distant melody from long before and from far away, which nonetheless echoed weakly through the notes that I was playing as I sat before him, offering him the only thing I had to offer.

I finished the melody and a few variations, to the extent that I could improvise on the composition, and I ended, begging his forgiveness for all the mistakes I had made. "No, no," he insisted, "I thank you! Your playing took me to a different world, a world in which the self gets lost in a greater harmony." As I packed up the sarangi in its case and got ready to leave, he said, "Bring your instrument again sometime—play for me again and again."

NEGLIGENCE

In the night, I stopped in at Pir Rasheed's house to deliver to him the new stationery for the Khanqah-e-Kaleemi Trust. I found Khalid there, but nobody else was at home. Pir Rasheed had just returned from the funeral of a neighbor. She had been a good friend of Pir Rasheed's wife, and so the whole family was there to pay respects after the funeral and keep their family company.

Pir Rasheed told me that everybody had been waiting for me the night before, when there was a fatiha ceremony in honor of Khwaja Ghareeb Nawaz, Muʿin al-Din Chishti. The ritual included qawwali followed by dinner. He said that "Every minute I was expecting you to show up!" But strangely, I did not know the event was happening on that night, or any night. Very strangely, I had suggested to Pir Rasheed two weeks ago that we have a mehfil-e sama' in honor of Ghareeb Nawaz, but nobody told me that it was actually happening. Pir Rasheed insisted that he had informed me and that I must have forgotten or gotten distracted by work. Yet that evening I had no work and do not remember him telling me it would happen. Khalid too said that for the last two days he was thinking of calling me to remind me but didn't bother, knowing that I would come. Strangely, my friend and Sufi scholar, Mauro Valdinocci from Italy, had written to me just one day before, asking whether I would be celebrating at Pir Rasheed's house. I wrote back saying

THE MERCIFUL DOOR

no. I had hoped an event would be organized but nothing was announced, so "we must all celebrate at our own places in our own ways."

Pir Rasheed simply said, "Sometimes Shaytan makes us forget the things we should be doing." But until now, I feel that I was never informed. Maybe this is a reminder that if I suggest that something should be done, then I should actually do it. Instead, I tell people what to do, and never bother to make it happen myself. In any case, Pir Rasheed would not let the matter rest. He continued to emphasize for me how wonderful the mehfil had been, and how great an event I had missed. Pir Rasheed's routine singer could not come, so a new singer was called who sang mainly Persian poems that were especially powerful. He sang poems of Ameer Khusro, like *Chashm-e mast-e 'ajabe*, whose lyrics pull you into a whirlpool of bewildering ecstasy.[87]

Intoxicating eye bewildering dangling locks bewildering Adoring wine bewildering weaving seduction bewildering!	چشمِ مستے عجبے زلفِ درازے عجبے مے پرستے عجبے فتنہ طرازے عجبے
He draws his blade to kill me I bow my head in prostration Bedazzling is his beneficence and my submission bewildering	بہرِ قتلم چو کشد تیغ نہم سر بہ سجود او بنازے عجبے من بہ نیازے عجبے
The arch of your delicate brow marks the direction I bow my head May envy-filled eyes be turned away from this prayer of lovers bewildering	طاقِ ابروئے تو سجدہ گہِ من بہ سجود چشمِ بد دور کہ ہستم بہ نمازے عجبے
In the spasm of sacrifice my open eyes behold his face Such tender undeserved kindness bestowed on a slave bewildering	وقتِ بسمل شدنم چشم بروئش باز است مہربانے عجبے بندہ نوازے عجبے
The wonder of beauty and splendor of downy cheek, black mole and curling hair The cypress stature bewildering the haughty height bewildering	بوالعجب حسنُ و جمال و خط و خال و گیسو سرو قدّے عجبے قامتِ نازے عجبے

Amorous Turk so fresh
with sleight of hand beguiling
Your cap awry bewildering
your tormenting me bewildering

ترک تازے عجبے شعبدہ بازے عجبے
کجکلا ہے عجبے عربدہ سازے عجبے

Don't reveal the truth, Khusro!
one word in this world is infidelity
The one who knows the secret is wondrous
he who keeps the secret bewildering

حق مگو کلمۂ کفر است در اینجا خسرو
رازدانے عجبے صاحبِ رازے عجبے

As if that were not enough, Pir Rasheed continued to elaborate on the beautiful songs that were sung in that gathering that I had missed. Each song was about giving one's head in submission. Pir Rasheed was narrating to me how powerful they were, as if he were wielding a sword, sharpened with my regret. Now he was playfully, almost cruelly, telling me all that I had missed. What a delicious pain!

The Qawwals, he told me, then presented one of my favorite poems, one that had attracted me to qawwali so long ago when I was a student and which pushed me to learn Persian, eventually drawing me close to Pir Rasheed. That song was *Khabaram raseeda im shab* by Ameer Khusro.[88]

This evening news arrived
that my beloved has come
Let my head lay as a gift
on the road along which he's come

خبرم رسیدہ امشب کہ نگار خواہی آمد
سرِ من فدائے راہے کہ سوار خواہی آمد

I'm about to give up my soul,
so come, that I might live
After I'm gone, what reason
would you have to come?

بلبم رسیدہ جانم تو بیا کہ زندہ مانم
پس ازان کہ من نمانم بہ چہ کار خواہی آمد

Despair and anxiety of your absence
I can bear if only I knew
That you, like my ill fortune,
would stick around once you come

غم و غصۂ فراقت بکشم چنانکہ دانم
اگرم چو بختِ روزے بہ کنار خواہی آمد

Your glance takes my heart and
soul, just pass the dice once more
Two worlds are yours if only
to the dice throw you might come

Your wine is the blood of
many slain, drunk in a single gulp
Don't drink this last cup
so the vintner himself might come

All the gazelles of the desert
lay their heads upon their palms
In hopes that someday near them
while hunting you might come

With one visit, you steal the heart
and soul of hundreds like Khusro
What all would happen if, perhaps,
a few more times you'd come?

All of these songs involve the image of laying one's head at the beloved's feet. Pir Rasheed said, "Usually in a mehfil, maybe one or two poems will touch the heart and give one some spiritual experience, but that night every ghazal was moving and each song stirred the heart." Hearing this made me want to cry with regret. What an opportunity missed.

Then Pir Rasheed spoke to me about *wajd* or ecstasy. He said that usually a person gets information from all sides through the five senses. This information lets us know who we are, where we are and what is happening around us. But sometimes, especially in the mehfil, one's reliance on the five senses is cut off. One does not receive information through these channels, for a moment or a minute or more. Then in that state, one receives information from other sources and through other channels—that is, through one's spiritual capacities and sensitivities rather than through the physical senses. Then it is as if one is not in the world, but in some other spiritual realm. One does not seem to know who one is, where one is placed, or what is happening. One senses things but not through the senses. One feels things but not through the routine channels. One is in a different state and therefore in a different realm. One does not even recognize oneself.

I told him I regret having never felt this before in samaʻ. He smiled and said that it is indescribable. Someone can tell you all about the meal they are eating, but that is not the same as tasting the food for yourself.

POWER

I went to the samaʻ-khana of Shah Khamosh today for qawwali that happens on the thirteenth day of each lunar month, on the day on which Shah Khamosh passed away. The darweshes there were very kind to me and very welcoming. But I could not fully enjoy being there, after having heard what Pir Rasheed told me of some Sufi leaders, descendants of Shah Khamosh, who played politics with the question of succession in his family. After the qawwali, they served a light lunch. Then I drove over to Pir Rasheed's house, where lunch was served for some mureeds gathered there.

Pir Rasheed reminded me about the teaching he gave me long ago, about the five senses. We think this world is natural, he said. It appears natural to our five senses. Yet in nature is a supernature, a super power, which allows nature to be as it is. "In *khudrat* there is *khuda*," he said. This is a pun that works in Hyderabad—meaning "in nature there is God." "As you know very well," Pir Rasheed told me, "in every religion there is Sufism—in Buddhist religion and in Hindu religion and in Christian religion and in Jewish religion there is mysticism. All these mysticisms teach the same thing about the five senses, that you have to learn to control the five senses and know what is beyond them. But in Islam there is a teaching about where the five senses come from, which is not clearly taught in other religions. The five senses come directly from God. Each sense is a reflection of God's quality. God sees, so we have the sense of sight. God feels, so we have the sense of touch. God hears, so we have the sense of hearing. These senses are not merely natural. They come directly from God, if you understand them correctly. In nature is a supernature. You come to understand that supernature which is God when you control your five senses. Then you begin to sense with your heart, to know that in your breathing is the divine spirit. When you control your senses, then you begin to focus on the heart. You hear the beating of your heart and you hear that it is really saying *alla-hu-alla-hu-alla-hu*; it is pronouncing the name of God. It is remembering the presence of God. Without that, you have no life. But you need to focus to realize this. When you begin to feel your own heart, and hear it saying the name of Allah, then your senses change. You begin to see with God's own seeing. You begin to hear with God's own hearing. You begin to will things with God's own willing. Things begin to happen around you that do not seem natural, that are beyond natural. You think something and then it happens. You remember somebody and then they call you. You wish for something and then it occurs. These are gifts and signs. You should just keep focusing on your heart and remembering God. But things around you will begin to change.

"You cannot do just anything you like. You begin to do things that God is willing you to do. I want to move back to the neighborhood where I grew up, where my ancestors lived, near the Kaleemi Astana. But I cannot, unless God wills that. You know how much I have tried. You know how much you have tried. We have looked at every plot of land. You put aside the money to purchase it. But no!" Pir Rasheed smiled, "No! It is not meant to happen. Not until and unless the superpower allows it to happen, it cannot. You see, I still desire things that are beyond me." He laughed at himself and smiled. "Still…"

PRESTIGE

The Kaleemi Astana is located just next to the dargah of Husayn Shah Wali. That is an enormous whitewashed building with a soaring dome in regal Deccani style. Its architecture is studded with carved plaster turrets in the shape of lotus buds. Before it is a monumental gateway, with an elevated chamber that houses kettle drums that are beaten on special festival days, a sign of royal authority. Husayn Shah Wali was clearly an important personality in Hyderabad. On one side of the dargah is the imposing house of the custodian and his family with a huge tract of land that they control. On the other side is an ancient mosque that was built for visitors to the dargah and local residents of Shaikhpet, as the neighborhood around the dargah. Adjoining the mosque is a chamber that is the Kaleemi Astana. It houses the grave of Pir Rasheed's great-grandfather who served as Imam of the mosque, when he migrated from Delhi in the mid-nineteenth century. The custodians of the dargah of Husayn Shah Wali appointed him as Imam, but local people revered him as a saint. As his reputation grew, the Kaleemi Astana grew in prestige and became

Photo 15: Pir Rasheed and his grandson Madani in qawwali

its own independent Sufi institution nestled within the shadow of Husayn Shah Wali.

When Husayn Shah Wali died in 1657 this locale was on the outskirts of Golconda, the fort city that first existed here. Starting with the reign of Ibrahim, the fourth Sultan of the Qutb Shahi dynasty who ruled from 1550 until 1580, Golconda experienced a period of peace and prosperity. These conditions attracted many scholars, literati and religious teachers from as far away as Iran and Iraq. The Qutb Shahi royal family consisted of Shi'i Muslims. At this time, Shi'i Muslims dominated in court administration and religious elites, but they were a minority among Muslims in the kingdom. For this reason, Shi'i rule depended upon developing a shared devotional and ritual culture which attracted Hindus and embraced Sunnis who were also devoted to 'Ali and the Prophet's family. The career of Husayn Shah Wali illustrates this dynamic.[89]

Husayn Shah Wali was a Sunni with a Sufi orientation. He was a descendant of Muhammad Husayni Gesu Daraz, who is considered the patron saint of the Deccan by Muslims in Hyderabad. Husayn Shah Wali moved from Bidar to Golconda as a young man. He was well-received by the king, Ibrahim Quli, who, though his courtiers were mainly Shi'i, welcomed this Sunni who had Sufi leanings and appointed him to a high position. Husayn Shah Wali became renowned as a builder and architect and he was in charge of building the reservoir north of Hyderabad that became known as "Husayn Sagar" in 1562. He married the Qutb Shahi king's daughter. One chronicler of Sufis in the Deccan explains his position in this way:

> Though the Qutb Shahi kings became openly Shi'i, it was their policy to treat Sunni and Shi'i Muslims as equals. Yet in their kingdom, Sunnis were more numerous than Shi'is so they feared lest any disturbance should shake their rule. In order to keep any conflict between Sunni and Shi'i from breaking out, Ibrahim Qutb Shah honored and praised the scholars and Sufis from among the Sunnis, giving them employment or grants. When Ibrahim Qutb Shah learned that Husayn Shah Wali had come to Golconda, the king offered him a noble position commanding 10,000 troops with provision to build residences and offered the hand of his daughter in marriage. Those who were Sunni were very pleased that the king had demonstrated his attitude of reconciliation and protecting the rights of all. It was the policy of the Qutb Shahi rulers to protect reconciliation between different sects and kept their distance from those who wanted to sow dissent and strife.[90]

This policy is partly the wisdom of the Qutb Shahi kings and partly the subtle influence of Sunni leaders like Husayn Shah Wali who, as Sufis, found common elements between their mystical devotion and Shi'i doctrine of rule in the name of 'Ali and his descendants.

Shi'i rulers and Sufis also came together in practical ways for projects to benefit the public. "Husayn Shah Wali chose to get close and intimate with the kings of his age so that by means of his influence, the common people might have their needs met and their rights protected, so that each one, whether rich or poor, can have his cares conveyed to the king. Outwardly he was a prince, but inwardly he was a Sufi."[91] As this Sufi Sunni courtier oversaw the building of the reservoir, there appears to have been friction between him and his patron. The king desired the reservoir be named "Ibrahim Sagar" after himself but the people called it "Husayn Sagar" after the builder. As royal proclamations tried to assert its proper name, a popularity contest ensued which neither side had instigated. The king proposed that the reservoir be named Ibrahim Sagar, but when laborers were asking where there were jobs to be found, others would answer that jobs were to be found at Husayn Sagar. No matter how hard the nobles and royalty tried to change the name to Ibrahim Sagar, none of their labor changed the situation. The tongue of common people proved to be the authoritative pronouncement of God, and Husayn Sagar remained its name."[92]

The story of Husayn Shah Wali reveals the power of the composite culture that was formed in Hyderabad, in which Sunni and Shi'i found ways of coexisting through Sufism and shared reverence for 'Ali and Husayn. Although the great early Chishti Sufi masters like Hazrat Nizam al-Din Awliya and Burhan al-Din Ghareeb insisted that Sufis minimize their dealings with rulers to keep aloof from those who hoard wealth and wield power, the Sufi family of Gesu Daraz did not follow this principle. Members of this family introduced the Chishti Order in Hyderabad, starting with Husayn Shah Wali and followed by other members of his family. By that time, they had already abandoned the principle of avoiding rulers; instead, they sought to get close to the rulers to influence them, to improve their moral values and refine their policies for the betterment of the common people. While Husayn Shah Wali was able to balance these ideals, some from his family in later generations settled into comfortable lives as landlords and feudal patriarchs.

Later Chishti Sufis had a hard time countering this trend, and there remains tension between Sufis who renounce power and those who stay close to the powerful. Pir Rasheed's ancestor, Sayyid Muhammad Hasan Jeeli Kaleemi, first settled in Hyderabad. He secured a position as the Imam of a mosque beside the dargah of Husayn Shah Wali. This position gave him the freedom to worship intensely while still supporting his family. His son continued the family's reputation as Sufi teachers, but did not serve as the Imam of a mosque, so the family fell on hard times. Pir Rasheed told me that once the Nizam of Hyderabad heard that his ancestor was living in poverty. The Nizam sent a farman, a royal order, stating that he was endowing a land-grant to support the Sufi teacher in perpetuity. The messenger arrived and handed over the order; the Sufi did not touch the paper but asked his follower to read it aloud. Everyone congratulated the Sufi that the ruler had so generously appointed a land-grant that would provide for him, his family and followers. The Sufi asked the messenger to take the paper back to the Nizam, "Tell him thank you, but I live on what God provides." The messenger, befuddled, took the royal order back.

When certain members of the Sufi's family heard this news, they ran to the Nizam and petitioned that there must have been a misunderstanding. They begged the Nizam to send the order a second time, assuring him that they would encourage their father to accept it. The messenger returned with the order in hand, and family members were sure to be present at its reception. They urged their Sufi patriarch to accept the Nizam's generosity, as so many other Sufis had done. The descendants of Husayn Shah Wali, for example, accepted huge tracts of land, the produce of which accumulated to them tax free, to support the dargah building, 'urs rituals, their expansive family and its expensive habits. This time, the Sufi asked for the paper himself.

As he gazed at his family members with mounting anger, the Sufi tore the paper into shreds. He handed them back to the messenger saying, "Since you refused to take this back to the Nizam in one piece, now take it back to the Nizam in tatters. God provides to those who rely on God. My ancestors never took land from kings." Pir Rasheed finished the story, sighed and smiled. "I still don't own any land. I am just a guest here."

ZAKAT—GIVING OF ONESELF

In the Chishti Order, wealth is the root of all evil while egoism is the fertile soil in which wealth sets its roots deep. In general, Muslims often value wealth as a sign of God's favor, and Islam has often been called a religion of merchants. Yet some of the Prophet's early companions, like Abu Dharr al-Ghifari, denounced the wealthy. Others more quietly renounced earning, like the "Companions of the Bench" or *Ahl al-Saffa*, who chose to sleep on the bench outside the first mosque in Medina and dedicate their lives to worship rather than save money and build households. These were models for the earliest Sufis, and the Chishti teachers propagated their suspicion of wealth and saving.

Of course, Muslims are legally allowed to work, earn and save. Yet we are enjoined to give of whatever wealth we have saved in an annual practice called *zakat*. Giving this percentage of one's savings is not "charity" but is rather to purify the wealth that one keeps for one's own needs. Zakat means purification rather than charity. Anything one gives above and beyond zakat is considered to be charity. As the Qur'an enjoins (Surat al-Layl 92:1–21).

> By the night when it covers over
> By the day when it shines forth
> By what created male and female
> Surely your strivings end up diverse
> As for the one who gives and stays aware
> And believes in reward for good
> We will incline him toward ease
> Yet the one who is stingy and thinks himself aloof
> And denies the reward for good
> We will incline him toward hardship
> His wealth will be no use as he perishes
> Surely, we must give guidance
> And surely to us belong the beginning and the end
> So I warn you of a fire that flames high
> In which only the miserable will burn
> Those who deny the truth and turn away
> yet they will be spared who stay aware
> Those who give of their wealthy to purify
> And confer no favor on others in expectation of reward
> But only to seek the face of God, the One most high
> Soon indeed they will be satisfied

All Muslims should give zakat to purify their earnings and savings. Yet Pir Rasheed uses the term zakat in a different meaning. It means to give a part of oneself rather than merely one's wealth. It means giving of one's time and attention to God, so that what one does in the world will be of pure intent. The Qur'an uses this same verb for "to purify one's wealth by giving" and to "purify one's soul" in the previous chapter (Surat al-Shams 91:1–10), as in many other places.

> By the sun and her morning light
> By the moon when he follows her
> By the day when it shines her forth
> By the night when it covers her over

By the sky and what raised her up
By the earth and what spread her wide
By the soul and what fashioned her
And inspired in her depravity and awareness
Those who purify the soul have prospered
While those who debase the soul have failed

Sufism is a method for staying aware of God's presence and purifying the soul. It is in this sense that Pir Rasheed uses the term zakat.

Many great Chishti masters of the past renounced wealth entirely. They took vows against saving and hoarding. Since they had no wealth at all, they could pay nothing in zakat, when the new year begins on the first day of Muharram. In the Chishti Order, a tradition developed to make zakat from one's time and attention rather than to give zakat from one's wealth, because they had no wealth to give! To make zakat means to do very intense *zikr* for the first ten days of Muharram, a holy month that starts the Islamic year. Pir Rasheed taught me and his other disciples to make zikr by reciting God's name along with the testament of faith (no god but God) 100,000 times over the ten days of Muharram.

The method of doing this is to recite the name Allah while extending the final letter "h" with a long "u" so that it takes on the sound of "hu."… Doing this does not employ the voice; rather, one lets the breath express the language of the heart… A sound may be generated in the nose while performing this meditation. That sound is known as "nasal sawing" (*arra-ye bini*). The friction and vibration of this sound creates zeal and passion but it can make the head hot and dry. Almond oil can be applied to the nostrils and forehead to avoid this and perfect this meditation with no hindrance. Perfection is attained when the breath of the seeker does this meditation without his knowing or choosing it.[93]

After every hundred times of reciting "Allahu" one recites the whole *kalima tayyiba* or testament of faith: *la ilaha illa 'llah* "There is no god but God" and *Muhammadun rasulu 'llah,* "Muhammad is God's Messenger." After every thousand times, one recites a small special prayer for concentrating on the divine presence.

O God, o God, o God! Guide me to you through you and grant me firm footing in your existence such that I can address you in your presence.
O God, o God, o God! By your greatness and magnificence, bestow upon me your love's incandescence.

> O God, o God, o God! Make the heart of your helpless servant to be a foundation for your signs and a manifestation of your essence.
> O God, o God, o God.

It was only after several years of being his disciple that Pir Rasheed gave me this practice. I found it to be a heavy practice that demanded a generous time, pointed concentration and firm determination.

During this practice, I feel that I'm coming apart at the seams. I'm entirely coming apart. I think this zikr practice in the first ten days of Muharram is going to kill me in the end. These ten days are called ʿAshura and they are days of atonement, like Rosh Hashanan for Jews. In the time of the Prophet, many Muslims fasted during these days in addition to giving their wealth as *zakat* before Muharram began. But after the Prophet died, another drama unfolded during the period of ʿAshura. Tribal strongmen were appointed governors and they tried to assert themselves as kings, leading the Prophet's grandson, Husayn, to denounce them. They tried to force him to pledge allegiance and legalize their usurpation of power, but he refused on principle. The self-appointed king, Yazeed, cornered him and his family and followers in the desert of Iraq, called Karbala. There a stand-off for justice happened, leading to the martyrdom of Husayn and many from the Prophet's family.

It is a particularly sacred time for Shiʿi Muslims, but Sunnis too revere Husayn and grieve for his ultimate sacrifice. From Sunni communities, Sufis especially honor Hazrat ʿAli and his son Husayn. The Chishti Order traces its chain of initiation—or silsila—back to ʿAli, and the Qadiri Order traces it back to him also through his son Husayn and his son, Zayn al-ʿAbideen, one of the only male survivors of the massacre at Karbala. Indeed, Khwaja Muʿin al-Din Chishti composed a poem lauding the brave sacrifice of Husayn, and it is inscribed on his tomb.[94]

Husayn is king and Husayn is king of all other kings Husayn is religion and Husayn preserves sacred things	شاه است حسین و بادشاه است حسین دین است حسین و دین پناه است حسین
Rather than place his hand on Yazeed's, he gave his head Because of Husayn "No god but God" in this world rings	سر داد نداد دست در دستِ یزید واللہ کہ بنائے لا الٰہ است حسین

Muʿin al-Din Chishti's short poem is also sung in qawwali and it gave rise to a long tradition of singing Husayn's praises, both to mourn his worldly loss and celebrate his spiritual victory. The twentieth century Sufi poet of Hyderabad, Kamil Shattari, wrote a much longer poem, a ghazal, in praise of Husayn that is still sung in qawwali all over the Deccan.[95]

I cry out, till the end from the start, "O Husayn!" Since the words are inscribed on my heart, O Husayn	ایک نعرہ سا نکل جاتا ہے اکثر یا حسین جب سے کندہ ہو گیا ہے لوحِ دل پر یا حسین
Boldly I assert that this world can never again witness Such a hero among men fighting an upstart, O Husayn	میرا دعویٰ ہے کہ دنیا پھر نہ پیدا کر سکی شیرِ میدانِ وفا تیرے برابر یا حسین
In Muharram, each new year begins with remembering you To the world does every tongue your tale impart, O Husayn	ابتدا ہر سال کی ہے آپ ہی کی یاد سے آپ ہی کا تذکرہ سب کی زباں پر یا حسین
O radiance of ʿAli's eye, beloved grandson of Muhammad, You alone enlighten masters of the mystic art, O Husayn	اہلِ عرفاں آپ ہی سے پا رہے ہیں روشنی نورِ چشمِ مرتضیٰ سبطِ پیمبر یا حسین
For the sake of your father, ʿAli, also grant spoils to us, who in the squad of that fearless lion take part, O Husayn	ہم بھی ہیں وابستگانِ حیدرِ کرّار سے کچھ اِدھر بھی صدقۂ دربارِ حیدر یا حسین
How miraculous is your generous gaze like a flowing spring watering your enemies who into friends convert, O Husayn	آپ کی چشمِ عنایت کا کھلا اعجاز تھا ورنہ حُر کا کیا بدل سکتا مقدّر یا حسین

> Let all swimmers learn
> from you who, in crossing over
> the whirlpools of sorrow,
> has no counterpart, O Husayn
>
> Those who place faith in
> Muhammad also revere Husayn
> Only infidels sever the whole
> from the part, O Husayn

Just as Kamil says in the poem, each new Islamic year begins with Muharram, when we remember Husayn's sacrifice. It is a time for commemoration and commiseration, when the fragility of life and the nearness of death come urgently to mind. As I try to focus on the strenuous zikr, I begin to feel that I am coming apart into pieces.

Making zakat it is called—giving away part of yourself so that the part remaining is pure. I'm not sure which part of myself I'm giving away. I'm staggering around like a drunkard, only half in this world. Today at noon, the birds were singing while I was struggling along with zikr and that helped. I'm so far behind I have no hope of being successful at completing this zikr, and maybe that is just the point. My situation reminds me of a poem by Hafez Shirazi, which is also sung in qawwali.

> Help me, masters of the heart,
> for my heart is out of control
> The pain that once a well-kept secret
> is now out in the open
>
> Our boat is broken, o wind,
> blow hard to reverse our course
> Such that I might once see
> my lover who is far out of sight
>
> In the two worlds, all comfort
> comes from these two phrases
> Be gentle with friends, keep the
> faults of enemies out of mind

THE DOOR'S HANDLE

They don't let me pass
through the alley of good repute
Go ahead and change my fate
if this sets you out of joint

در کوئے نیکنامی ما را گذر نہ دادند
گر تو نمی پسندی تغییر کن قضا را

O master with a pure white robe,
accept my apologies
This wine-stained cloak
Hafez is wearing out of necessity

اے شیخ پاک دامن معذور دار ما را
حافظ بخود نپوشید این خرقۂ مے آلود

It is a leaky boat I'm sailing. If Hafez were here, he could help us but he long ago floated away over the horizon into the realm of open secrets.[96]

How fitting for 'Ashura to come in the long, dark days of late December. If we can make it through this, we can make it through anything. I've had to stop playing music now, in the last five days of 'Ashura. My sarangi teacher came on Thursday for a last lesson, before the strings have to be silent. Not that I'm any good, but it was a pleasure to have something to keep my fingers and mind occupied, and now that too is gone. The city is draped in black. The *matam*, or mourning processions, are going on nightly in the old city. The new city has been closed down with strikes called by political parties angling for a separate Telangana state, and even the petrol stations are closed. There is nowhere to go, no distractions to be had. There is nothing to do but zikr. I'm not made for this, let me tell you. It's going to kill me.

There are moments when I'm doing this, losing all hope in any sense of self-sufficiency, and I suddenly feel that Pir Rasheed is doing the zikr for me. It is a very strange feeling, but my fingers aren't mine anymore. They feel cool and even translucent. Like the bone belongs to me but the living flesh belongs to someone else. Does that make any sense? Of course not. Yet it is there, it comes and goes, and when it comes it is such a relief. He told me to practice tasawwur-e shaykh when doing zikr: I used to imagine his face when I began, but it quickly faded or faded back in or I got distracted. I never expected this *tasawwur*, this imagination, to become more real than me, the one imagining. Yet that is exactly what happens. The zikr courses along under the careful watch of someone else and I'm just there as a witness, or not there at all, or not quite me who is there. Words have a hard time trying to capture this.

SEPARATION

What a blessing to be back in Hyderabad and to meet Pir Rasheed again. I had returned to America to renew my Indian visa. The process was long and grueling and took six weeks because of all the bureaucracy. In the meantime, I had to send away my passport to the Indian Consulate, and that was the only valid ID I had in America. I had no driver's license anymore and no USA address. Once or twice I showed my Indian driver's license as identity proof to cash a check or board transport, and that was a total failure! I felt trapped, exhausted and very unhappy there, even though I was with my family in Hawaii. My friends laughed at me when I said I was stranded in Honolulu. Poor me! It is worth laughing at.

In the end, I returned to Hyderabad. When I called Pir Rasheed, he just said, "Ah, my son, my son, my son. You've come back." What a lovely relief it gave me to hear that. Pir Rasheed invited me to come the next day to share lunch with him. When I went to his home, Pir Rasheed greeted me with a hug and sat me down next to him on the rug. It is a dirty rug, with its faded designs in black and red and green. But I loved sitting on that rug, despite the bits of food trampled into it and the ants that crawl across it, back and forth, from the balcony through the room.

Pir Rasheed chided me for having left Hyderabad, especially for having not given any word of my leaving. But then he told me, "You should go anywhere God takes you. Hyderabad is no special place. It is my place only because my ancestors are buried here. I am merely a servant of the Kaleemi Astana where they are buried." He recited one of his favorite lines of poetry.[97]

> I am the priest, I am the statue, I am the temple, I am the idol
> So whom do I worship? To whom do I offer incense of sandal?

Pir Rasheed said, "Who am I? I am nobody! I am nothing but them working through me, so I stay here. But if you worship God then know God is anywhere. Go wherever you want to go."

A while later, I was heading north to Delhi for some work. The 'urs of Shaykh Kaleemullah was approaching, and Pir Rasheed was busy getting the invitation cards printed and distributed. When I told him that I was going to Delhi, his eyes lit up. "Will you be going to Nizam al-Din Awliya?" Of course, I replied. "Then please take one of these invitation cards with you, and when you go to the dargah of Nizam al-Din please stop by the home of Khwaja Hasan Sani Nizami, which is just around the corner from the dargah. Please convey my salams to him and invite him to celebrate the 'urs with us." I agreed but observed, "Pir Sahib, isn't Khwaja Hasan Sani suffering from heart trouble? I hear that he just had heart surgery! Do you really think he would come to Hyderabad for the 'urs?" He looked at me with an expression of pity, at a person so overcome by reason that he can't see what's in front of him. "Of course, he can't come but still you should invite him. How much better it is to hand an invitation to him yourself than for me to send it by post—and don't forget to convey my salams."

So off I went to Delhi. Khwaja Hasan Sani Nizami is a very learned elder in the Chishti Order, and he also belongs to the Kaleemi branch. He is a font of knowledge and the music programs he organizes are interwoven with lectures and edifying stories and moral advice. He is really an admirable Sufi. After paying my respects at the dargahs of Nizam al-Din and Hazrat Inayat Khan, I walked down the narrow alleys of the basti neighborhood—past the butchers and the beggars and the perfume sellers and the *Tableeghi* missionaries gnawing on their huge sticks of miswak like pious troglodytes. In a few minutes, I arrived at the imposing mansion that Khwaja Hasan Sani inherited from his father, Khwaja Hasan Nizami, and his ancestors who have been upholding Sufism from there for many generations. I knocked on the door.

After a long time, an elderly servant came and let me in. He sat me down in a chair in the courtyard and disappeared. Almost a half hour passed while I sat there in total silence, wondering whether the servant forgot me or if he had ever intended to tell his master that someone had arrived. Just as I was entertaining the idea of leaving, Khwaja Hasan Sani walked into the courtyard. He was a very tall and imposing man, though now he was visibly feeble and walked with a cane. Yet his eyes glimmered with wisdom and he greeted me warmly, though I had never met him before. I conveyed to him the salams of Pir Rasheed and he smiled widely to hear that name. I gave him the invitation card and asked him to please come to Hyderabad and celebrate with us. He said that he would do his best to come, but shrugged and smiled, as if to say that his heart might give out at any moment, so who knows?

I was ready to leave but Khwaja Hasan Sani was still engaging me with small talk. Then he became serious and asked me, "What are you doing in Hyderabad?" I explained that I was a disciple of Pir Rasheed, so I was staying close to him while doing some research projects, giving some lectures, and writing a book. He said, "But you are from America! Why are you wasting your time in Hyderabad?" I was taken aback, but he continued. "You are American and your real work is there in America—that is where people need you to give lectures. Of course, it is alright to come to India, and to visit Hyderabad now and then because your Pir is there. Pir Rasheed is a very fine man. You did well to find him. Come here to India whenever you need to, but go back to America." I think Khwaja Hasan Sani could sense the shock on my face, as his voice softened a bit. "Look here, see my situation. I have thousands of disciples in America—in Chicago, in New York, in Houston, everywhere. I have gone to America several times to visit with them and speak with them. But I always come back here." He tapped his cane on the packed earth of his courtyard. "Here, where I belong. Yes, it is time for you to go back."

With that unsolicited advice, he shook my hand and bade me farewell—"Please convey my salam to your Pir Rasheed." I walked out of the ancient house and the heavy wooden door rattled shut behind me. My head was reeling and brain was in a daze, unable to absorb the advice he gave me. Who was he to tell me where to go and what to do, I thought to myself. He is not my Pir, after all, no matter how much I respect him. I walked back to the dargah of Nizam al-Din, entered the marble tiled courtyard. I found a quiet place to sit on the raised platform that surrounds the tomb shrine. I sat near a pillar, offering salams and praise for the Prophet, and then quieted my mind. In the shadow of the dargah, I found there a blissful quietude as it seemed my mind completely slowed down and slipped into a delicious silence.

I have no idea how long I sat there in that state. My awareness returned reluctantly because somebody was poking me in the ribs. I came to my senses and turned to see what was going on. From behind me, a darwesh was poking me to get my attention. He seemed to be one of the many destitute fellows who hangs around the tomb—some are simply beggars and some are majzubs, holy fools, who find a haven at the dargah. When this fellow got my attention, he said to me in Urdu, "You don't belong here." I answered him, "Yes, I do." I turned back to face the dargah, hoping to revive whatever state I had been in which was so comforting and spiritually nourishing. Another poke in the ribs. "You don't belong here." Now I started thinking that maybe this was a place on the platform near where the women often come to sit, and he was telling me that men should not sit here. I answered, "There are no women nearby, I'm not in anybody's way." He just said again as he shuffled off, "You don't belong here. You're not from here." I turned back to the dargah and closed my eyes, but the state of deep concentration would not come back to me. I was merely sitting in front of a building's wall. I sat there for some time until I got stiff. Then I asked Hazrat Nizam al-Din to give me leave, bade my salams to him and to Ameer Khusro on the other side of the courtyard, and walked away.

When I arrived back in Hyderabad, I went to see Pir Rasheed. He welcomed me warmly and inquired about whether I delivered the invitation to Khwaja Hasan Sani Nizami. I told him about my visit to the haveli and how upset I was when he suggested—no, rather commanded—that I should be back in America. I asked, "Who is he to tell me this? I am here because of my connection to you, so how does he think it right to meddle in this?" Pir Rasheed was quiet for a moment. He muttered under his breath, as he always does when he is deep in thought, "*Subhanallah wa bi hamd-ihi, subhanallah al-azeem, astaghfarullaha, la hawla wa la quwwata illa bi' llah*—Glory be to God and praise be with God, glory to God the great One, I seek forgiveness with God, there is no power and no means except with God." He continued looking down at his hands for a long moment, then looked up at me. "If Khwaja Hasan Sani says this, you can be sure it is not Khwaja Hasan Sani saying this." I looked at him blankly, wondering what he meant. Pir Rasheed clarified it for me, "This is a message conveyed by Khwaja Hasan Sani but it is not from him. What does he have to do with whether you stay in India or go someplace else? No, if this message comes from Khwaja Hasan Sani you can be sure it is a message from Nizam al-Din Awliya." Pir Rasheed raised his hand to hold his earlobe when he said the name, in a gesture of respect for one's teacher, and he bowed his head.

I thought for a moment and then answered, "If it is a message from Hazrat Nizam al-Din, then I need to pay attention." Pir Rasheed replied, "Yes, you need to listen carefully. It is not what I want but it may be what he wants, and he is the teacher of us all. Let us wait and see." I left him that day mystified and bewildered. One month later, I received an email from Emory University in Atlanta, offering me a position as a professor. It seems that a lecture I had given there was actually a job interview, though I did not realize that at the time. There had been no job announcement or formal interview process. They called it an "opportunity hire" that came up suddenly, as the university decided it needed someone to teach about religion, spirituality and sexuality and the Department of Middle Eastern and South Asian Studies leapt upon that opportunity to suggest my name.

I returned to Pir Rasheed to give him this news, and to ask his help in making a decision. "Ah ha," he said when he heard the event, "that is what was going on! But do you want to go to America?" I answered, "No, I do not. I want to stay here with you." He chuckled, "See now, Mr. Scott, I also do not want you to go to America. I also want you to stay here close to me. You are like my right hand. What can I do without my right hand?" We sat quietly for some time. Then I said, "But perhaps he wants me to go." Pir Rasheed answered, "Definitely he wants you to go." Silence again. I implored, "Won't you tell me what to do?" Pir Rasheed laughed, "I cannot tell you want to do. You must decide for yourself what is best. Whatever you decide, I bless you in your decision. You see, Mr. Scott, distance does not matter. Separation is not reality. Unity is the reality. In Sufism, that is the basic teaching. The relationship between you and me is a spiritual connection—it is not limited through time and space. I am just as close to you when you are in America as I am to you when you are here in front of me. I have many disciples and followers who live here in Hyderabad, even in this very neighborhood of Yaqutpura, but they are not close to me. They come to me when they need something. They come out of their own greed. They are *matlabi*, self-serving people even if they are living near me, in my neighborhood, even in my own family. Yes, that is true. They think they are close to me but they are very far away! Do not imagine that if you are in America and I am here in Hyderabad, that you will be far away from me. No, I will be here," he pointed to my heart. "I will be closer to you than you are to yourself. Never fear—you should go anywhere God takes you. Hyderabad is no special place."

With tears in my eyes, I bade Pir Rasheed farewell. I drove home to start planning how to shift to Atlanta, a place I had never intended or even imagined I would call home.

CONCURRENCE

One year later, I woke one morning at my home in Atlanta. It was a crisp and sunny Saturday. I ate breakfast and thought about what tasks to finish during the day, but a strange mood came over me. My head felt heavy. I took a shawl and lay down on the couch. I covered my head with the shawl and faded out. A strange state came over me, and I traveled through a different place. I have no idea how long I lay there. I believe I got up at some point and took a long walk through Piedmont Park, a few blocks from my home. But I was completely in a different place. I cannot write now what happened to me or what I learned. Later I realized that the ʻurs of Inayat Khan was underway in Delhi. At that moment, it was evening time in Delhi, when samaʻ was happening at the dargah, where Pir Rasheed and Pir Zia were together in one gathering. How could I have missed that?

Two weeks later, I arrived back in Hyderabad after having left my teaching duties aside and taken my spring break one week early. I am afraid that I cannot shirk my duties like this often for fear of getting fired, but I longed to reach Hyderabad for Shaykh Kaleemullah's ʻurs. I arrived in Hyderabad, on the very day of the ʻurs. I just had time to unpack my bags, dress and get to the old city to reach Pir Rasheed's house in the evening.

I arrived there in the middle of the qawwali mehfil. I found another foreigner there, Mikko Viitamäki from Finland, whom I had met previously in Delhi. Mikko is an eminently qualified scholar and gentleman with a profound love for qawwali and a good knowledge of poetry in Urdu and Persian, which is all disguised by his stern and cool countenance. Pir Rasheed calls Mikko by his Islamic name, Sajid 'Ali, and gave him initiation (*bay'at*) one week earlier; tonight, he received authorization (*khilafat*), so this was an important day. I felt like Pir Rasheed had called me to come and be present. He had me sign the *khilafat-nama* as a witness after the qawwali was over. Thank God, I arrived in time to participate.

How long Mikko searched for a Sufi guide suitable to his nature and temperament! How hopeful he was that the great scholar Khwaja Hasan Sani Nizami would give him initiation, during the time he spent in Delhi doing his PhD dissertation. I do not know why Mikko never directly asked Khwaja Hasan Sani, but maybe there was no easy opportunity. That is hardly important, since it just was not to be. Now Mikko is sitting with us in Hyderabad, having become the mureed of Pir Rasheed, who has no scholarly pretensions at all. Pir Rasheed always says with a note of regret, "I'm an unlettered gentleman."

PURIFYING THE HEART

As I was sitting with Pir Rasheed, my fellow mureed Zakir 'Ali showed up. We had a long rambling conversation, driven mostly by Zakir's inspired diatribes. He is a bit manic, but also a majzub and his words deserve attention. Among many poems, he recited for us in full this ghazal of Watan.[98]

You find the true One when you discover the secrets of your Shaykh You see God's truth when you truly see the face of your Shaykh	پائے حق کو پائے جب اسرارِ شیخ دیکھے حق کو دیکھے جب دیدارِ شیخ
You can speak to God freely just as did the Prophet Moses When the ear of your heart can hear the speech of your Shaykh	حق سے باتیں کر لو موسیٰ کی طرح گوشِ دل سے گر سنو گفتارِ شیخ

As long as the thread of breaths
weaves in and out concealed
Never will be severed the cord
that binds me to my Shaykh

جب تک تارِ نفس ستار ہے
ٹوٹنے پائے نہ مجھ سے تارِ شیخ

Who could desire to tarry near God's
throne above the heavens?
I am content to take shelter
by the wall of the home of my Shaykh

عرش پر رہنے کی ہے کس کو ہوس
بس ہے مجھ کو سایۂ دیوارِ شیخ

They have purchased preparation
for judgment day, O Watan
Those who do their shopping
in the busy market of my Shaykh

حشر کا سودا ہوا کرتا ہے یاں
اے وطن سرگرم ہے بازارِ شیخ

The basic point of Zakir's sermon is that one must melt away while imaging the image and form of one's own Pir. Zakir even said that he sees himself as a dead body laying horizontal, while the doing self is that of his Pir standing over that body. This is what he imagines as he rises to pray. "Pray as if you are seeing your Lord, and if you cannot see the Lord then know that the Lord is seeing you."[99]

The next time I went to see Pir Rasheed, I was joined there by Mikko and Ahmad. Pir Rasheed gave us a talk on *zikr-e ruhi* and *pas-e anfas*. He explained, "The heart is the seat of understanding, and it controls the mind and the senses. But you must realize that Khannas resides near the heart, whispering seductive thoughts to mislead the heart. Doing this zikr cleanses the heart and makes Khannas and his inciting whispers subside."

Pir Rasheed directed that, "One should learn this zikr and practise it until the heart itself begins to beat with the words of the zikr, as explained in the book, *Kashkul-e Kaleemi*, the Alms Bowl." In that precious book, Shaykh Kaleemullah explained:

> This is the method of meditation by observing the breath (*pas-e anfas*)… This meditation is sometimes taught such that one only recites the name Allah. The method of doing this is to recite the name Allah while extending the final letter "h" with a long "u" so that it takes on the sound of "hu." [In Arabic grammar, this is called pronouncing with ashba' which extends the final vowel sound which is not an inherent part of the word and pronouncing it audibly; saying God's name as Alla-hu gives it the implied meaning of "God is".] While inhaling, one recites

Alla- and when exhaling, one recites -hu. Doing this does not employ the voice; rather, one lets the breath express the language of the heart... One does this with each breath exhaled and inhaled while keeping one's concentration upon the navel as it is drawn in and extended out during breathing. After one does this meditation continuously and extensively, the meditation continues with one's breathing even if one is asleep or awake.... Perfection is attained when the breath of the seeker does this meditation without his knowing or choosing it.[100]

Pir Rasheed taught us how to do this zikr in precisely the same way that Shaykh Kaleemullah had written about it three centuries ago. Pir Rasheed owned a copy of the *Kashkul-e Kaleemi*, a valuable book about meditation practices, but he never took it out to read from it, at least never when I was present. It was always buried, along with the other books by Shaykh Kaleemullah in Urdu translation, deep in his almirah under piles of other papers, photographs and prayer beads. No, Pir Rasheed taught us this zikr practice from memory, as he had learned it orally from his Pir and his ancestors. It was a living tradition. It just so happened that it corresponded to what was written down by an authoritative guide, who established our Kaleemi Order, long ago.

Surely, the zikr practice predates Shaykh Kaleemullah. As a living tradition, it reaches far back into the remote past, probably even further back than Khwaja Muʻin al-Din Chishti and Shaykhʻ Abd al-Qadir Jeelani, the founders of the Sufi Orders that are the foundation of our Kaleemi tradition. Pir Rasheed told the story of how zikr began. Once, Hazrat ʻAli and his wife Bibi Fatima were living in Medina near her father, the Prophet Muhammad. They were among the muhajirun or Muslims who left Mecca in exile to emigrate to Medina. The Prophet tried to get the people of Medina to help them settle by giving them houses to live, business partnerships to prosper, date palm oases to cultivate, and marriage proposals to integrate. Soon most of the emigrants were living well, in comfortable homes and many had servants to help with the housework and business. Hazrat ʻAli did not get any such help, but rather strove along with the Prophet to help everyone else. He and his wife were living very simply, almost in poverty. Bibi Fatima had to do her own housework—carry wood, fetch water, prepare meals—and it was very exhausting. One day, she complained to her husband, "You are the closest person to the Prophet and I am his beloved daughter, but we are living in poverty. I'm worn out and tired! Please go to the Prophet and request him to give you some money so we can hire some help." The next day, Hazrat ʻAli went to the Prophet, but he was too ashamed to ask, and he went home empty-handed. Bibi Fatima urged him to ask the next day. Again, he approached the Prophet, but was overcome by humility and could not ask. Bibi Fatima was really angry, but the next day Hazrat ʿAli again came home with nothing.

That night, as the people of Medina settled down to sleep and all was quiet, the Prophet knocked on the door of his daughter's home. Hazrat ʿAli was in bed with Bibi Fatima. When they realized it was the Prophet, they told him to come in. He came into their room and sat on the bed with them, his closest companions and his beloved family. He told Hazrat ʿAli that he knew something was on his mind but was ashamed to speak of it, so he himself had come to inquire. Bibi Fatima elbowed her husband, and Hazrat ʿAli finally spoke up, "Dear Prophet of God, we are living in poverty and it is very hard on my wife, your daughter. Could you give us something valuable so that we can ease our hardship?" The Prophet smiled and suggested, "Would you like me to give you both the most valuable thing I have?" Their eyes widened and they nodded. Then the Prophet said, "The most valuable thing I have is this zikr. Each day before you go to sleep, say thirty-three times 'Glory be to God' and then thirty-three times 'Praise be to God' and then thirty-three times 'There is no god but God.' In that alone can one find comfort in any trial and ease in every hardship."

That was the origin of zikr, which the Prophet taught in private to his closest companions, those who were attuned to it. He taught it to Hazrat ʿAli and Bibi Fatima. He taught it to Abu Bakr Siddiq. He taught it to Salman Farsi. Through dream visions he taught it to Owais Qarani, who never could meet the Prophet in person but who loved him more than those who lived nearby and saw him every day. All the Sufi Orders trace their origins back to these few companions. As the zikr was passed along from generation to generation, it grew more varied and more elaborate, until now there are countless and colorful ways of doing zikr. All these ways were collected and documented by Shaykh Kaleemullah in his book, *Kashkul-e Kaleemi*, along with the essential elements and foundational principles that unite them all in their common roots.

Pir Zia contacted me by email and commissioned me to translate *Kashkul-e Kaleemi* into English. I went to Pir Rasheed to ask his advice and permission. "You must do it!" he exclaimed. "And blessing to Pir Zia and his publishing house for requesting that you do it. Many years ago, the custodian of the dargah of Shaykh Kaleemullah in Delhi published the *Kashkul-e Kaleemi* in Urdu. That is the book that I have, but it is long out of print. In any case, the Urdu version is very old-fashioned and difficult for people to read nowadays, and worse, very few people are learning Urdu anymore. All our Indian Muslims are learning English to secure a livelihood. Look, even I had to learn English to survive," he said with a laugh. "But my grandchildren are not reading in Urdu anymore, and the generations are changing. You know, many years ago I tried to get it translated into English! You don't know that, since it was before you came to me, long before. I asked one of my disciples to make a translation so we could get it published in English, and he did it! Yes, I still have it in my almirah."

Pir Rasheed got up and unlocked the drawer where he kept his valuable papers. Shuffling through decades of documents, he pulled out a notebook. In it, written in exquisite cursive script that is not taught in schools anymore, was a version of the *Kashkul* in English. I was amazed. Perhaps this project would be easier than any of us imagined. I asked, "Why didn't you get it published?" He answered, "I didn't have anyone to tell me whether it was a good translation or not. You see, I am just an unlettered gentleman. But now here you are! Sit down and take a look... tell me what you think." I opened the notebook and started to read. The letters were English. The words were English. The sentences started with capital letters and ended with periods, but that is about the extent of its resemblance to an English translation. To be generous, it was gibberish. The man who had done this put his whole heart into fulfilling his Pir's request, but did not have the courage to tell him that he did not have the skills to do the job. It was very sad. Pir Rasheed was watching carefully for my reaction. I closed the notebook and handed it back to him. He paused for a moment, then put the notebook back in his drawer and locked it up. He turned to me and asked, "Shall we begin again afresh?"

I smiled and said, "It is always good to begin afresh." He affirmed, "Yes, put this precious book into English and let Pir Zia publish it in America!" This episode showed me how intentions, once put into the world by being voiced, have a power all their own. It must have been decades ago that Pir Rasheed tried, with what few resources he had, to give new life to *Kashkul-e Kaleemi*. The first attempt failed. But the intention coursed along its non-linear route toward becoming reality. It lodged itself in Pir Zia's mind, and he had contacted me, and I had circled back to Pir Rasheed, across several decades and continents, to ask his permission. Pir Zia sent me the Persian text so that I could render a new translation from the original.

It was a joy to read *Kashkul-e Kaleemi* with Pir Rasheed, once the project got moving. We would sit together and he would read from his Urdu translation, interjecting comments and explanations like a madrasa teacher. It was beautiful to hear his explanation of the abstract theological ideas or obscure technical terms for spiritual anatomy and breathing patterns. I realized that the *Kashkul-e Kaleemi* is almost impossible to really understand without a living teacher to explain it. Shaykh Kaleemullah probably wrote it this way on purpose, since he warned readers that one can't learn meditation and zikr from a book—even the book he was writing—but that one needed a living teacher to impart the knowledge effectively. Our study of this book got continually interrupted by mobile calls by mureeds soliciting advice or visits from those afflicted with ailments, physical and psychic. I never finished reading the whole book with him, but we read enough together for me to understand its key concepts and terms. The translation flowed along after that, effortlessly. Pir Zia and his publishing house, Omega Press, transformed it into a lovely and useful book. All thanks and praise be to God, *the One who teaches by the pen, teaches humanity that which they knew not* (Qur'an 96:4–5).

REELING IN THE SENSES

I spent my spring break in Hyderabad—extended by playing hooky from university—but eventually I needed to return to my new home in Atlanta. I woke up this morning to a warm and bright Sunday during a Georgia spring. While having breakfast, I thought about what tasks to do during the day. Then a strange mood came over me. My head felt heavy. I finished eating and crawled back into bed, but I did not sleep. The experience that came to me was similar to what I had experienced back in February, which I was unable to write down. It was an unfolding of a certain knowledge through intuition, a learning of something through experience without observing anything in the sensory world.

The five senses are like kites which we release and let fly far out into the world. They catch the winds of phenomena—they pull and tug, they drift and dart. We struggle with them and think that we control these kites, but they pull us and play with us. If we would only reel them in! In fact, we can reel in the string of the senses, through concentration and practice. The more we reel in the string, the closer the kite comes to us and the closer it comes to us the less it catches the wind, the less it tugs and pulls, the less it plays of its own accord, the less power it exerts over us, the less distracted we become. As the kite draws near to us, we find that it loses the power that it seemed to have, when it appeared to be animated by phenomenon far from us and beyond our control. What an illusion!

As the kite draws very near to us, it simply floats down to the ground. Flat on the ground it rests, perfectly tranquil. Perhaps there is a ripple as a breeze blows over it, or a flutter, but it stays on the ground, still and at peace. If one can reel in the strings of the five senses, they will lay peacefully at our feet. To reel them in, we need to turn the spool. To turn the spool, we need to find the central axis. We find the axis and then turn and turn and turn, and that means grasping the breath with our awareness and then guiding it through zikr.

I did not do any zikr this day or yesterday; this experience was not caused by my doing zikr, as suggested by this metaphor of reeling in the kites. No, this experience was given to me as a gift, undeserved. It is Pir Rasheed's state that is casting its shade over me, and granting me this experience through him. Indeed, I felt him there with me, standing near me. Together we were facing a very formidable presence, a huge man, very voluminous and dense. I understood that this was Shaykh Muhammad Ghaus Gwaliori, a great saint of the Shattari Sufi Order, and I was afraid of him.[101] I wanted to reach out to learn from him, but I was uncertain if I should because his density and enormity were very threatening. I asked Pir Rasheed to stand in front of me to shield me if I was not to meet Muhammad Ghaus, and I asked him to stand behind me and support me if I was to meet Muhammad Ghaus. As I thought this, Pir Rasheed stood beside me to my right. He let me greet Muhammad Ghaus and pay respects to him and touch his feet. The things that I write here I learned through this encounter and Muhammad Ghaus's presence was confirmation of them and Pir Rasheed's presence enabled me to be there and learn what was learned.

The experience did not happen in this order: it did not happen in any chronological order. As I remember it, I am placing it in an order because I must. I must put one word before the next, and after that comes a next word. Yet it did not happen through words. I have written that the senses are like kites, and then that I was with Pir Rasheed, and then that I met Muhammad Ghaus, and then that he taught me something, but it was not like that. I was with Pir Rasheed before I knew that he was with me. Things were taught to me before, while and after I encountered Muhammad Ghaus, and these things took on his form and appeared through him like an image of light appears through a lens. The metaphor of the kites became clear to me only as I was returning to my routine senses. But that is where the experience started right where it ended. I can say nothing more about how and why.

This is some of what I was taught. The central axis was established when God created heavens and earth. This creation makes the axis and the axis is of seven levels which together make a harmonious whole.

> Blessed be the One in whose hand is dominion and who has power over all things, who created death and life to try you and see which of you is better

in deed. That One is mighty and forgiving, who created the seven heavens in levels, one above the other (Surat al-Mulk 67:2–3).

Of seven levels is heaven and of seven levels is earth. The human being stands between them, being of earth and being of heaven, within and without, mirroring above and below. The human being is also of seven levels or stages.

> Why do you not place trust in God who has created you stage by stage? Do you not see how God created the heavens in seven levels, and made the moon glow within them and set the sun to light them? Thus has God nurtured you from the earth like plants growing gradually and you will return into the earth and raise you forth again (Surat Nuh 71:13–18).

These stages we must pass through as we journey to God. These levels we must rise through as we ascend to God.

> I swear by the twilight and night what it calls to return, and by the moon as it waxes full—surely you must travel from stage to stage (Surat al-Inshiqaq 84:16–19).

You can call these stages *lata'if* or subtle energy centers, located along an axis from the base of the spine to the top of the cranium, which nourish the body, guide the psyche and energize the soul.

When your awareness moves along the axis through the seven subtle centers, then you come to know all things that are essential. Then your awareness can move back down the axis, knowing its centers and feeling its harmonics, like the seven notes of a musical scale until one returns to the base note. Then your awareness can sense God's presence in the heart. Your meditation and prayer then focuses the heart and clears it of all darkness and obscuring veils. One feels this by a vibration that is established within the heart, between the heart and all the other limbs, so that one becomes integral and whole and harmonious and serene.

This was inspired to me and I have recorded it as best that I can in words, of which I can share just a little here. To know this is one thing, but to put it into practice and persist with it is another thing altogether. God alone knows best.

HEALING

All kinds of people come to Pir Rasheed for guidance and healing. Local Hyderabadis come in abundance. I was always impressed by the gentleness and generosity of Pir Rasheed who would stop whatever he was doing to listen to their complaints, give advice, and pray for them and with them and over them.

Pir Rasheed had specific rituals for healing. Honestly, I was not interested in that aspect of our Kaleemi Order. I never investigated these cases, to see if the healing rituals actually worked and people's practical problems got solved, though one of my colleagues from Emory University had written a fascinating book about such practices in Hyderabad.[102] I was rather impressed that Pir Rasheed never asked for anything in return—no money or favors. Some Sufi masters in the city make healing into a business; other religious scholars or *mullah*s have reputations as *'amil*s or "practitioners" who turn prayer into incantations for practical benefits. Pir Rasheed was following the example of his grandfather, of healing as a service to the people and a way of worshipping God by comforting others. He never took money, as that was strictly against his principles and those of his ancestors.

I once received an email from a Sufi in America named Hafizullah. He was from the community of Pir Zia. Hafizullah wrote that he wanted to do a forty-day spiritual retreat, a chilla, in Hyderabad, just as Pir Vilayat Khan had done. Pir Zia had recommended that he write to me to ask if Pir Rasheed would guide him through this experience. I was happy to help and Pir Rasheed agreed, but we were in a quandary over where Hafizullah could stay. He needed only a small spartan room and should come out only for Friday communal prayers. Pir Rasheed was very apologetic that he could not accommodate him in his own home. His own room was the khanqah, and the rest of the house was bustling with family. Hafizullah wanted to stay in at the dargah of Fakhr al-Din Pahari, where Pir Vilayat Khan had done his chilla in Hyderabad so long ago. Yet that place was very remote and now a family was living in the room beside the dargah, acting as its caretakers. Finally, Pir Rasheed worked it out for Hafizullah to stay in a room at the dargah of Husayn Shah Wali, just near the Astana Kaleemi. He arranged for the dargah custodian to take care of his meals and cleaning, and the Husayni mosque was just across the alley for communal prayers. Pir Rasheed agreed to guide Hafizullah through the zikr and meditation exercises, just as his father had done before for Pir Vilayat Khan.

I never got to meet Hafizullah, since I was away in America by the time he came to Hyderabad. It was an honor to help set up this visit. I learned later that he is a skilled calligrapher, among his other talents. Pir Rasheed showed me the beautiful Arabic calligraphy that Hafizullah had made for him, and he hung it on the wall of the khanqah with great pride. "You see what they can do in America? This is better calligraphy than our Muslims are doing here in

Hyderabad! That Hafizullah—so clever." However, Pir Rasheed noted with displeasure that the custodian at the dargah of Husayn Shah Wali demanded rent from Hafizullah. "Just imagine, a Sufi comes all the way from America to do a chilla, a strenuous forty-day retreat, and all these people think about is how much money to demand from him. It is shameful. I regret that I do not have a proper khanqah with guest rooms so that visitors can come, stay, eat and pray at their leisure. Someday, inshallah, we will build such a khanqah."

I was more fortunate to be present when Imam Saleem Chishti and his wife Tara visited. They live in Pir Zia's community in America, where Imam Saleem works in urban planning and serves as the prayer leader and his wife works as a therapist and healer. They came for a week to learn healing rituals from Pir Rasheed, armed with a video camera, notebooks and an array of questions. Pir Rasheed requested me to recommend a hotel for them and arrange to drive them to his home. For the week, I became chauffeur and sometimes translator, whenever Pir Rasheed found it more convenient to switch from English to Urdu. Tara and Imam Saleem are delightful and joyful people, with a great deal of love for Pir Rasheed and respect for Indian ways, along with a healthy dose of skeptical pragmatism. They represent the best of American-style Islam.

By the end of the week, they had learned different prayers for relieving pain, anxiety and suffering of many sorts. They also spent a great deal of time learning the healing ritual that involved lemons. Pir Rasheed would use lemons to remove negative forces from people who were suffering misfortune, rubbing a lemon over the person's body in different patterns while silently praying. They videoed Pir Rasheed doing the ritual, learned it, and then did it themselves. On their last day, as they said goodbye to Pir Rasheed, Imam Saleem hesitated. "I have one last question," he said as he turned to me to translate. "The lemons that you are using here in India are these small and perfectly round lemons—you know, the little limbu. In America, we don't get those lemons. Our lemons are really big and they are oblong, shaped like eggs. Do you think we should buy a bunch of Indian lemons to take back with us so that the ritual will work?" Pir Rasheed listened carefully as I translated. "Don't worry, Imam Saleem! The size and the shape of the lemon does not matter. It just has to be a lemon. God will take care of the rest."

Weaving through the congested lanes of the old city, Tara and Imam Saleem commended me on my driving skills. Imam Saleem peered out the window anxiously and said, "I can't understand how people aren't smashing into each other all the time—it is so chaotic." Tara said, "I cannot believe that you actually drive here—it is total madness!" I replied, "One just has to be as mad as everyone around you, and then it somehow all works out!" I shared with them my theory about driving which was taught to me by my friend Salahuddin, who happens to be a professional driver. He helped me to buy my car in Hyderabad. As Salahuddin was driving me out of the second-hand car showroom in my new purchase, he warned me, "Now Scott, you are from America so you are used to driving in the lane system." I asked, "What do you mean, the lane system?" He replied, "I mean the system where there are lanes painted on the road and everyone drives straight in the middle of the lane—you all have that system in America. Here we have lanes painted on the road, but no lane system in people's brains. Whatever you do, don't drive your car by the lane system." I asked, "If there is no lane system to driving here, then what other system is there?" He thought for a minute, then replied, "Actually, there is no system!" That is certainly how it appears at first.

I told Tara and Imam Saleem that in fact there is a secret system. There is the "lane system" that does not work here, and then there is the "school of fish system." Here, lanes mean nothing. Lanes are for people who believe in private space, personal rights, elbow room and the adage "Good fences make good neighbors." In Hyderabad, all of that is worthless. People drive like a school of fish swims. One nudges a bit and the others adjust so the tiniest of spaces becomes a place to squeeze through. Looking at any individual it seems chaotic, but looking at the mass of it as an organic whole it just flows around obstacles in a very elegant way. You just have to drive with a communal sense and not an individualistic sense. Doing silent zikr while driving in Hyderabad helps tremendously, I told them. They laughed, "You don't have a diesel-powered jeep, you have a zikr-mobile!"

PLEASE WRITE OUR BOOK

I had the pleasure of sitting this evening with Pir Rasheed. All evening people were coming to consult him. Whatever he was doing he would interrupt, except for his obligatory prayers, and turn immediately to aid whoever came. He called it khidmat-e khalq or serving the people. People came to be healed and blessed. He sighed, saying, "This is my responsibility to give them holy water and rub them with lemons and pray for them. Everyone wants lemons and water! This is why the saints used to live in the wilderness, to get away from the demands of people, because it is their responsibility always to give and never to refuse. It becomes a burden and a distraction, so they would go and live in the mountains, like Baba Sharf al-Din and Baba Fakhr al-Din Pahari."

But despite these sighs and apologies, Pir Rasheed was following a well-trodden path in the Chishti Order. Hazrat Nizam al-Din Awliya was fond of quoting a little-known hadees report that the Prophet said, "The person most pleasing in the sight of God is the one who give others the most happiness."[103] Pointedly, the person most pleasing to God is not the one who worships the most. Nizam al-Din explained this to his followers using the analogy of direct and indirect verbs in grammar. Devotion that is direct is called mandatory, and devotion that is indirect is called supererogatory. Nizam al-Din taught this way:

> There are two forms of devotion. One is mandatory and the other is supererogatory. Mandatory devotion is that from which the benefit is limited to one person, that is, to the performer of the devotion, whether it be canonical prayers, fasting, pilgrimage to Arabia, invocations, repetitions of the rosary, or the like. But supererogatory devotion is that which brings benefit and comfort to others, whether through the expenditure of money or demonstration of compassion or other ways of helping one's fellow man. Such actions are called supererogatory devotion. Their reward is incalculable; it is limitless.[104]

Helping, healing, counseling and comforting are the best forms of worship, even if many Islamic leaders and jurists do not recognize them as such. That is due to their narrow vision!

For this reason, Pir Rasheed was seldom at rest and was often interrupted. All the Chishti leaders who lived in big cities had to face this challenge, being continuously called into the tumult and trials of the world by common people. For instance, Pir Rasheed recounted the story of Kale Miyan, "The Black Master." He was the leader of the Kaleemi Order in Delhi who gave initiation to Pir Rasheed's great-grandfather, Sayyid Muhammad Hasan Jeeli Kaleemi. Kale Miyan's given name was Ghulam Naseer al-Din. He also served as the spiritual advisor to the last Mughal emperor, Bahadur Shah Zafar, even as British colonial rule was overtaking the land. In the capital of Delhi, Kale Miyan was fated to help others out of their problems.

For instance, the famous poet Ghalib had been thrown in a British jail for running up debts while gambling. Kale Miyan secured his release by promising to keep Ghalib in his own home. When his friends met Ghalib on the street, they congratulated him on getting release from jail. He replied wittily, "Who has been released from prison? I was just shifted from the white's jail to the black's jail!" It seems that Kale Miyan, "The Black Master" had allowed Ghalib to stay, but only if he promised not to drink wine in his home, making it seem like a prison to the pleasure-loving poet.[105] Telling this story, Pir Rasheed quoted one of his favorite couplets by Ghalib.[106]

> One mention of that beauty and again you declaim without rest
>   He is now your persecutor whom you once held to your chest

I answered with two of my favorite couplets by Ghalib, which also uses the same word bayan to mean declaiming with eloquent speech.[107]

> Achieving union with my beloved, it seems, is not my fate
>   If any life is left to me at all, it will just be more of a wait

> These Sufi teachings and your eloquent speech, Ghalib
>   You seem a saint, though your thirst with wine you sate

Kale Miyan introduced Ghalib into the court of Emperor Bahadur Shah Zafar, who was an eloquent poet and patron of poets. Ghalib eventually got a stipend from the Emperor and served as his poetry teacher, allowing him to live independently again.

Why is it that serving the common people, whether they appear as sinful or pious, is the best kind of devotion? Pir Rasheed said, "God's essence is within every person. God gives to each person regardless of what that person is like. Muslim or non-Muslim, good or bad. What a large-hearted being is God!" To illustrate this, Pir Rasheed told a story about his grandfather, who was his Sufi guide. Once Sayyid Muhammad Zia al-Hasan Jeeli Kaleemi heard a cock crowing as if saying "Alla-hu, Alla-hu—God is the One, God is the One!" Hearing this, Zia al-Hasan went into an ecstatic state, cried out and fell unconscious. Coming back to consciousness, Zia al-Hasan exclaimed about the crowing cock, "*Mere satna-pir hai*—It is my true spiritual guide!" Even in the simplest and lowliest things, he would hear the voice of glorifying God and find the presence of God. Yet it is especially in those who are weak, vulnerable and downtrodden that the presence of God appears, and reaching out to them in aid and compassion is the best kind of worship.

As I was leaving, Pir Rasheed must have sensed that I was admiring his spirit of selfless service. He decided to challenge me to live up to that myself, in at least one little way. He said to me, "I have one last request. Why don't you write a small book about our Sufi Order and your experiences in it? Just a small book, so that people can learn what our Order is about. The Wahhabis, the Jama'at-e Islami people, the Tableeghis and the Ahl-e Hadees are trying to extinguish it in any way they can, but they don't understand it. It is mere jealousy on their part that drives their hatred. Anyway, write that small book, I ask of you."

I am now writing the book that he requested of me; I pray that it will be a small demonstration of khidmat-e khalq. Many people in America, Europe and even India are searching for a spiritual guide and some are drawn to Sufism, but it is very hard to find a satna-pir, a true guide. Maybe this book will help them to see what such a guide is like, so they can better find one in their own environments and avoid those who prey on others and exploit them in the name of religion. May those who find help, healing, counsel and comfort in this little book offer blessings on Pir Rasheed and pray on his behalf for God's compassion, forgiveness and peace.

CHAPTER 6
THE DOOR'S LOCK

HEART ATTACK

In 2012, I was blessed to receive a university fellowship that let me take a year off from teaching to study in India. In the summer, I first settled in Kerala to do a small project related to Islam in this far southern corner of India. I spent the holy month of Ramadan and celebrated Eid in Trivandrum, the capital of Kerala, while the rainy season poured in earnest. I looked forward to returning to Hyderabad soon thereafter. Just after the Onam festival in late August, I drove north from Trivandrum up the coast to visit friends and the tombs of several Chishti Sufis in Kerala. It is little known that some of the most famous Sufis of Kerala, like Makhdum Zayn al-Din Ma'bari the Elder, belonged to the Chishti Order, along with his son Makhdum 'Abd al-'Azeez and his grandson Makhdum Zayn al-Din. They are revered but nobody recognizes their lineage anymore. After stopping at the coastal ports of Ponnani and Mahé to pay my respects to them at their tombs, I drove over the Nilgiri mountains, through the Wayanad jungles and across the Deccan plateau, which was unusually vivid green just after the monsoons.

It took me ten days to drive north, slowly through the monsoon rains, to the Deccan. I arrived last evening in Hyderabad but went directly to my friend Kumar's house to eat dinner and rest, since my flat was not cleaned or arranged yet. Kumar's home was my home, and my home was his: we have been friends for two decades. He lives in a simple two room house with smooth stone floors and a tumbling tile roof, out beyond the Secunderabad Cantonment. His father had been in the Indian airforce, and raised the family from low-caste roots in the countryside, through conversion to Christianity, up into English education. But Kumar liked to keep close to the soil—living simply, growing his own vegetables, and traveling by foot or bus. Still, he had been all over the country, visiting temples and dargahs and churches while gathering stories from everyone he met.

Kumar was so full of love that one could never find a better friend, so it was natural to confide in him. I complained to him about a nagging feeling of pain and constriction in my chest that had been coming and going for the past two weeks. It is foolish to ignore a chest pain, he admonished me. I had never experienced anything like it in the past, and it did not seem to be related to activity or fatigue. I actually went to a hospital once in Trivandrum, but during the Onam festival the doctors were on leave for the holiday. There was no time to see a doctor before packing up my car and setting out from Trivandrum to drive to Hyderabad.

I arrived at my flat the next day and called up Pir Rasheed to tell him that I had arrived safely. He was out on the road and could not talk. The sounds of traffic swirled around his voice. He said to call back in the evening when he would be at home, so I refrained until after sunset, knowing he would be busy with the maghrib prayer. When I called around 7:30 pm, he answered in a voice that sounded dazed, confused and distant. I had never heard that quality in his voice before.

He said with much hesitance and repetition, "I received the phone call about your heart attack, and just now after maghrib prayer, during the prostration, I prayed to God for your health and safety." I said, "What phone call?" He said, "Did you have a heart attack? I received a phone call from America this evening telling me that you suffered a heart attack, so I was praying for your health." I told him, "But I called you in the afternoon and I didn't say anything about a heart attack." His voice began to gain clarity, and he said, "Really? If you didn't call me about your heart attack, then who did? It was a call from America! I was so upset. Tears were coming to my eyes as I thought about how young you are and how good is your health. So I prayed during the prostration for you."

I was stunned to hear this. He said, "You are well then? Ok, good, very good! You didn't call me? Then it must have been someone else calling to tell me about your heart attack. Who was that who called?" I told him incredulously that I did not know who called. But then I said, "It is very strange. I have been feeling pain in my chest for the past ten days. I was afraid that it might be something wrong with my heart, but I didn't tell anyone about it." He said, "That is fine. Then you are well. You didn't have a heart attack? Very good. Someone else must have called me to inform me about that. Who was it who called? It was from America. I assumed it was you. Then it is fine."

I told him not to be sad. I was feeling fine, and I would come to see him the following day. He invited me to come for lunch, and I promised to be there. I wanted to deliver to him his copy of the newly-published *Sufi Meditation and Contemplation*, the English translation of *Kashkul-e Kaleemi* or "The Alms Bowl", that includes a foreword by him. I hung up the phone. I rushed to say isha prayers, in gratitude for all that has come to me.

The next day, I saw Pir Rasheed at his home. "I am so happy to see you, Mr. Scott, to see that you are in the best of health. I was so anxious about you when I heard that you had a heart attack. I felt like my right arm had withered away at the thought that you were no more, but here you are looking just fine!" he continued to say, amazed. "What badmash is that who called from America, playing tricks on me? That is very strange. Maybe someone else in America has suffered a heart attack. We should call Pir Zia and Imam Saleem to ask if everyone is alright." I realized then that he was continually receiving messages along unseen wires about the psychic and physical and spiritual condition of his disciples and followers and loved ones. He was receiving messages the way we might receive phone calls. He was intervening in our affairs also by sending out messages. A Pir's work and service is never done. I am surprised now that he is not continually distracted and disoriented!

CLIMAX OF A LIFETIME

It was the 'urs of Hazrat Nizam al-Din Aurangabadi. I had been in Delhi giving lectures and flew directly from there to Aurangabad upon finishing my work. I checked into a hotel, rested, took a bath and ate. Pir Rasheed was scheduled to arrive earlier in the day by train along with four disciples. Of these, I was closest to Mustafa 'Ali, a kindly, middle-class gentleman from Hyderabad who had worked as a driver and clerk for ICRISAT, the International Crops Research Institute for the Semi-Arid Tropics, a federal government institution which has a big center in Hyderabad. From there, he drove Japanese agricultural scientists all over the dry and dusty Deccan plateau as they studied millet and barley cultivation in the arid zone. For this reason, Mustafa 'Ali was comfortable with foreigners and full of stories. He and I got along fine, though now he was "retired" and always looking for odd jobs, fixing up used cars or helping to manage milk dairies or some such scheme with friends which always seemed to end in disaster. I could not reach him or the other mureeds by phone. Both of Pir Rasheed's numbers were not working, and Mustafa 'Ali's phone was switched off. I was worried that they had not arrived and wondered how I would find them. I hopped in an autorickshaw to bounce over potholes through the old city neighborhood of Shahganj, to reach the dargah of Nizam al-Din Aurangabadi.

As I stepped through the gateway into the courtyard of the dargah, there was Pir Rasheed standing at the head of the stairs with Mustafa 'Ali. I greeted them and Mustafa was laughing—"Just now we were remembering you and wondering when you were going to arrive. Pir Rasheed just insisted on stepping out of our room at this moment—and there you are!" I still don't know why their phones were not working, but I was relieved at the serendipity of meeting them. We went into the tomb to visit Nizam al-Din Aurangabadi and recited *Fatiha* for him. I had brought some rose petals to scatter on the tomb.

Then we returned to the small lime-washed room in which the five of them were staying. We sat around and talked. Pir Rasheed told about his receiving the durud and wazeefa, his special way of invoking blessings on the Prophet Muhammad. "When I was younger, my family fell upon hard times. I finished school and then went directly to work at the State Bank of Hyderabad in 1950. I worked there until I got a better job at Saudia Airlines, so I moved to Jeddah. There I worked for about 25 years. All that time, I used to say so many durud. I used to love reciting *Dala'il al-Khayrat*, which gives so many beautiful durud for each day of the week. Yet in my heart, I longed to have a durud that was more beautiful and rare that is not found in *Dala'il al-Khayrat* or any other book.[108]

"Then once I went to Medina to the tomb of the Prophet and I was longing for some gift, some durud that would be mine forever. As I was coming out of the tomb, I was called over by one Shaykh al-Tabrezi who lived at the tomb. He was *ra'ees al-fuqara*, the one responsible for all the *faqeers* who lived there at Medina. He called me over, 'Ta'ala, ta'ala!' Now I am an unlettered man. I don't speak any Arabic. I can read the Qur'an alright, but I can't speak or write Arabic. Still, this man called me over and insisted on giving me a durud. In Arabic he said, 'Take out a pen and paper and write it down!' I didn't have pen and paper. I ran to the market to spend one riyal on pens and one riyal on paper. He wrote out for me the durud, and signed it, and recorded the date. He also wrote out the wazeefa that I received:

> Dear God, grant blessings and peace to our Prophet Muhammad. Bless him to the extent of your boundless love for him and increase our love for him. O Lord, by his greatness in your estimation, remove from us all obstacles that impede us. Grant peace to him and his family and followers, bless and keep them. We do not ask you, our sustaining Lord, to revoke what you decree but ask only for grace in accepting it. Amen.[109]

THE DOOR'S LOCK

"He was commanded by the Prophet to give these to me. What a blessing that is! These are the only things that I cherish. I had no other desires in the world when I visited the Prophet's tomb. I had given up everything. But I was asking to just have a durud that no one else had. On the Day of Judgment, I will offer up only these two things—a durud and a wazeefa. I have nothing else and nothing else will matter.

"That day was the climax of my life. From the tomb of the Prophet I went to Jannat al-Baqeeʿ, the graveyard where the Prophet's family is buried. Bibi Fatima is buried there and Imam Hasan is buried there and many others. The Saudis destroyed the shrines and buildings that were built there by the Turks. They razed it all to the ground. Now they have built walls around it. But there is a concrete grill where you can see inside to where the tombs are. There I stood to offer Fatiha for Bibi Fatima, just near her tomb. When I looked up, there was the Prophet standing just behind her tomb! What beauty was radiating from his face, full of light! I saw him as clearly as I am seeing you. His hair was long and loose and his beard was short and trimmed. His face was round and glowing. He stood facing me and for several minutes I stood there rapt, watching him. I don't know how long I was there—several minutes perhaps. But then a Shiʿi lady who was coming to that place bumped my shoulder from behind, and at that moment, the Prophet disappeared from my vision. How happy I was that day. I didn't need to live any longer. I did not need anything else in this world. I remain only to say this durud and wazeefa and to give it to others. That was the climax of my life."

Pir Rasheed told this story and then fell silent. This very durud he had taught to me and all his followers long ago, but I had never heard the story of its inspiration. Much later, I noticed a text in Persian calligraphy framed and hanging on the wall of the Kaleemi Khanqah, a text that commemorates one of Pir Rasheed's many visits to Medina, to the green dome of the Prophet's tomb. It begins by writing out the text of Pir Rasheed's durud, and reads that it "presents a poem offering a chronogram of the date on which our Pir and Murshid, Sayyid Muhammad Rasheed al-Hasan Jeeli Kaleemi, came to the two Holy Cities, by which he attained the happiness of circumambulating the Kaʿba in Mecca and visiting the noble Prophet's tomb in Medina." The poem reads like this…

> May your thirst to see the Prophet be blessed
> May your radiant halo of selflessness be blessed
>
> O Pir Rasheed Kaleemi, both Qadiri and Chishti
> May your visit to that ruler of the pious be blessed

Receive his welcome as you see his lofty green dome
   May your bowing at the beloved's threshold be blessed

Be happy, leader of the righteous, as you are called
   May Muttaqi's measure of the stars' conjunction be blessed

A star enters the joyous assembly on your journey's date
   May your stay at the world leader's home be blessed!

The poem is a qaseeda for praising a hero or leader, and its last couplet encodes a chronogram. In Persian, this is an arcane system in which every letter of the alphabet has a numerical value; this system, called *abjad*, is used also in Urdu and Arabic, and it comes from Hebrew and ancient Syriac. In these languages, you can make a chronogram, meaning a phrase that is crafted such that the numerical value of the letters adds up to the date of a memorable event. In this case, the phrase "May your stay at the world-leader's home be blessed" should add up to 1430 Hijri, which in Islamic years corresponds to 2009 CE. Reading chronograms is a dying art, let alone having the skill to compose them! The text concludes by saying "This poem was composed by the lowliest of God's servants, Dr. Sayyid Abbas Muttaqi in 1430 Hijri, may God pardon his faults," giving the reader a helpful hint, at both the name of the poet "Muttaqi" (meaning the Pious One) and the encoded date of 1430 Hijri / 2009 CE.

Having heard Pir Rasheed's story of his visit to Medina and receipt of this precious durud, all of us on the journey to Aurangabad decided to take some rest. The qawwali would begin at 3am and the sandal ceremony would follow at 4am, so everyone needed sleep now in preparation for a long night of wakefulness. I left to sit in the mosque, to give everyone a chance to stretch out on the cotton mattresses spread across the floor of the small chamber.

Meanwhile, in the mosque I met Salim, an Italian dervish from the Jerrahi Order who was visiting India to learn to play the harmonium. We were joined by the majzub from Hyderabad—I don't know his name, but I had seen his antics before. During qawwali, he sometimes goes into a manic state that makes him leap and land on his back, over and over again, in a sort of self-punishment that never seems to injure him. I saw him do this in Bahadurpura, a neighborhood of Hyderabad, at the 'urs of 'Abd al-Qadeer Siddiqi. It was quite startling, though nobody reacted to it at all. This majzub came up to us and demanded that Salim give him the white cap he was wearing. Salim declined saying, "This cap has been given to me by my shaykh." The majzub insisted. Salim told him, "You will have to go to Istanbul and ask for one for yourself. This was not my property but rather it belongs to my Order. I am not at liberty to give it to anyone else."

The majzub argued with him, "If one experiences fana fi'l-shaykh and the shaykh is present with one in the heart, then what use is it holding on to a topi, a mere cap? One can give it away to others, who may benefit from a spiritual bond with the shaykh who had given it in the first place. Then you would get the benefit of confirming that the shaykh is in your heart and also the benefit of helping someone else by giving the cap!" Salim did not accept this logic. I tried to defuse the discussion so that Salim would not feel pressured, since he was a guest, after all, and a stranger in our gathering. In the end, I had to insist that they both leave so that I could get some peace and quiet. Strange people sometimes gravitate to Sufism like moths to a candle; like moths, some get singed and damaged.

COUNTING

It is the last night before 'Ashura. I have been counting down the ten days from the beginning of the month of Muharram to this tenth day. Ten holy days of atonement at the beginning of the new Islamic year.

I promised myself and Pir Rasheed that during these ten days, I would make zakat, giving the self to devotional practices. He had directed me recite 100,000 times the divine name "Allahu" directed toward the heart. I resolved to recite 10,000 on each day for 10 days. I tried my best, but I allowed other commitments to get in the way. I accepted an invitation to join a conference at EFLU, the English and Foreign Languages University, about translation studies. I allowed Moshem, my housekeeper, to take two days off to travel to Tirupati to help secure his friend's nursing school certificate. During those two days, I stayed at EFLU campus to eat and sleep. I tried to give minimum attention to the conference and spend time in my room, doing the zikr, but it was not enough. My worldly commitments became entanglements that snared me and I fell behind. I missed an entire day's zikr. Bravely, I thought I could slowly catch up, but it was a struggle to just keep up 10,000 each day.

I used my *tasbeeh* with 99 beads to count to 100 repetitions. With each round of 100, I would place one maulsary seed in a brass bowl that my friend Kumar had gifted me from his trip to Ajmer, that has the *Ayat al-kursi* inscribed in the inside. I had a pile of 100 seeds, so that 100 times 100 would give me a count of 10,000. But soon, I got so distracted that I was not sure whether I had completed 50,000 or 60,000. I just forgot. I hoped it was 60,000 but I feared it was 50,000. I kept going during the last days approaching 'Ashura, assuming I had done 60,000.

Sometimes, my zikr recitation was anxious and fearful. Sometimes, it was hurried and ragged. Sometimes, it just resolved into a tranquil buzz. Sometimes, I pronounced the words clearly and sometimes, they blurred into a devotional hum. Sometimes, I found myself falling asleep but mostly, I observed myself thinking and planning other things related with the world's ambitions and pleasures, as if I were not doing zikr at all! Often, I recalled the directive to keep the image of my Pir in mind, tasawwur-e shaykh. Sometimes, I imagined his face and his form sitting before me. Sometimes, I fell at his feet and he was standing above me. Sometimes, I felt that he was doing the zikr and I was just reflecting the actions that he had already done. Sometimes, it was not his zikr resounding through me, but that of his guide and others before him.

I felt a vibration arise in some part of my body, as if it were doing zikr itself. I felt this in my rear left hip once so strongly and distinctly that I reached over to check if my mobile phone was ringing on vibrate mode. There was no phone in my pocket. My phone was lying on the floor five feet away from me, and it was not ringing or vibrating. This was most disconcerting of all, but I remembered the instructions of Shaykh Kaleemullah in his book, *The Alms Bowl*. I tried to keep my awareness on my heart and ignore the vibrations of my body, knowing that they were merely an echo of what was resounding in my heart. Sometimes I felt like I was drowning in the ocean, other times that I was floating on its surface, other times that I was caught up in its waves of foam. You cannot drink foam. You can only drink water. To begin to drink the ocean is to drown.

Tonight, I resolved to finish. As I pushed hard to complete 10,000, I forced myself to hope that it was my last 10,000. Almost to the end of that cycle, the thread holding together the beads of my tasbeeh broke. I didn't realize it until the beads were lolling in my lap and rolling across the floor. I tried to finish counting on my fingers, which is entirely tedious. But I did finish at 2:30 am. I was convinced that the tasbeeh broke as a sign that my work had been completed and there was no need for more.

I went to sleep. When I woke up in the morning, I had breakfast with Amina Wadud, a colleague and friend of mine. She is a renowned scholar of Islamic feminism from the USA whose reputation spread globally with her fiery lectures and incisive books that challenge patriarchy. She is an African-American Muslim who has spent considerable years in Asia, and for this year she was living in Kerala. From there, she came up to Hyderabad to visit me and it was a joy to have her as my house guest. She went to bathe and dress, to get ready to go to Pir Rasheed's house, and said she'd be ready in an hour. Spontaneously, I asked to borrow her tasbeeh. I decided to do zikr for the remaining hour, even though I thought I had finished my commitment to 100,000.

When I sat and began to recite, everything was different. The words did not emerge from my lips or throat. They were not distinct. They were like a buzzing or a drone. It was a continuous vibration that rose and fell in oscillations as my fingers ran through the beads. The buzz emerged into words only at the end of the beads to say *la ilaha illa 'llahu muhammadun rasulu 'llah*, and then it began again. It was recitation not from my tongue or my throat but from my heart. It did not emerge from my mind but engaged the resonant space where my nose meets my brow. This was recitation beyond words, and the real meaning of the words became clear to me as it progressed. Does the resonant skin of a drum belong to the wooden frame that holds it tight or to the hand that plays upon it? It is an extension of one, but it is an activity of the other. The zikr that welled up inside me this morning made me into the skin of a drum. It made me into the writing that flows out from the love play between tablet and pen.

I realized then that the ego is like a drowning sailor clinging to flotsam which is the navel. The navel is the ego's source and its vehicle. It depends upon the navel and hangs from the navel like a sailor clinging to a floating beam, trying desperately not to look down into the depth of the sea. Yet the log is floating on the sea and moves at its whim. Still the desperate sailor thinks the log will save him and conceives of the log in counter distinction to the sea. So, the ego's existence has its source in the navel and depends upon the navel, and the navel is that scar which gives witness to a person's emerging into being from other than itself. What sad desperation is the ego's misperception, to think that the navel is somehow independent from the umbilical cord that gave rise to it, that fed it and formed it, that nurtured it and empowered it.

From this zikr emerged the knowledge that the ego depends upon the navel and clings to it while the navel floats upon the seething ocean of existence, giving shape to the body that is enlivened by the spirit. This flash of knowledge came from the zikr that was coursing through me. It was a continuous zikr that did not start or stop. I dropped into it and I fell out of it. I did not do the zikr, but rather the zikr did me. It pre-existed my awareness of it and it continues when I am distracted from it. Even as I write down this experience and inscribe this knowledge I received in words, I am so saddened that I am distracted from this zikr. I hope it is still there, just as intense, when I put all this behind me and turn to it again.

My alarm rang. It was time to take Amina Wadud down to the old city to visit Pir Rasheed. She had given me an hour while she was getting ready. That hour was up. I looked down at her tasbeeh beads in my hand and the pile of maulsary seeds before me. About half were in the bowl and the other half were still heaped on the floor, waiting to be counted. I had not finished the last 5000. But I had finished my commitment to do the zikr completely: its worth was not counted by numbers. I scooped up the remaining seeds and poured them into the bowl with the others, and put them away on the shelf. I got up unsteadily as if drunk, and gave Amina back her tasbeeh. I would have to buy some strong silk thread to re-string the beads of my tasbeeh, but I would never again imagine that counting on them measured the worth of what I was doing.

DANCING TO THE EXECUTION GROUND

It is the climax of 'Ashura, the tenth day of Muharram. At 1:30 pm is the moment when we believe Imam Husayn was killed in the battle of Karbala. The Sufi understanding of Husayn's sacrifice is best expressed in this poem by Shah Niyaz Ahmad Barelvi, who also belonged to our Kaleemi Order. His poem is often sung in qawwali.[110]

O heart, cling to the hem of the leader of God's friends That is, to Husayn, son of 'Ali, the spirit of God's friends	اے دل بگیر دامنِ سلطانِ اولیا یعنی حسین ابنِ علی جانِ اولیا
For him came a special taste of martyrdom's cup From him comes rapture of wisdom of God's friends	ذوقِ دگر بجامِ شہادت ازو رسید شوقِ دگر بمستئ عرفانِ اولیا
His form is a mirror to beauty divine, such that Toward him turns the prayerful faith of God's friends	آئینہ جمالِ الہیست صورتش زانرو شدہ است قبلہَ ایمانِ اولیا
Because he stands in for both Muhammad and 'Ali He is pride of the prophets and glory of God's friends	چوں صاحبِ مقامِ نبی وعلی ست او ہم فخرِ انبیا شد و ہم شانِ اولیا

THE DOOR'S LOCK

His lovely face is the radiance
of salvation's dawn
His brow is the candle in
the chamber of God's friends

روئے نکوست مطلعِ صبحِ سعادتست
سیمائے اوست شمعِ شبستانِ اولیا

On judgment day, Niyaz
will rely on Husayn because
Lovers of God's friends rise
in the company of God's friends

دارد نیاز حشرِ خود امید با حسین
با اولیاست حشرِ محبانِ اولیا

On this momentous day, Pir Rasheed invited me for lunch at his home. I asked whether Amina Wadud could come along with me, as she was my guest in Hyderabad at that time. I was terribly excited for her to meet Pir Rasheed and was anxious about what her experience would be and what her judgment might be. I feared she might judge him as just another patriarchal Muslim leader. I was also anxious that she might do something that others in Pir Rasheed's family might misinterpret or they might say something that she would find offensive or off-putting, because she does not accept cultural norms that she finds unjust or inequitable, while gender segregation was the norm in Pir Rasheed's family. I should have known better than to entertain such fears.

Pir Rasheed welcomed us upstairs in the Khanqah room. Amina Wadud sat with us, for it was the custom for Pir Rasheed to welcome female visitors there among the men. I had bought some Osmania biscuits to give him so that he could host his visitors who would surely show up in the evening when the roads cleared after the matam processions that filled Hyderabad's roads on ʿAshura day. Before I could give him the biscuits, he presented me with a bag containing a prayer carpet and tasbeeh that he had brought for me from Medina, when he was last there on ʿumra.

At 1:30 pm, Pir Rasheed excused himself to go down to the living room and join his family to say Fatiha over the food and consecrate it in the name of Imam Husayn. We visitors didn't go downstairs because Pir Rasheed's family and women members would be present there for the ritual. Amina Wadud and I stayed upstairs, and we recited fatiha and durud ourselves at 1:32 pm. At 2:00, we were called downstairs to join Pir Rasheed for lunch, along with his grandsons, the teenage Asrar and the toddler Muneer, his disciples Ahmad Bhai and his son, and two girls whose names I don't know. He generously served us kebab with roti and fresh sliced radish, then rice with kofta curry, and then two kinds of *sharbat*—one with milk and almonds and one with sweetened water and pistachio. Amina mistook the milk sharbat for raita and poured a little on her rice to eat. Ahmad Bhai instantly reached over for a clean plate and took hers away, and gave her new food to eat, asking her to drink the sharbat after eating. Amina handled it with consummate grace, but I fear she was hoping for some raita with curds to cut the chilies!

After lunch, we retired upstairs to the Khanqah room for tea and biscuits and conversation. Pir Rasheed's disciples Mubeen and his brother Hamid joined us there. Mubeen was wearing his white peaked cap, his char-kohne topi, and he looked radiant. He informed Pir Rasheed that he had successfully completed his zikr and had made 100,000 repetitions of *la ilaha illa 'llah*. Pir Rasheed congratulated him and blessed him, and Mubeen's face glowed with satisfaction. Ahmad also reported that he completed his 100,000. I said that I had completed mine. He was quiet for a while.

Then he looked up at me and recited a line of Persian poetry *"Man-am 'Usman-e Haruni keh yar-e Shaykh Mansur-am* (I am 'Usman Haruni—the friend of Mansur Hallaj am I)." He glanced at me expectantly, so I recited the second line of the couplet, *"Malamat mi-kunad khalqi o man bar-dar mi-raqsam* (Let others hide their sanctity—allow me on gallows to dance)." He smiled and his eyes lit up. I recited a few more couplets from this ghazal by 'Usman Haruni, the Sufi master of Mu'in al-Din Chishti, what few I could remember.[111]

I don't know why the moment I catch sight of him I begin to dance My only boast is that I'm inspired before my beloved to dance	نمی دانم که آخر چوں دم دیدار می رقصم مگر نازم به آں شوقے که پیشِ یار می رقصم
You keep singing different tunes— I keep up with dance Whichever way you like to spin me, my dear, I love to dance	تو ہر دم می سرائی نغمہ و ہر بار می رقصم بہ ہر طرزے کہ می رقصانیم اے یار می رقصم
From head to toe I've sacrificed myself to utter selflessness Like a compass around an absent center I'm left to dance	سراپا بر سراپائے خودم از بیخودی قرباں بگردِ مرکزِ خود صورتِ پرکار می رقصم

THE DOOR'S LOCK

Like a joyous drunk, I trample
underfoot self-righteous caution
My piety is insisting, decked out
in cloak and turban, to dance

خوشا رندی که پامالش کنم صد پارسائی را
زهے تقویٰ که من با جبّہ و دستار می رقصم

You're such a killer that you
spill my blood just for show
I'm such a victim that beneath
your dagger I long to dance

تو آں قاتل کہ از بہرِ تماشا خون می ریزی
من آں بسمل کہ زیرِ خنجر خنخوار می رقصم

Come, my love, and see me
among this throng of stricken lovers
As I, in the public market with
my riches of ruin, take to dance

بیا جاناں تماشا بیں کہ در انبوہِ جاں بازاں
بصد سامانِ رسوائی سرِ بازار می رقصم

Though one finds dew nestled
in roses not clinging to thorns
I am a drop of dew that
on a thorn-tip quivers as if to dance

اگرچہ قطرۂ شبنم نہ پاید بر سرِ خارے
منم آں قطرۂ شبنم بہ نوکِ خار می رقصم

I am 'Usman Haruni—
the friend of Mansur Hallaj am I
Let others hide their sanctity—
allow me on gallows to dance

منم عثمانِ ہارونی کہ یارِ شیخ منصورم
ملامت می کند خلقے و من بردار می رقصم

What does the ecstasy of 'Usman Haruni have to do with counting beads? He is dancing with Mansur Hallaj—who is mentioned explicitly in the poem—and with his friend Shibli. Shibli is not mentioned by name, but there he is in the image of a Sufi master dancing in public in his cloak and turban. Isn't it Shibli who declared, "There is none in this robe of mine but God"? When Mansur Hallaj was executed for heresy in Baghdad and all the Sufis of the city were silent in fear of persecution, it was Shibli who threw a red rose up to him on the gallows. Then Pir Rasheed quoted an Urdu couplet.[112]

> I have no desire for wine and its potency
>   I want only night and day that kind of ecstasy

He then quoted the Persian poem that God "is the pot and he is potter, he is the clay and the drunken reveler." He glanced over at me to complete the couplet for him, and I said that God is also the one "reeling up to the wine-vat to buy a cup, he smashes it and disappears." He was overjoyed to hear the couplet. I mentioned that this was a poem of Maulana Rumi. He turned to the others and quoted from another poem by Rumi, declaring, "Who was Maulana Rumi before he met Shams? He was only a maulana—a mere professor. But once he fell in love with Shams and his teachings, then he became Maulana Rumi!"[113]

I'm a lowly nobody but you, a generous noble, carry me With one glance from you, full of grace, you nourish me	تو کریمی من کمینہ بردہ ام لیکن از لطفِ شما پروردہ ام
Life has come so that we can play the service game A life led without serving others is a mere shame	زندگی آمد برائے بندگی زندگی بے بندگی شرمندگی
If one's Pir doesn't appear as God to the eye's pupil Then one is surely no disciple, No disciple, no disciple!	ہر کہ پیر و ذاتِ حق را یک ندید نہ مرید و نہ مرید و نہ مرید
He was a mere professor stuck in his arrogant ways Not Maulana Rumi, till he served Shams-e Tabrez	مولوی ہرگز نشد مولائے روم تا غلام شمش تبریزی نشد

Pir Rasheed said, "It is strange that God is such a being that 'He who knows himself knows his Lord—*man ʿarifa nafsahu fa-qad ʿarifa rabbahu.*' God is present in everything, but we are directed to look deep inside ourselves to find knowledge of God. How strange it is, and how wonderful!"

BEFORE BIRTH AND BEYOND DEATH

While this conversation was going on, Pir Rasheed called me by my Islamic name, Siraj al-Haqq. He translated it as "the one who illumines the truth for others." Amina asked me whether Pir Rasheed had given me my Islamic name. I replied, "No, I received my name before I had met Pir Rasheed. I got it in Morocco from the sister of a friend, a Sayyida named Hamida. She asked me what name I like and I said Siraj. She suggested I take the name Siraj al-Din. I told her that I was less concerned with *din* (religion) and more concerned with *haqq* (truth). She said, "Then take the name Siraj al-Haqq!" I replied, "I've never heard of anyone with that name." She said, "I haven't either but it has a good meaning." I accepted that and took it. It is partly a name she gave me and partly a name I gave to myself.

Pir Rasheed smiled and said, "When I was born, my father made an Urdu poem whose letters encoded the date of my birth by the abjad system. This couplet was: *Sari 'alam ko siraj-e hidayat* meaning 'a light of guidance to the whole world.'" He laughed and said, "You see, we are linked by a name!" I said, "You mean I was there in you even from your birth?" He laughed again and said, "Yes, from birth and before that, too!" Then he quoted the poem by Ameer Khusro, *Man tu shudam tu man shudi* (I have become you and you have become me). I finished the couplet while he smiled...

> I became you and you became me, I will be body if soul you will be
>   So none can claim that there be any difference between you and me

Pir Rasheed asked why I did not bring along my sarangi. "I was hoping you would come with that sarangi and play some music." Perhaps it was the poem by Khusro that made him think of music. I was flattered that he would think of me playing music for him in any way that approached Khusro playing music for his master, Hazrat Nizam al-Din Awliya. I replied that my music Ustad commanded me to stop playing during the days of Muharram. "If you like, I will bring it next time." He gave his characteristic smiling shrug that said, "Of course!" and "Why not?" and "Whatever you think best," all at the same time.

Turning to Amina Wadud, Pir Rasheed said, "Music is the very backbone of our tareeqat." Earlier they had talked about the differences between the Naqshbandi Order which Amina belongs to and the Chishti Order. The Naqshbandis favor *muraqaba* over zikr, and favor silent zikr over vocal zikr. But the Chishtis favor music over zikr and certainly appreciate vocal zikr with voice and resonance over silent zikr. Then he turned to Mubeen and his brother and said, "When I die and they take out my corpse for the *janaza* funeral, I want there to be music! Make a note of that." They both nodded dutifully. "There should be Qawwals leading the procession," he insisted. I asked, "What song would you like them to sing?" He paused for a moment. Then he replied, "Why not those very lines—I became you and you became me?"[114]

Your beautiful face makes even
Azeri idols seethe with jealousy
Whatever metaphor I employ
surely falls short of your beauty

Never will I see a vision finer
than your face's luminous beauty
I know no sun or moon as radiant,
as lovely no human or fairy

Beyond the horizons I have traveled,
enchanting idols I pursued
Many beauties I witnessed but
the likes of you none will ever see

You have looted the world,
you drive people of God insane
With your bashful dark eye,
you've set the custom of idolatry

More delicate than roses you are,
than fairies more appealing
Whatever I may say falls short,
bewildering is your sorcery

Why, o my soul's rest and respite,
did you stroll by like a cypress
With so many men begging of you,
why steal away my tranquility

You resolve to show yourself
then charge off into the wilderness
You steal my heart and soul away,
a fine display of trickery

I became you and you became me,
I will be body if soul you will be
So none can claim that there be
any difference between you and me

> Khusro has come knocking on doors
> begging in this town of yours
> For God's sake he's on all fours,
> "Look to the poor" is his only plea

خسرو غریب است و گدا افتاده در شہر شما
باشد کہ از بہرِ خدا سوئے غریباں بنگری

ONE GREAT SPIRIT

Today I was invited along with Pir Rasheed to a *niyaz* function. One of Pir Rasheed's mureeds, Ahmed Pasha, hosted the event in the memory of his father's death anniversary. His father was a mureed and khaleefa of Pir Rasheed's father. Pir Rasheed called him a *buzurg* or great soul. The niyaz function consisted of dinner, then some religious speeches on faith and hope, a prayer, and then qawwali.

I arrived at Pir Rasheed's house just before sunset and we prayed the maghrib prayer together. Then Mustafa ʿAli arrived and sat with us, while we waited for Mubeen to come, who was to show us the way to Ahmed Pasha's house. But Mubeen never showed up and didn't answer the phone. We chatted a while, waiting. Pir Rasheed asked me how my travels were, and I told him the best part was presenting a lecture at Mumbai University. There is a class there on mysticism, organized by the Sanskrit and Hindu Philosophy department. Though most of the students were of Hindu background, they were very interested in Sufism and invited me to speak as a guest lecturer.

Pir Rasheed nodded and said, "There is Sufism or mysticism in every religion. Hinduism is very old—over three thousand years old. Hindus believed from the earliest times in the great spirit that rules over the world, creates it, nourishes it and sustains it. Different groups have given different names to this great spirit or pure essence. Jains, Buddhists and Hindus have given it different names and called it by different metaphors, but every group believes in the creative and sustaining spirit. Some people later made idols and statues in human form, and claimed that the great spirit resided in them or could be reached through means of them, but this is a later development. Then along came Islam just 1400 years ago—very recently. Islam, too, teaches the worship and reverence of the one great spirit that is called Allah. Yet Islam is very focused on maintaining the original purity and oneness of the spirit, in hopes to guide people back to the original belief that all shared. The Sufism in Islam is the same in principle as mysticism in other religions," he explained.

Our discussion was interrupted by phone calls, family agitations, and worry over how to get ourselves to the niyaz function. Finally, we decided to drive ourselves to Shah Ali Banda and wait at the Pista House restaurant for someone from Ahmed Pasha's house to meet us and guide us there. We arrived late, but the food was delicious though the speeches were much too long. When qawwali began, the singers started with a poem by Hasrat Hyderabadi in praise of God's essence. And then they sang Jami's beloved ghazal in honor of the Prophet.[115]

My body is worn and frayed in separation from you, o Prophet of God My heart is weary and wild in negligence of you, o Prophet of God	تنم فرسوده جان پاره ز هجران یا رسول الله دلم پژمرده آواره ز عصیان یا رسول الله
All that happened to me, poor wretch, out of my own ignorance Let me sacrifice all for the imprint of your sandals, o Prophet of God	چو سوی من گذر آری من مسکین ز ناداری فدای نقشِ نعلینت کنم جان یا رسول الله
I am bewildered by my deeds, my face is darkened by forgetfulness I am ashamed, so ashamed, entirely ashamed, o Prophet of God	ز کردهٔ خویش حیرانم سیه شد روزِ عصیانم پشیمانم پشیمانم پشیمان یا رسول الله
I am drunk by your cup, my heart is bound by your chain I don't say I'm the best of those who praise you, oh Prophet of God	ز جامِ حبِّ تو مستم بزنجیرِ تو دل بستم نمی گویم که من هستم سخندان یا رسول الله
When the strong arm of intercession sweeps over us sinners Don't let Jami be excluded from that blessing, o Prophet of God	ز بازوئے شفاعت را کجا این بر گنه گاران مکن محروم جامی را دراں آن یا رسول الله

ENDING AND BEGINNING

As was my routine since 2010, I returned to the USA to teach. I enjoyed working with my students and hosting zikr for a small circle of Sufi friends in Atlanta who meet every Sunday. But still, I was waiting eagerly for Winter break holidays so that I could return to Hyderabad and see Pir Rasheed. This year, I flew into Delhi to see my auntie and some friends. I visited Hazrat Nizam al-Din Awliya's dargah again, and I spoke with Pir Rasheed by phone.

He asked when I was coming to Hyderabad and sounded relieved when I said I was headed toward the Deccan in a few days. He did not mention that he was gravely ill.

I leisurely made my way south to Gwalior for the Tansen Music Festival that happens every year in mid-December beside the dargah of Muhammad Ghaus. There, between the astounding music presentations that go on for four days continuously, I visited the dargah of Khwaja Khanun Chishti. Then I moved further south to attend the Sawai Gandharva Music Festival in Pune, which happened the next weekend. From there, it was a short journey over the Deccan plateau to Hyderabad. But when I arrived, I found that I could not reach Pir Rasheed by phone. Finally, his son Mukarram answered and told me that Pir Rasheed had been admitted to the hospital, but he was in the Intensive Care Unit where non-family visitors are not allowed. I waited anxiously to hear back from Mukarram whether he would be moved from the Intensive Care Unit to the general ward.

The next day, with still no news, I contacted my fellow disciple Mustafa 'Ali and planned to pick him up in the evening so that we could go together to the hospital and see for ourselves. However, that evening the traffic was so snarled, tangled and stalled that we grew frustrated, and when rain fell so heavily that it obscured the view in my car's windows, we turned back in despair. I could not make it to the old city that day.

The following evening, I ventured to the hospital alone. I found that Pir Rasheed had been shifted that day from the Intensive Care Unit to the general ward, where visitors could enter. His extended family was arrayed in the waiting room, and his grandsons informed me that his condition was critical. When they ushered me into his room, Pir Rasheed could not speak but he was conscious. Connected to IV tubes and monitors, through a tangle of wires he still managed to communicate through his eyes. He recognized me and reacted startled, as if he were surprised that I had made it to his side. Then his gaze beamed satisfaction, with even a twinkle of mischievousness, and he held my hand for a long while as we held a long discussion without words. I left for home, praying that he would recover as he did routinely from such bouts with ill-health.

Just after midnight, I got a call from Mukarram telling me his father had died. Pir Rasheed was gone. I could not help but feel that he held out a little longer than he needed to in the hope that I might get to see him once more.

That was December 22, 2013 or Safar 21, 1435 AH. The days that followed were full of pandemonium. The calm center of this community, which kept everyone in some sort of harmony, quietly faded away. People began to spiral out of control. I suppose it must only be expected amid the grief, pent-up family drama, and uncertainty over how the community would move forward now that Pir Rasheed had passed beyond this world.

The next day, I drove through the Old City to Pir Rasheed's home. Downstairs in the main living room, I found his body in a refrigerator casket. The room was full of women in black, family members and friends and neighbors, with the men spilling out into the street. I entered the room for a minute, to gaze upon his body, visible through the glass of the casket. His wife, Piranima, was weeping inconsolably and gesturing futilely at the casket. I was hardly moved to look upon his body. There was no resemblance to the radiant man I knew and loved. It was useless to cling to a lump of cold flesh when the soul has moved on, so I said a quick prayer asking God to grant him mercy in death as God granted him mercy in life and to let us live up to his example. I left the room.

Outside, the men were agitated because we could not bury Pir Rasheed immediately, as demanded by Islamic custom. Instead, we were waiting for his second son, Mujahid Baba, to return from Saudi Arabia where he was working. It was not easy to get leave, as his employers held his passport, forcing all migrant employees into bonded labor. Mujahid Baba is the designated successor of Pir Rasheed, so as sajjada-nasheen the funeral prayers should not be recited without him, but how long would it take for him to get permission, take his passport, and return to Hyderabad? Anxiety gathered around us like dark clouds.

The next day was Christmas Eve. We were still waiting for Mujahid Baba to come from Saudi Arabia, amid confusion about whether he would get permission to come or not. Pir Rasheed's eldest son, Mukarram, was succumbing to pressure from some men in the community to just go ahead and bury the body—after all, how many days can a corpse wait in the refrigerator casket in the living room, giving more grief to the ladies and in danger of the electricity going off in a black-out? Mujahid Baba had sent his brothers a message threatening dire consequences if anyone dared to move the body out of the living room before he arrived, but there was no actual news about whether he would arrive or not to attend the funeral prayers or murder anyone.

I was waiting at home on tenterhooks, ready at a moment's notice to leap into the car, fight the traffic and get myself to the Old City. In the midst of all this tension, I receive an email from Tariq, a law student at Aligarh Muslim University who had corresponded with me occasionally after reading one of my books. This time he didn't have a philosophical question. Instead, he wrote expressing condolences since he had seen a Facebook post that Pir Rasheed had died, and he asked me to give him bayʿat, initiation into our Sufi lineage.

THE DOOR'S LOCK

I was stunned. Just one day after Pir Rasheed had died, I am now being asked to give initiation? I did not know how to answer. I asked Tariq for some time to see the funeral through to its conclusion and ponder where I am going now.

The next day was Christmas Day, which is fast becoming a popular holiday in India. I got word that Mujahid Baba finally arrived early in the morning, so the funeral was scheduled for the time of noon prayers at the Chowk Masjid. I drove down to the Old City just at the time when churches were letting out. Santas were out on the streets in red fur suits, leading processions of drummers and singing Christians. Kids were wearing pink Santa masks in a bizarre mixture of Christmas and Halloween. Traffic inched along amid the jovial celebration.

I arrived at Pir Rasheed's house as the men of his family were giving his body its ritual bath or *ghusl*. I waited patiently outside, for that is a job fit only for his closest relatives. Then his body, wrapped in its white shroud and an ochre shawl wafting perfume, was lifted on a bier and loaded onto a truck waiting outside. The men followed behind the truck as it slowly started off toward the mosque. Mujahid Baba was slumped over in a feverish stupor. His eyes were completely unseeing, as if his soul had been temporarily pulled from his body. Some men dragged him along so that he could also participate in the procession. Amjad Bhai trotted along behind holding Mujahid Baba's red velvet cap on his head, as it bobbed this way and that. Then everyone loaded up into cars and onto motorbikes and into autorickshaws as the truck pulled away into traffic. In the bustle, Pir Rasheed's grandson had pushed into my hands a plastic bag full of bottles of *zamzam* water, dirt from Medina, and bottles of attar—ripped down one seam from being stuffed so full. Carrying my precious cargo, I perched on the back of Mustafa 'Ali's battered scooter, trying to balance and keep the cheap plastic bag from ripping further. We all sped toward Chowk Masjid, to arrive before the truck and welcome Pir Rasheed's body into the mosque.

The *janaza* prayer was short but the mosque was crowded with Pir Rasheed's admirers. Men pushed to get into the front row: I don't think Pir Rasheed would approve of that, but their zeal showed me how many people had been touched by his persona and how many families attributed healing to his interventions. A plastic lawn chair was carried to the front row, and then Mujahid Baba was dragged to the chair, barely conscious but murmuring the words of the prayer. Then everyone pushed to the side courtyard of the mosque where Pir Rasheed's corpse was laid in state. Two rows of men filed past on each side of the coffin, offering last prayers and wishes, and I have never seen so many men weep together. Then the truck pulled up and we all rushed to our vehicles to drive in procession from the Old City to the Kaleemi Astana, where Pir Rasheed would be buried beside his ancestors.

The truck stopped in the narrow alley near the dargah of Husayn Shah Wali which leads further to the Astana. As Pir Rasheed's body was gently lowered onto the bier and borne on men's shoulders, the singers assembled to fulfill his last wishes. True to his prediction, they led his body with songs to the grave. Some men walked backward carrying the harmoniums, while others played upon them walking forward. Dhols were strapped about the drummer's necks. I had never seen qawwali performed standing in procession. The procession went painfully slow, so that they could sing as many songs as possible in the short stretch of alley up to the Astana. The tears flowed as the Qawwals sang some of Pir Rasheed's favorite songs, and rupee bills were stuffed into their pockets all along the way.

The Qawwals sang a na'at by Jami, "O Muhammad, I am without reputation or goods, come to my aid—Focus of my prayer, center of my faith, come to my aid."[116] Without name, reputation, wealth or fortune he was going back to the earth, just as how he came. Then the beloved na'at poem by Bedam Warsi, *Adam se layi hai hasti mein arzu-ye rasul*—"God brings forth from nothingness through longing for the Prophet," with hopes that Pir Rasheed's longing to meet the Prophet would bring him back from material nothingness into a fuller spiritual being in the world beyond. Pir Rasheed loved the poems by Bedam Warsi so much that the Qawwals continued with another ghazal by him.

In your subtle hidden way, you render me senseless I'll give you my heart— just once appear, my beloved	بے خود کیے دیتے ہیں اندازِ حجابانہ آ دل میں تجھے رکھ لوں اے جلوہٴ جانانہ
It's my fate, you who criticize, that I bowed before this house I never left nor will leave the threshold of my love	زاہد میری قسمت میں سجدے ہیں اسی در کے چھوٹا ہے نہ چھوٹے گا سنگِ درِ جانانہ
I have given up my awareness and my sense Since you said, laughing, here comes that crazy one	میں ہوش و حواس اپنے اس بات پہ کھو بیٹھا ہنس کر جو کہا تم نے آیا میرا دیوانہ

Since you have made me yours in this world In the next be sure to mention, yes, this is my madman	دنیا میں مجھے تم نے جب اپنا بنایا ہے محشر میں بھی کہہ دینا یہ ہے میرا دیوانہ
Why did you meet my eye, why did you set me aflame? Now you sit with face covered, driving me wild	کیوں آنکھ ملائی تھی کیوں آگ لگائی تھی اب رخ کو چھپا بیٹھے کر کے مجھے دیوانہ
I don't know who I am, o Bedam, or what I may be A friend among friends or a stranger among strangers?	معلوم نہیں بیدمؔ میں کون ہوں اور کیا ہوں یوں اپنوں میں اپنا ہوں بیگانوں میں بیگانہ

    The burial was chaotic. I felt more like a stranger among strangers than a friend among friends. Family politics and pious machismo took over, as the men began yelling commands and critiques at each other.

    Everyone was pushing and straining to watch the body go down into the earth. Sandalwood paste and attar perfume were poured over his body as it went down. After the body was lowered into the pit, the men pulled out the carpet on which he was carried and the pale ochre shawl that covered his body, drenched in perfume; these were haphazardly tossed onto the ground. Long stone slabs were laid over the body, then dirt was shoveled over, spadeful by spadeful, making a mournful rattling sound.

    I needed to get away from that chaotic and competitive scene. The ochre shawl and carpet caught my eye, tossed to the ground. I picked them up to keep them from getting soiled by careless feet, and took them into the courtyard of the mosque behind the Kaleemi Astana and its tombs. The courtyard was empty, and I needed a quiet moment to collect my thoughts and sort out my muddled feelings. I folded the carpet carefully and laid it on the wooden bier, to keep it off the dusty ground. Then I folded the ochre shawl that had covered his body. A powerful fragrance of sandalwood and rose attar wafted from its simple weave. At first, I laid the shawl over the carpet, but then picked it up again and held it to my chest. I stood there wondering whether I should keep the shawl for myself or whether it belonged to someone else. I put it down and picked it up several times. Just then, a disciple of Afsar ʿAli, the son-in-law and a khaleefa of Pir Rasheed, came walking through the courtyard. The disciple walked over and looked at the shawl. I handed it to him, saying, "Keep that safe." He asked, "Keep it with whom?" "Keep it with you," I replied. "Yes, that's why I came for it," he whispered and slipped it under his waistcoat as he walked away.

Everyone here seemed to know what they wanted to take away from this burial: prestige, honor, or shawls. It seemed that I was the only one who was bewildered and leaving empty-handed.

CHAPTER 7
THE DOOR'S HINGE

TYING CONTINUITY

The next evening everyone in the community came to Pir Rasheed's home for a dinner of chicken biryani and tomato curry. Life must go on. The community needs a leader. This was the Dastar-Bandan or turban tying ceremony for Pir Rasheed's successor. As a senior khaleefa and son-in-law, Afsar 'Ali, took charge. He took in his hands a bright yellow cloth and tied it as a turban, loop after loop, on Mujahid Baba's head while everyone recited durud aloud. Then Mustafa 'Ali approached and placed a garland of jasmine and roses around Mujahid's neck, as a sign of blessing and congratulations.

The Qawwals who hereditarily serve Pir Rasheed's family, and have done so for several generations, came again tonight. They are Wasi-uz-Zaman and his family, the same group that sang to lead the funeral procession. They started with the saucy Persian lyrics, *Bar tu in majlis-e shahana mubarak bashad*, by Sarmad Shaheed.[117] That song is for auspicious beginnings, to celebrate a new year at a birthday or a new dispensation. The song begins by invoking the blessing of the mysterious letters in the Qur'an:

> Blessed be now and now be blessed
> I begin with N and Y S to be blessed

These letters indicate Muhammad both as a person and as a cosmic force. They reference the beginning of three chapters of the Qur'an that affirm Muhammad as an honest man, a messenger and a warning Prophet. "Letter N, sworn by the written line and the pen, by the blessing of your Lord you are not insane!" (Qur'an 68:1). Another chapter begins, "Letters Y S, sworn by the clear Qur'an, indeed you are from among the messengers, sent by the One mighty and wise" (Qur'an 36:1). And another begins, "Blessed be God who revealed the criterion to God's servant that he might be a warner to all nations" (Surat al-Furqan 25:1). By these letters and the persona whose presence they invoke, the gathering begins as an outpouring of blessings, a bewilderment of love, a drunken reveling in beauty.

With your presence, may this royal gathering be blessed Begin pouring it out, may wine and cup be blessed	بر تو ایں محفلِ شاہانہ مبارک باشد ساقیا بادہ و پیمانہ مبارک باشد
By the bank of a pure stream of scintillating colors Let the pourer's lip and the cup's lip both be blessed	بر لبِ جوئے مصفّا بہ ہزاراں انوار لبِ یار و لبِ پیمانہ مبارک باشد
If I have no relation with you, ruler of this world's beauties Then let a flirtatious wink from any lover be blessed	با تو نسبت نبود اے شہِ خوبانِ جہاں اے پری غمزۂ ترکانہ مبارک باشد
If there is no jug or liquor in the wine-pourer's hand Let circling his bashful intoxicating eyes be blessed	ساغر و بادہ اگر نیست بکفِ ساقی را گردشِ نرگسِ مستانہ مبارک باشد
Take your seat before the throne of eternity O Sarmad, let this fortune of lovers be blessed	بنشین بر سرِ تختِ ازلی تا بہ ابد سرمد ایں دولتِ جانانہ مبارک باشد

The Qawwals sang many of Pir Rasheed's favorite songs, and their music swept away the sorrow of yesterday's burial like a broom sweeps dust out of the room. They sang the poem by Jami, *Wa salla Allahu ala nurin*—"May God bless that light" with which Pir Rasheed would start every qawwali gathering. They also sang songs by Bedam Warsi that Pir Rasheed had loved so much, like *Aye naseem-e bu-e Muhammad*.[118]

THE DOOR'S HINGE

A breeze came bearing the scent of Muhammad
May God bless him and give him peace
the heart gets pulled by yearning for Muhammad
May God bless him and give him peace

His name is generosity's doorway
You see the sanctuary's niche of prayer
When you see the arch of the forehead of Muhammad
May God bless him and give him peace

O you who tire on the journey to Medina
Open your eyes and shake yourself awake
Gaze on the heart-captivating form of Muhammad
May God bless him and give him peace

We all set our faces toward the Kaba
But the Kaba sets its face toward Muhammad
The Kaba's prayer faces the abode of Muhammad
May God bless him and give him peace

Gentle fragrance spread, o Bedam,
Making fragrant the world of the heart
When loose flowed the tresses of Muhammad
May God bless him and give him peace

Then the Qawwals sang a *manqabat* for Shaykh ʿAbd al-Qadir Jeelani, praising his prowess and beseeching his help, knowing that Pir Rasheed's family traced its ancestry from him. The song's dense rhyme and militaristic beat have a powerful spiritual quality that stirred the room.[119]

O Jeelani, whose will
is the will of God
Help us, with
the permission of God

In my heart
is a lack of good
I am bad, badder,
worst of all

You are the very goodness of good 'Abd al-Qadir, ruler of all	تو اچھا ہے تو اچھا عبد القادر شاہنشاہ
O Jeelani, whose will is the will of God Help us, with the permission of God	یا جیلانی شیاء اللہ المدد باذن اللہ
I am bad but still I'm yours I am still yours in my dejection	میں ہوں برا پر تیرا ہوں ہوں رسوا پر تیرا ہوں
Whatever I may be, I'm yours I'm yours so give me protection	ہوں کیا کیا پر تیرا ہوں تیرا ہوں دے مجھ کو پناہ
O Jeelani, whose will is the will of God Help us, with the permission of God	یا جیلانی شیاء اللہ المدد باذن اللہ

The Qawwals were honoring the foundations of our Sufi order, which is both Qadiri and Chishti. After this song in honor of 'Abd al-Qadir Jeelani, a song was requested in honor of Khawaja Mu'in al-Din Chishti. The Qawwals sang an introductory couplet that is plea for protection, which Pir Rasheed recited every Sunday during our *Khatam* ritual. This anonymous Persian couplet is actually inscribed on the entry to Mu'in al-Din Chishti's tomb.

Our raft is sunk, of drowning we're afraid You support the helpless and dismayed	بہ گردابِ بلا افتادہ کشتی ضعیف و ناتوان را تو دہ پشتی

For the sake of ʿUsman Haruni, your master O Muʿin al-Din Chishti, come to our aid	بہ حقِّ خواجہ عثمان ہرونی مدد کن یا معین الدین چشتی

This short introductory petition was followed by a ghazal attributed to Muʿin al-Din himself.[120]

I see the reflection of his beauty in my soul's mirror, just like I see the blazing sun reflected in a pool of pure, still water	اندر آئینۂ جاں عکسِ جمالی دیدم ہمچو خورشید کہ در آبِ زلالی دیدم
The gaze of reason is stunned by rays from my beloved's face I see his image despite the obscuring of a hundred veils	خیرہ شد دیدۂ عقل از لمعاتِ رخِ دوست با وجود از پسِ صد پردہ خیالی دیدم
The light shining from my soul's mirror is of the essence I see it, however, as a metaphor representing the truth	ایں چنیں نور کہ در آئینۂ جاں بنمود عینِ ذات ست ولیکن بمثالی دیدم
Let me be excused for acting so bewildered and drunk I see his beauty and goodness in my amazement's mirror	من اگر والہ و مدہوش شوم معذورم کہ در آئینہ عجب حسنُ و جمالی دیدم
I am a drunken lover since I heard "Am I not your Lord?"[121] I see reason and intelligence as impossible for me	عاشق و مست من از روزِ ازل آمدہ ام عقل و ہشیارے خود امرِ محالی دیدم
My being is gone and all that's left is absolute cosmic being I see all this as exile endured in hopes of some future union	ہستیم رفت و کنوں ہستیِ مطلق باقیست ایں ہمہ ہجر بہ امیدِ وصالی دیدم

Through a painful narrowness
I've entered the party of oneness
I see nothing as impossible
after passing through such an ordeal

بزمِ وحدت کہ مرا تنگتر از تنگ نمود
چوں ز تنگی بگذشتم چہ محالی دیدم

In the expanse of "all is he"
this whole world and cosmos
I see as less than a crowing cock
unable to even fly

در بیابانِ ہویّت ہمہ ملک و ملکوت
کمتر از پشہ کلی بے پر و بالی دیدم

Since Muʿin left phenomena's dust
for eternity's light
I see no impending dawn
and no sunset and no high noon

تا معیّن ذرّہ صفت رفت پئے نورِ ازل
نہ طلوع و نہ غروب و نہ زوالی دیدم

I leave Pir Rasheed's house thinking that all I sense is sunset. There were moments of joy when I witnessed the community come together around Mujahid Baba. There were glimmers of hope when I saw continuity asserted in the face of loss. There were notes of ecstasy, when Muʿin al-Din Chishti's own poetry sang of a oneness that is beyond dissipation and an eternal light that is beyond obstruction. I cling to these words but in my heart, all I can sense is a sun that has disappeared below the horizon and everywhere lurks an impending darkness.

EMPTINESS

Mujahid Baba called a group of Pir Rasheed's disciples—Mustafa ʿAli, Ahmed and me—for a meeting at the family house. I arrived and found him sitting upstairs, speaking sternly to Mubeen and his brother Hamid and some other mureeds.

The room seemed so much bigger and emptier now that Pir Rasheed's bed was removed. I don't know where it has gone. That single bed used to be a whole world. His tasbeeh was under the pillow, along with his copy of the wazeefa that he would recite every evening. Under the pillow was also his shoulder cloth that he would use to wipe his face or clean up spills, and his mobile phone that was always lost in the fold of the sheets. His box of pills was kept under the bed, along with his iron knife for cutting lemons to cure the people who came to him at any time of night or day with complaints. Under the bed was the suitcase that he locked to store his important papers

THE DOOR'S HINGE

for administrating the Khanqah along with pictures of the Prophet's tomb in Medina. On top of it was the box with scissors on top, where he would store the daily hadees that was printed in the *Siyasat Daily* Urdu newspaper—he would not want any words of the Prophet to be thrown into the trash, so he would carefully clip out the little hadees and store it in a box. Only then would he let the newspaper go downstairs to the wider family and into trash where it would be used to wipe the dishes clean or dry chillies in the sun on the roof. God knows whether anyone ever read the little scraps of paper with the text of hadees printed on them. Pir Rasheed trained his young grandson, Hasan, to help him cut out the hadees carefully and store it in the box. Now there were no boxes and no scissors. Where were all these objects that I hardly noticed until now, now that they are gone?

The room seemed wider and more expansive, as we mureeds sat in a row facing Mujahid Baba. He was busy giving a stern speech. He said, "You all loved my father and he loved you. He would mention you by name all the time. He loved you mureeds more than he loved his children. I'm saying that even though I'm his son, but it's true. Yet now he is gone, so you should consider me as you considered him and come to me as you came to him. Everything that he had, he gave to me. I'm not myself anymore—that is true! The day of the funeral, you saw my condition. I was not there in my body. I can't say where I was, but I was with him and then he sent me back. So now I am here, sitting in front of you, and whatever was your love for him, you should give that love to me. However, you considered my father, so you should consider me. Whatever problems you have, you should share with me. We have to be like one person."

Before we could finish the meeting, some of Mujahid Baba's relatives came in and sat down beside him. He turned to speak to them and they watched us. The conversation faltered. Mujahid Baba addressed us, "I will speak with you all another time. Come back soon to visit." We were dismissed and filed down the narrow stairs toward the gate.

We all scattered in our different directions. I stayed back for a moment as the others left, to ask Mujahid Baba whether I should give initiation to mureeds or not. I told him how someone had contacted me by email just one day after Pir Rasheed died and asked me for initiation, but I was confused as to the proper path. Mujahid Baba listened carefully then paused for a minute, as if to consult with his father's soul. He then turned to me and say, "Yes, go ahead with confidence. Give initiation into our lineage. That is what my father would like you to do." I was leaving Hyderabad the next morning, heading back to the USA. So that night I called up Tariq, the fellow who asked for initiation, and granted this to him over the phone the way Pir Rasheed had granted it to me face to face. It would be a whole year until I had the chance to meet him face to face, my first mureed.

As I was leaving Pir Rasheed's house that night, I caught a glimpse of Piranima standing in the doorway, peering out from behind the curtain. She called me over and took my hand. Beginning again to cry, she said to me, "He left us! He left us here and went away! But don't worry, he is fine. He is more than fine—he is full of joy there, full of light. No, don't worry about him. But what about us? He left us here! How could he leave me behind?" She started to weep again, and her sons came to embrace her and pull her back from the doorway into the house.

She did not let go of my hand, but said, "Don't you leave us, too! Don't stop coming back to us!" as she disappeared inside. I never did get the chance to go again to Yaqutpura to see her before I left for America.

SHIFTING GROUND

I returned to Atlanta to teach, and found that the zikr circle that we started there has begun to take on more depth. Now some members of that zikr group have asked to take initiation through me into Pir Rasheed's Kaleemi Order. From beyond the grave, his blessings continue to flow into this world.

During the summer, I took vacation from teaching so I could return to Hyderabad. It is the month of Ramadan, so it is a good time to be back. It is the first time I am returning to Hyderabad without Pir Rasheed here, and I am apprehensive about how I will feel. Will the city still feel like home? My friends are here and my music teacher is here, but my Pir seems far away. Still, he told me when I was leaving to take up my job in the USA, that distance means nothing in this Sufi relationship, and I found that to be true. Perhaps what held true between two continents will also hold true in a relationship between two different worlds.

When I return to Hyderabad, I find that Mujahid Baba has gone back to Saudi Arabia to fulfill his work contract. The community in Hyderabad seems rudderless and restless. I speak with Mujahid Baba by phone, and he tells me that he is now all alone. He tells me how, when Pir Rasheed went on 'umra three months before he died, he met Mujahid Baba in Medina. He took Mujahid Baba aside, with much difficulty as family members were always lingering nearby, to have a private talk. Pir Rasheed told him that he would be isolated and alone, yet he would be always protected if he kept his anger in check. Yet if he allowed himself to get angry, that would be the way that others would destroy him. If he let himself become like fire, then they could throw water on him and put him out. He has taken this to heart, and is keeping cool and aloof from their provocations. But he has an angry nature, and has no patience for people who are disrespectful, so it is hard.

As for his angry nature, Mujahid Baba says that people have told him that his great-grandfather, Sayyid Zia al-Hasan Jeeli Kaleemi, was also of the same angry nature. He could stand no disrespect or deceit. Pir Rasheed by contrast was always forgiving and patient, and withstood all kinds of nonsense around him, without critique. Mujahid Baba said, "His nature was like a river that always flowed slow and even. My nature is like the ocean that, when whipped up by winds and tides, rises and destroys people that are in its way."

When I visited the Astana to pay respects to Pir Rasheed's tomb, I found the whole place to be in a sparkling state. Before he left for Saudi Arabia, Mujahid Baba had taken pains to make new grave clothes with fine calligraphic writing of the name of each deceased leader, ending with Pir Rasheed. Mujahid Baba ordered Mubeen and the other mureeds to meet every Sunday to clean the Astana and recite the Khatam there, before Pir Rasheed's grave. His mother, Piranima, had objected and asked why the people were not coming to the house in the Old City anymore to recite the Khatam, as they used to in Pir Rasheed's room. Mujahid Baba told her that Pir Rasheed is not there anymore. He always said that Khatam should be recited before one's Pir, so the people should do that now at the grave site. She is refusing now to speak with him.

Mujahid Baba sighed as we concluded our phone conversation. "A man cannot live two lives at once. He cannot live in two places. I cannot stay in Saudi Arabia and take care of mureeds and the Astana in India. Just pray to God that I can earn as much money in India as I earn in Saudi so that I can return to Hyderabad." Mujahid's saying this mirrors my own dilemma. I cannot live in two places at once, both in Atlanta and Hyderabad. When Pir Rasheed was alive, those two places seemed juxtaposed somehow. But now that he is gone, these two places seem very far from each other.

THE KA'BA OF THE HEART

I was back in Hyderabad to observe Ramadan. As the holy month drew to a close, Eid al-Fitr dawned, a celebration of breaking the month-long fast, announced at the sighting of the new moon. In Delhi at the dargah of Nizam al-Din Awliya, the Qawwals will be singing the famous ghazal of Ameer Khusro.[122]

THE MERCIFUL DOOR

Poor me, on Eid I make prayers
in this alley of yours
For me, the joy of Eid is
in glimpsing that face of yours

For you, I would give
a hundred crescents of Eid
The new moon for me is
that arched brow of yours

O Nizam al-Din Awliya,
O beloved of God
All other loves are sacrificed
for this life of yours

Ka'ba of the heart, I turn in prayer
toward the face of yours
The niche where lovers bow
is that forehead of yours

Broke and busted,
I wander your alleyway
Good Lord, to beg for a glimpse
of that beauty of yours

Hyacinth gets perplexed
by the tangles of your locks
Enchanting are these sorcerous
narcissus eyes of yours

I know nothing of the Ka'ba
or the idol's temple
I simply prostrate wherever I
find that face of yours

Some may ask,
"What has killed that poor Khusro?"
Your wink, your eye,
that graceful brow of yours

THE DOOR'S HINGE

Khusro did not care for the sighting of the crescent moon and could not decide which way was the Kaʻba to orient his Eid prayer. His view was fully occupied by the face of his spiritual guide, Nizam al-Din Awliya.

I got a call from Zaida today, who used to live near the dargah of Nizam al-Din Awliya. How fortunate she was to have been able to visit there any day she pleased. I've not spoken with her since Pir Rasheed passed away. She was so kind to call on Eid to wish me warm greetings. She is living in Pondicherry now, at the spiritual ashram-town of Auroville on the Tamil Nadu coast. She informed me that she's training to become a third-grade teacher in the International American school.

During the call, she told me a story. Back in 2013, just before Pir Rasheed passed away, her parents had come to visit her in India. She took them to Hyderabad to show them a new place, and she visited Pir Rasheed's home with them. He treated them kindly, and then suddenly turned to Zaida and asked her whether she wanted to take initiation with him into the Kaleemi lineage. She said yes, and he initiated her. He gave her a signed paper and a booklet with our tareeqat's chain of initiation and prayers in it. She would always say after meeting Pir Rasheed, "He is such a beautiful human being!"

Tonight, Zaida informed me by phone about this initiation. She also said, "Just after he passed away, a strange feeling came over me. I felt that Pir Rasheed was there with me in the room, and he was connecting me through himself to a long chain of spiritual teachers. He was fastening me to this chain of all the masters in the Order," she explained. Her American husband also realized that something was happening. He is American but has lived in Pondicherry for almost half a century, and describes himself as spiritual but not religious. Sensing something strange, he asked Zaida who it was that was in her presence there in the room with them, saying, "It is as if someone is here working on your heart." Zaida explained that this presence lasted for about half an hour, and then faded away.

DREAM GUIDES

I went to the dargah of Yusufayn for the weekly mehfil-e samaʻ that happens every Thursday night. I invited my friend Zohaib Qadiri to join me. He is a law student who had contacted me over Facebook wanting to talk about Sufism; though he claimed to have encountered it only a few years ago, he already knew much about its teachings and its poetry. He suggested we meet a little early to chat and before going to the mehfil together. We met around 11 pm and talked while sitting on the steps of the courtyard of the dargah. All around us blew the chaos of children, cats, poor ladies lining up for the new sari giveaway for Eid, flower sellers and hawkers of all kinds, and a girl who kept begging while meowing like a kitten. Zohaib was joined by his friend Aditya, who has recently gotten interested in mysticism and has been reading books about Sufism and Vedanta.

We spoke of many things, but I was struck by Zohaib's dream. He shared with me that he had a dream just one week ago. He saw a khanqah and out from it came Pir Rasheed along with another man, as they were conversing. Pir Rasheed was reciting the durud called Salat al-Fatih. This durud is ascribed to Shaykh Ahmad Tijani, and it goes like this:

> Dear God, grant peace and blessings upon our master, Muhammad, the opener of what has been closed and the seal of what had come before, who aids the truth with the truth and who guides to your direct path, bless him and his family and his companion as his power and his great stature deserves to be blessed.[123]

In Zohaib's dream, Pir Rasheed recited this durud and then approached Zohaib and gave him a very stern look. Zohaib called the look jalali, full of wrath and power, and commented that he was surprised that Pir Rasheed would give a stern look because he has heard that Pir Rasheed was very *jamali*, full of beauty and grace. Zohaib had never met Pir Rasheed, and the dream set him to thinking whether he had done anything to anger the Pir.

I asked him how he recognized Pir Rasheed if he never met him. It turns out Zohaib had read the short "In Memoria" I had written, which Pir Zia posted on his website along with Pir Rasheed's photo, so from that he recognized Pir Rasheed's face. I asked who was the person Pir Rasheed was talking to in the dream. Zohaib looked embarrassed, then slowly said, "It was Shah Rukh Khan." "The Bollywood actor?" I asked. "Yes, exactly," he replied, "but why would they be talking? It is very strange. The famous actor gave Pir Rasheed a hundred rupee note and turned to leave." Pir Rasheed seems to be visiting many people in dreams. I told Zohaib, "Don't feel bad about the stern look—Pir Rasheed sometimes did get that fiery look. I got that look several times in my life, and it is terrifying!" He said, "You are very blessed to have elicited that look from such a jamali man!" In the mehfil, we listened to the Warsi brothers sing about Shaykh Naseer al-Din Chiragh-e-Delli, for it was his 'urs day yesterday on 17 Ramadan. It was a joyful song about his being the bride and the marriage procession coming to take him away.

A few days later, Zohaib invited me to attend a mehfil-e sama' at the khanqah of Shah Murtaza Qadiri, near the dargah of Shah Musa Qadiri in the Old City neighborhood of Husayni Alam. We met a little early at Muazzam Jahi market and sat for tea at Empire Hotel. At this sitting, Zohaib finished the unfolding story about his dream. He informed me that he wrote to Pir Zia Inayat Khan by internet to ask about this dream, because he did not know to whom to turn. Pir Zia asked if he had done anything to anger Pir Rasheed, but Zohaib answered, "No, that is not possible because I never met him or had any interaction with him." Pir Zia suggested that perhaps it was possible someone else in Zohaib's family had done something to anger him. So Zohaib asked his father whether he knew anything about Pir Rasheed, but his father was distracted and gave no firm reply. So Pir Zia simply replied that Zohaib should be patient until maybe another clue would come in the near future.

Meanwhile, Zohaib asked his father again about Pir Rasheed, and this time received the answer that his father had been friendly with him long back and in fact they were related. Thinking hard, Zohaib went to his mother to ask whether she knew Pir Rasheed. "Yes," she answered, "he is a distant relative of ours, for their family consists of Qadiri Sayyids." A few weeks later, Zohaib had another dream, in which he saw Pir Rasheed, who gave him a look that was utterly jamali, full of kindness and love. Zohaib smelled a fragrance of pure musk coming from his direction. He told me, "I've never smelled real musk but only its fragrance in perfumes, yet I imagine that this strong and sweet smell is exactly what pure musk must be like."

Zohaib then turned to me and asked, "What did I do wrong that I got that look of anger?" I replied that the question ought to be, "What did you do right to get the look of utter kindness!" He thought a moment, and then said, "Before this, I didn't know of my relationship to him through my family, but now I do." I replied, "Yes, perhaps the angry look was to spur you to discover this—now that you have, it will lead you a little deeper to your goal, whatever that may be."

We arrived at the mehfil by motorcycle around midnight. At the entrance, we met the Warsi Brothers qawwali troupe where they were loitering and chatting. The rhythmic beat of qawwali was coming from the hall a short distance away. I asked if they were about to play or had just finished, and Nazir Warsi answered that they were waiting for their turn. I said, "Ah, then we are fortunate tonight to get to listen to you." He replied with a Persian couplet, haltingly remembered, "*Khush-bakht-am keh man-am sana-khwan-e rasul*—Fortunate am I to be one who sings the praise of the Prophet." I waited for him to finish the couplet with the second line, but he just smiled bashfully and said, "I myself composed that line in Persian!" I commended him.

Walking into the assembly, Nazir Warsi's Persian line was circling around in my head. Then suddenly, a partner line came to me to complete the rhyme: *Fakhr-e man-ast keh man-am qadar-dan-e rasul.*

> Fortunate am I to be one who sings the praise of the Prophet
> Honored am I to be one who values the ways of the Prophet

The mehfil lasted until just before dawn, when a meal was served that would tide everyone over through the day-long fast. Everyone, the singers included, sat in rows around the long red dastarkhwan cloths laid out on the floor the length of the hall. After washing my hands outside, I ran into Nazir Warsi and shared with him the line that came to my mind. His eyebrows shot up as he repeated it, weighing the rhythm and rhyme on his tongue, and he walked away happy.

NIGHT OF UNION

In December 2014, the one-year anniversary of Pir Rasheed's death approached. I struggled to rearrange my teaching schedule to get free one week early, so I could arrive in Hyderabad for the commemoration of his first ʿurs. This year, the date of his death, twenty-first of Safar in the Islamic lunar calendar, would fall on December 12. Like a gift from heaven, I managed to get off from teaching in time. I arrived to find that Mujahid Baba had also managed to settle his affairs in Saudi Arabia and had permanently shifted back to Hyderabad. His celebrating the first ʿurs of his father would mark the beginning of his taking up the mantle of the sajjada-nasheen of the Astana Kaleemi.

On the night of his ʿurs, the Qawwals sang Pir Rasheed's favorite songs, and I realized that his favorites had become the favorite songs of the whole community. When he would go into ecstasy, it gave a chance for the community to grow closer, rising to care for him, make sure his cap stayed on his head, helping him back to his seat, offering nazrana and blessings to cool him off. Pir Rasheed's favorite songs became the community's songs, and that repertoire is passed on in continuity after his death. Perhaps they were passed to him in this way from his father, Sayyid Fakhr al-Hasan, and to him from his father, Sayyid Zia al-Hasan Jeeli Kaleemi.

However, a song I had not heard before at an ʿurs at Pir Rasheed's Khanqah was requested, so some variation and change does happen. That is only right, for flowing water is clean to drink while stagnant water causes illness. Someone requested a ghazal by Watan, a modern Sufi poet from Hyderabad.[124]

THE DOOR'S HINGE

I am merely a mirror—
form and image belong to you
I do not really exist—
facing yourself is you, only you

Where is there a heart
in which you do not reside?
Where is the rose
whose fragrance isn't from you?

I am filled from head to toe
with *Allah-hu Allah-hu*
Vision is *hu*, heart is *hu*,
soul is *hu* which means you

The goal was attained
the moment I understood
There is no you without me,
there is no me only you

Ask the seekers what they
want to strive to do
When desire itself is sought,
what's demanded of you?

Wherever I bow my head,
that direction is the qibla
Since wherever I turn, I only
see the face of you

He is present in me
when I am dissolved in him
You smell the rose but
can't see its aroma, can you?

On judgment day, o Watan,
whom will you beseech
When your beloved every moment
is already with you?

Listening to this song, I realized that I was no longer full of sorrow at the death of Pir Rasheed. At first, I had been at a total loss. He had occupied such a large place in my life and my heart, that his no longer being present felt devastating. But now, I realize that his physical and embodied presence was just one aspect of Pir Rasheed. That is gone but he is not gone. His virtues live on, still challenging us to live up to them. His spiritual presence still comes to our aid.

When I first took initiation with him, he said to me, "Now it is like your second birth. You are like a child of my spirit. We will be connected forever and, even on the Day of Judgment, I will be there with you." I accepted that but did not understand it until now. On the Day of Judgment whom will I beseech when my beloved every moment is already with me?

Photo 16: Mujahid Baba and family reciting prayers at the tomb of Pir Rasheed

After the qawwali was over, dinner was served, and after that I went to Mujahid Baba to thank him and ask permission to leave. Others were milling about, chatting and helping clear away plates. Mujahid Baba shook my hand smiling slyly, and I was taken aback to find something in his hand as he shook mine. He would not let my hand go as I looked at him questioningly. He said quietly, so nobody else could hear, "Keep this. It is for you. My father wants you to have it. Do not show it to anyone." His eyes held a stern warning about jealousy from others, as he released my hand. I took whatever it was in my hand and surreptitiously set it in my coat pocket. I thanked him and walked out.

After I got home, I reached into my pocket and pulled out a tasbeeh, a string of prayer beads which were very small and delicately carved of wood. The tassel of the string was tangled and worn out, and the wooden beads were smooth and oiled from long use. It was the string prayer beads that belonged to Pir Rasheed. I gave thanks to God, for when my Pir died I felt that I had nothing of his to keep for myself—the shawl that had covered his corpse I had given away to someone else. I had nothing in a physical sense. The physical sense is actually very important. Relics make tangible and embody the psychic and spiritual presence of a person that continues on after his or her death. There is great comfort to the heart to have a small relic, a sensory reminder, of someone you love.

That shawl that I had given away was a relic of his death, but the prayer beads that I held now in my hand represent a relic of his life. Pir Rasheed had once told me, "Sometimes you want something so badly, but you do not get it. The response to this is to pray, saying, 'Dear Allah, what I wanted you did not want for me, so give me something better that you want for me.' Always remember that the disappointment you feel is because of some narrowness in your vision or some shallowness in your understanding. Give that up to God, and ask God to give you what God knows is best for you. Then you will always be satisfied."

PEACE BE UPON YOU

Tonight, the 27th night of Ramadan, is *Shab-e Qadr* or the Night of Power, the holiest night of the year. I went to meet Zohaib and his friends in the Public Gardens to pray in the evening at The Nizam's Mosque. Rain was pouring this evening, as Ramadan came in the heart of the monsoon season, and the breezes were cool. There could not have been a better evening for the Imam to recite during our prayer from the Chapter of Power (Surat al-Qadr 97:1–5).

> Indeed, we sent it down on the night of power
> How can you know what is the night of power?
> The night of power is better than a thousand months
> The angels and spirit descend in it by leave of their Lord to each command
> Peace it is until the rising of the dawn.

After praying, we shared *iftar* as the mosque's custodians served large plates of dates, cut fruit, and boiled salty lentils to the hundreds of worshippers gathered to pray and break the fast. We drank a spot of tea while admiring the mosque's delicate architecture—much expanded with a tin shed roof and garish modern improvements to accommodate today's crowd. The rain pounded out rhythms on the tin roof as we spoke of the poet Ghalib. When the rain let up, we whisked off on motorcycles to Grand Hotel for biryani, which never disappoints.

We bade farewell to the other friends, as the rains had let up. Then Zohaib, Aditya and I took off to the Kaleemi Astana. We got there late and missed meeting Mujahid Baba there at the night-time prayer, but he called us to his home. Before we left, we quickly paid our respects and Zohaib sang in Urdu a beautiful *salam* by Sayyid Ahmed Reza Barelwi.[125]

> On the Chosen One, spirit of compassion,
>   may there be countless blessings
> On the candle in gatherings of guidance,
>   may there be boundless blessings
>
> On the sun in the skies of Prophethood,
>   may there be limitless blessings
> On the rose in the garden of Messengers,
>   may there be countless blessings
>
> On the king of splendors that shine,
>   on the ruler of the sacred shrine
> On the spring of intercession divine,
>   may there be countless blessings
>
> On the beloved of the nightly journey,
>   may there be peace everlasting
> On the groom of heaven's assembly,
>   may there be countless blessings
>
> In service to his most holy presence,
>   Yes, Reza, somehow try to say
> On the Chosen One, spirit of compassion,
>   may there be countless blessings

The genre of salam poems is very poignant. The salam offers greetings of peace and blessings upon the Prophet from afar. These poems express the yearning to go to Medina, which is a physical embodiment of the longing to be in the Prophet Muhammad's presence. They picture the Prophet as a great ruler, a protecting friend, or a distant beloved. Sufis sing these poems with a great deal of nostalgia, longing for a homeland they never will have.

At their deepest level, these songs are not about lands and geographical distance, but are rather metaphorical, about the soul's longing to return to its source in God. But the imagery of a human beloved—the Prophet Muhammad—and the beauties of his distant town—Medina—make that deeper meaning accessible and emotionally moving. In our Sufi order, Sayyid Zia al-Hasan Jeeli Kaleemi also wrote many poems in this genre, and the most famous is his salam that is often sung by the community over his tomb and those of his followers.[126]

O morning breeze, when you pass by Medina
Give my salam and politely convey
This restlessness I feel to meet him,
The beloved of God, do fully convey

گزر مدینہ میں جب صبا ہو ادب سے میرا سلام کہنا
جو میری دیکھی ہے بے قراری حبیبِ حق سے تمام کہنا

I am rapt with longing to kiss his foot
But have no way to get near
To his lofty essence beyond compare
How can a slave attain, kindly convey!

ہے پائے بوسی کی بس تمنا ولے رسائی نہیں ہے ممکن
کہ ذاتِ عالی ہے بے مثالی ہو کیسے حاضر غلام کہنا

My spirit is fallen into such turbulence
As I oppose my lower soul's urge
With sighs and cries, this state of mine
To the best of humanity quickly convey

پڑی تلاطم میں جان میری ہے نفسِ بد کی مخالفت سے
بآہ و نالہ یہ حال میرا حضورِ خیر الانام کہنا

No patience has my heart to bear separation
How long can I stay away from him?
"I give my soul, my mother and father too!"
Such speech my lips continuously convey

نہ تابِ فرقت نہ صبر دل میں رہوں قدم سے جدا میں تا کہ
فداک روحی ابی و امی یہی ہے لب پر کلام کہنا

The fires of separation blaze higher
As my heart and guts burn on the grill
But to demand the reviving cup of union
my tongue will never complainingly convey

بھڑک رہی ہے وہ آگِ فرقت دل و جگر ہیں کباب بھن کر
نہیں زباں پر ہے شکوہ کوئی عطا ہو وصلت کا جام کہنا

"The one who lies in ruins with separation
whose spirit writhes within his body
If only a glance of compassion would grace him!"
Convey this message and weepingly convey

ہوا جدائی سے حال ابتر ہے جان تن میں بہت ہی مضطر
ہو اس کی حالت پہ نظر رحمت کہا ہے رو کر پیام کہنا

> His holy essence intercedes for our community
> So be not afraid of judgment day
> But still, Zia, I wish to face the judge
> And "I am your servant" lovingly convey

شفیعِ امت ہے ذاتِ اقدس نہیں ہے خطرہ بروزِ محشر
مگر تمنا ہے پیشِ داور ضیاؔ کو اپنا غلام کہنا

In our Kaleemi Sufi Order, these salam poems are very powerful. This is portrayed by the story of Shaykh Yahya Madani, which Pir Rasheed told me several times. Yahya Madani was the Sufi guide of Shaykh Kaleemullah, after whom our order is named.

Yahya Madani lived in Ahmedabad, in Gujarat near the busy ports on the Arabian Sea. After his mother died, he fell into a spell of deep sorrow and depression, and he began to long for the chance to visit Medina and offer salams to the Prophet at his grave. His story is told like this.

> One day, on the eighteenth of Ramadan, Yahya Madani went to the graveyard to recite Fatiha over the tomb of his dear mother. A Qawwal named Mustafa was accompanying him. He knew of Yahya Madani's ardent desire to go to Medina. He saw this as a great opportunity, and began to sing for him a poem of Maulana Jami.[127]

> How would it be, o Lord, to turn
> toward Yathrib and Batha its plaza
> To stay for a time in Mecca and then
> Make my place in beloved Medina

کے بود یا رب کہ رو در یثرب و بطحا کنم
گہہ بہ مکہ منزل و گہہ در مدینہ جا کنم

> Listening to this ghazal sung lit a fire in Yahya Madani's heart. Rubbing his hands on his face, he intoned, "There is such grace in this poem! O Mustafa, may you find eternal success!" With this encouragement, Mustafa the Qawwal sang the ghazal a second time. In an ecstatic state, Yahya Madani called out, "Not today or tomorrow but right now I am going!" Without giving anyone advanced warning, he left home in 1087 AH to stay in Medina forever.[128]

Surely his family and followers were upset, but he became famous as the Axial Saint of Medina (*Qutb al-Medina*) and the Master of the Holy Cities (*Shaykh al-Haramayn*). In accord with the couplet he heard sung, which lit a fire in his heart, he lived alternatively for a year in Mecca and a year in Medina, until he died in 1689. When Shaykh Kaleemullah was young, he went to Mecca and Medina, met him and took initiation from him there, then returned to India to start the Kaleemi branch of the Chishti Order.

THE DOOR'S HINGE

    Yet even before Yahya Madani, the Chishti masters loved this form of poetry, the salam. One of the only full poems that we have of Hazrat Nizam al-Din Awliya is a salam in the form of a qaseeda. This poem is sung every evening at his dargah, as the doors are shut for the night.[129]

Turn toward Medina, o morning breeze, and go convey salam from one who offers this petition With a hundred humilities, render his salam To that king of all sent on the prophetic mission	صبا بسوئے مدینہ رو کن از یں دعا گو سلام بر خواں بگردِ شاہِ رسل بگرد و بصد تضرع سلام بر خواں
Wash for me the grave over his exquisite form Offer for me a graceful prayer then recite from Qur'an the chapter called Muhammad In your voice's most melodious rendition[130]	بشو ز من صورتِ مثالی نماز بگزار اندر آنجا بہ لحن خوش سورۂ محمّد تمام اندر قیام بر خواں
Passing the Door of Mercy and bowing at the Door of Gabriel At the Door of Peace give divine salam from me To the Prophet, that's your commission	بباب رحمت گہے گزر کن بباب جبریل کہ جبیں سا سلام ربّی علیٰ حبیبی گہے بباب سلام بر خواں
With impeccable respect, lay your willing head Down in the dust of that alleyway Give copious salam to the pure spirit Of that exemplar of the human condition	بنہ پچندیں ادب طرازی سر ارادت بخاکِ آں کو صلوٰتِ وافر بروحِ پاک جنابِ خیر الانام بر خواں
With a harmony like the Psalmist David With a heart infused with pain and longing In the Prophet's court, sing this poem of Nizam His servant, steeped in sins of omission	بہ لحنِ داؤد ہمنوا شو بہ نالۂ درد آشنا شو بہ بزمِ پیغمبر ایں غزل را از عبدِ عاصی نظام بر خواں

    Zohaib only needed to sing a few verses of one salam to recall in my mind the depth of this tradition. Even a few notes conjure up the long chain of beautiful associations and ancient longings that are expressed in the salam poems. His strong and mellow voice echoed over the tombs in the otherwise silent Kaleemi Astana, as Aditya and I tried to join with him in the refrain.

    From the Astana, we headed to the neighborhood of Tolichowki—just a short drive away—to visit Mujahid Baba at his home. He met us with great hospitality and waxed eloquent this evening. Zohaib told him about his dreams of Pir Rasheed, and Mujahid Baba told us many stories. Mujahid Baba reminded us of how Pir Rasheed would never call himself sajjada-nasheen, the "One who Sits on the Prayer Carpet" and is the authorized leader of the order. Rather he would say, "I am merely the servant (*khadim*) of this Astana." Mujahid Baba said, "I don't even have the courage to say that I'm a servant, because serving implies that I have choice in the matter and it is given freely. No, I am merely the slave (*ghulam*) of this Astana."

Mujahid Baba told us about his many run-ins with Wahhabis and Salafis and Tableeghis in Saudi Arabia while he was working there. They get so agitated about Sufi poetry and songs, partly because they resent the power of music and partly because they misunderstand the poetic imagery of wine. We discussed the feeling of intoxication and ecstasy. Mujahid Baba said, "I have never drunk alcohol—I'm simply not able to do it! My ancestors would never allow me to do such a thing. But I admire drunk people because they are never dishonest. A drunk will say exactly what he thinks and feels and cannot hide the truth. That is a wonderful thing about drunk people! I don't criticize them, even though it is forbidden in the sharee'a to get drunk. That is between them and God, and who am I to interfere between them and God? But the question to consider is how can you achieve that state of simple honesty without drinking alcohol?"

CHAPTER 8
THE DOOR'S KEY

Pir Rasheed passed away in body but he remains with us in spirit. Most concretely, he has left successors who follow his principles, and those principles remain in the world as guideposts for any who want to follow in his footsteps. These principles are the key to unlock the door of mercy.

Pir Rasheed belonged to the family of Shaykh 'Abd al-Qadir Jeelani and his Kaleemi Order fused the Qadiri and Chishti Orders. In the Qadiri Order, eleven is a very special number, and many of its devotional rituals incorporate the number eleven. In honor of him, I extracted eleven principles to follow from Pir Rasheed's life and teachings, as explained above in this book. Those eleven principles are: being, awareness, purity, unity, insight, respect, love, music, remembrance, intimacy and mercy. Look into each one briefly as we close this book and open the door of mercy.

BEING

Pir Rasheed said, "God's essence is within every person. God gives to each person regardless of what that person is like—Muslim or non-Muslim, good or bad. What a large-hearted being is God!" God is the essence that brings into being all things and all forms of life. From the vast cosmos to the microscopic atom, from the smallest gnat to sentient creatures like us, God gives each its foundation and its being is permeated with God's own being. Being is one. Being brings all diverse entities into oneness. This is radical monotheism which questions the conventions of routine experience based on the ego's distinction between me and other-than-me.

God is the foundation of every being, but more than this, God is present in the human heart which is the core of our particular being. The human heart is the most comprehensive quintessence of being which can comprehend the whole universe and God beyond it. When the heart is refined and purified, it reflects reality like a mirror.

Pir Rasheed was invited to a follower's home for a meal but declined to come. The follower boasted, "Our house is big and our hearts are big!" Pir Rasheed laughed, "The big One is in my heart, what need have I for anything else?" The big One, al-Kabeer, is one of the many names of God as described in the Qur'an. God can be present in the refined heart in the same way the image of a beloved person can be seen in the mirror. Yet how difficult it is to refine the heart and keep it polished with continual awareness and worship.

AWARENESS

True worship means maintaining constant awareness and not just performing ritual acts. Pir Rasheed used to teach, "Doesn't the Qur'an tell us that God says, I created the jinn and human beings only to worship me?" (Surat al-Dhariyat 51:56) How is it possible for a human being to spend each moment worshipping God through ritual prayer? Only Sufis can give the real explanation of this verse in the Qur'an, because they know that each breath—inhaling and exhaling—can be prayer if it is done with sincerity and mindfulness. This is the only kind of prayer that one can do in every moment, while still fulfilling one's other duties in the world."

This internal prayer consists of staying constantly aware. This awareness is called *taqwa* in the Qur'an, and it is the mindfulness which is at the root of conscience. It means awareness that God's presence is overwhelming and that your own existence is fragile, flawed and contingent. Keeping this awareness always alight in the heart allows one to stay pure, to be guided in every moment, to steer clear of the ego's pitfalls, and to trust in God's ever-present mercy.

PURITY

One maintains awareness by purifying the heart. This requires cultivating virtues in our social interactions, practising zikr or meditation in our breath and voice, and engaging in muraqaba or contemplation with our mind and imagination. Sufism is purification of the heart's intent, and any tradition that purifies the heart is related to Sufism no matter what its name and form. Pir Rasheed taught that, "There is Sufism or mysticism in every religion [that believes in] the great spirit that rules over the world, creates it, nourishes it and sustains it. Different groups have given different names to this great spirit or pure essence. Jains, Buddhists and Hindus have given it different names and called it by different metaphors, but every group believes in the creative and sustaining spirit… Islam, too, teaches the worship and reverence of the one great spirit that is called Allah. But Islam is very focused on maintaining the original purity and oneness of the spirit, in hope of guiding people back to the original belief that all shared."

UNITY

Sufism is the essence of Islam, the religion that urges us to move from fragmentation toward unity. In the social world, we are divided by language, ethnicity, race, gender, sexuality, religion, nation and other identities, but these dimensions of the ego are all partial and divisive. This diversity is ordained by God through creation's principle of multiplicity, and it is meant as a challenge for us to overcome apparent divisions and achieve a greater unity. Indeed, the Qur'an teaches, "O humanity, we created you from a male and female and made you into nations and tribes that you should come to acknowledge each other, and to understand that the most noble of you in God's sight is the one with most constant awareness" (Surat al-Hujurat 49:13).

How can we acknowledge people who differ from us and who may conflict with us? One begins to do this through respecting others with adab, by upholding their dignity in one's outer interactions. One continues to do this by cultivating virtues like compassion, forbearance, forgiveness and generosity in one's inward intentions. One completes this effort by abandoning selfish concern and egoistic pretensions altogether, bringing one's outward interactions and inward intentions into complete harmony. One nullifies the lower self in order to realize a greater unity. Sufism teaches us to delve below surface appearance and perceive with insight the ultimate unity between people, between religions, and even between this world and the next.

INSIGHT

Spiritual refinement depends upon our abandoning selfish concern and to do this, we must gain insight into the nature of the self. Pir Rasheed taught, "We must understand the five senses and where they came from. We experience the world through seeing, hearing, feeling, tasting and smelling and we can do no work in the world without them… By means of these five senses, we experience the world. We come to know things. We are enabled to think about things, not only what is happening now, but what has happened in memory or could happen in our rational deliberation. God has given us thought, reason and mind in order to perform acts in the world. We have used the mind to create atom bombs or to fly to the moon… We have the freedom to use our ability for good or for bad, and that choice is given to us by God as well."

Sufis uphold the nobility of human choice and its weighty consequences, as the Qur'an teaches: "God does not impose burdens on the human soul more than it can bear—for the soul is the merit of its good deeds and against the soul is the acquisition of its bad deeds" (Surat al-Mu'minun 23:62). Indeed, Sufis admire Eve and Adam for their choice to disobey; theirs was a fortunate fall from paradise to earth, where, despite their suffering and alienation, they became the locus for repentance, forgiveness and mercy. There is no original sin—there is merely negligence followed by deeper intimacy, as Adam became a prophet. He is not just the primordial human being but is also the first prophet in the series of 124,000 prophets—some of whom are named in the Qur'an and most of whom are unnamed, some of whom are known in other traditions and most of whom are unknown—which culminated with Hazrat Muhammad, the final Messenger of God and the Seal of Prophecy.

Although they spoke different languages, used varying metaphors, and adapted to diverse societies, all of the prophets came with the same essential teaching: to worship the one divinity, uphold the most noble of virtues, and overcome the divisive ego. They all taught us to generate insight rather than rely on sight, to stay aware of the essence rather than rely on commonsense, and to oppose the lower self rather than compete with our neighbors for power and prestige. In short, they all conveyed the nobility of human choice and its weighty consequences, and the final message of the Qur'an expresses this most succinctly and purely—"I swear by soul and what created it, and what gave it insight into its deceit and its awareness. Whoever keeps the soul pure has triumphed and whoever lets the soul tarnish has failed" (Surat al-Shams 91:8–10). Indeed, those who know the real consequence of choice abandon their selfish impulse to impose their own will and submit to God's choosing for them. They chose to abandon choice and drift willingly in the current of God's decree for them. This is the real meaning of renouncing the world and relying upon God.

RESPECT

Pir Rasheed strictly followed the sharee'a but never imposed rules on others. He followed sharee'a as an expression of good manners and respect with regard to God. He used to say, "Sufism is in its entirety good adab. It is how you treat people and the environment and all things around you. Sufism is not about rites and rituals, customs and ceremonies… Sufism is an attitude of respect and benevolence toward all people and all things around you. It is adab and it comes directly from the heart. The person with the better adab is the better Sufi. It is in being kind and compassionate in all situations, being forbearing and forgiving with all people, and putting aside your own wants and needs to serve others. Everything else is a means toward this goal."

The Prophet Muhammad brought these teachings in their Sufi form. Out of respect and love toward him, Pir Rasheed would follow the sharee'a, trusting that the sharee'a expressed the Muslim community's consensus about how the Prophet Muhammad behaved. These outer rules are not to be followed blindly or imposed coercively, but rather one should follow them out of respect and love, in the light of one's own conscience and to the extent of one's own capacity.

LOVE

Pir Rasheed said, "Love is the single most essential thing in Sufism, without which nothing one does is of any benefit. Love for God is the main thing, as expressed in awe and humility in prayer. Without this emotion, prayer is just movement, like exercise. It is not beneficial in that case; in fact, it could be very harmful. Love for other people is also crucial, just as I love you, and you have come to love me and place me in the circle of your love." One of God's ninety-nine most beautiful names is al-Wadud, the loving One. Many Muslims forget this and imagine that obedience is the highest virtue.

Yet obedience could come from fear or from love. Love which buds from the branch of sincerity is a much bigger challenge. In the Qur'an, God makes divine guidance and favor dependent upon our love, "If you turn away from God, God will bring forth a community in your place whom God loves and who love God" (Surat al-Ma'ida 5:54). The Prophet Muhammad also taught that, "Your faith is not complete until you love for your brothers and sisters what you love for yourself."[131] In Pir Rasheed's teachings, love is the very principle of creation. God felt love and thus overflowed divine singularity and generated the cosmos with everything in it—and especially the human being which is its most conscious element—so that it could serve as the reflection of divine love. Life is the potential to love, while to live without loving is to waste away in darkness.

Pir Rasheed said, "You should burn with love, like a candle. Its nature is to burn down, slowly dwindling away toward death but giving off so much light. Wherever it is, in whatever environment or surroundings, the candle gives off light. It may be in a mosque or temple, it may be in a party where people have gathered to celebrate, it may be in a bar where people come to drink in oblivion. Wherever it may be, the candle burns and in burning it gives others light. That is the way you must be."

LISTENING

Pir Rasheed used to say, "Music is the very backbone of our tareeqat." The Kaleemi Sufi Order advocates and thrives on music. Even though it fuses four different Sufi Orders, the Chishti Order predominates in its love for music.

Once I asked Pir Rasheed permission to learn Indian music and he responded by reciting a couplet by Maulana Rumi: "Dried skin, brittle wood and strung gut, from this how does my beloved's voice come? Not from skin, not from wood or from gut, from beyond these does my beloved's voice come." Then he said, "You should not only study music, but you must learn to play music! ... It is the very foundation of the Chishti Order. Without music, there would be no energy and no light in the Chishti path. The better one understands music, the better one can progress in the Chishti Order."

Pir Rasheed loved qawwali, especially songs about visiting the Prophet in Medina. A favorite song was by Bedam Warsi and he would rise in ecstasy and tears upon hearing its powerful final couplet, "Gentle fragrance spread, O Bedam, making fragrant the world of the heart/ When loose flowed the tresses of Muhammad, may God bless him and give him peace." He used to say, "I am no musician. I don't know even the basics of a raga with its notes and intervals and patterns, but I feel music intensely. When I listen to qawwali, I feel that I am flying from this world to a different world, a world much closer to God." In Sufism, one is not required to become a musician, but one is required to become an ardent and expert listener. Active listening is not merely the basis of musical sensitivity, but is also the foundation for receiving the Qur'an. God's speech praises those "who listen acutely to the discourse and follow that which is best in it" (Surat al-Zumar 39:18).

Indian music, like modern Western music, is based on scales that divide an octave into seven tones. Ascending along the intervals of these seven tones, one arrives at the octave which resonates with the base note at which one began. Just as there are seven notes in the musical scale that makes up a raga, there are seven lata'if or subtle energy centers in the body. These energy centers are found in intervals along the inside of the spine, from its base to the crown of the skull. Keeping these lata'if pure and in sync is like tuning the notes of an instrument before playing a melody in a particular scale. In music, tuning the notes is done by adjusting the body of the instrument or tightening its strings. In Sufism, purifying and refining the lata'if is done by adjusting the breath and intention through zikr, either with the voice or silently. How can one practise Sufism without understanding music, when the body and its breath must be forged into a well-tuned instrument?

REMEMBRANCE

The literal meaning of zikr is remembrance of God, but its practical meaning is meditation. One remembers God by meditating on God's names and contemplating God's qualities that are manifest in this world. Otherwise, how can we directly remember God whom we cannot see, hear, touch or comprehend with concepts?

Pir Rasheed used to teach about doing zikr in every breath, "When you begin to feel your own heart and hear it saying the name *Allahu* then your senses change. You begin to see with God's own seeing. You begin to hear with God's own hearing. You begin to will things with God's own willing. Things begin to happen around you that do not seem natural, that are beyond natural. You think something and then it happens. You remember somebody and then they call you. You wish for something and then it occurs. These are gifts and signs. You should just keep focusing on your heart and remembering God but things around you will begin to change." By doing such meditation, we are among "those who believe and whose hearts are tranquil with the remembrance of God—for surely, human hearts only become calm through remembrance of God" (Surat al-Ra'd 13:27).

Doing zikr gives us awareness of the eternal axis around which all being circles in its bewildering diversity. All things are transient but the face of God abides, looking directly at us through all circumstances. As Pir Rasheed used to say, "Death could come at any time without any warning. One moment you are healthy and happy, the next moment you are dead... With breathing in and out, the soul is tasting death for a moment. Death is as close to each person as the space between one breath and the next... After breathing out, what guarantee is there that you will once again breathe in?" Let each breath be filled with awareness, so that its going will be a prayer and its coming will be a reminder that God's presence is always nearer than we can possibly imagine.

INTIMACY

Pir Rasheed used to say, "God has imposed limits. This is to force our minds to restrain and not to give into any old path that the five senses open up for us as a possibility. This is to preserve our nobility, for the human being is the best model and image of God in this world. Our senses are reflections, though dim, of God's power of perception and our reasoning is a reflection of God's own knowledge and thought. Therefore, we must keep these reflected qualities pure, clear and full of light… The power of electricity comes through all the wires in this room from a generator, and it powers the lights and fan here. If the generator is turned off, then it doesn't matter how many of the switches in this room we turn on or off, no power will come and none of our appliances will work." It is God's presence with us that provides us with our five senses. These senses bring us knowledge and through them, we are able to think about experiences and conceive of an essence that is beyond our direct experience.

God's presence with us is the very foundation of our being and our sensing. Pir Rasheed said, "We think of our senses as belonging to our body in our anatomy. Sight is in the eyes. Hearing is in the ears. Tasting is in the tongue. Smelling is in the nose. Feeling is in the skin. We think these parts and their powers belong to us, constitute us. But in fact, God is closer to us than these. God is with you and in you, and that is what gives you the senses and their powers. Without acknowledging that, the five senses and the thoughts which arise from them will mislead you." The whispering tempter of egoism works deep within our consciousness. As the Qur'an says, "We created humanity and we know what is whispering inside every human soul—indeed we are closer to the human than the artery in the neck" (Surat Qaf 50:16). Yet God's presence is even deeper, more pervasive and more intimate in our conscience and our bodies. God is the foundation for our very being.

MERCY

The better we come to know our selves, the more intimately we come to acknowledge God. Indeed, there is no way to draw close to God except through one's own being. Pir Rasheed said, "It is strange that God is such a being that 'He who knows himself knows his Lord.' God is present in everything, but we are directed to look deep inside ourselves to find knowledge of God." One must venture deep inside, into the darkness within the self, through the sharp shards of the wounded ego, in the very hurt of the darkened heart that is you and also is me. "Every being in the heaven and earth approaches the merciful One as a worshipful servant. God accounts for each of them with a precise reckoning and all of them come to God on the day of judgment as unique individuals. The merciful One will establish those who believe and do beautiful deeds in loving intimacy" (Surat Maryam 19:93–96). Each being is unique, and embracing the emptiness of yourself is the key to opening the treasury of the fullness of the divine.

God promises to love us with intimacy, if we believe and do beautiful deeds of compassion, kindness and forgiveness with others and to our own selves. In fact, that intimacy is already there in our very being, for God is the subtle One (*al-lateef*) the One that pervades all things (*al-khabeer*). Our being and all being resounds with mercy. Mercy is the very foundation of being. As the Qur'an in hymnic grandeur proclaims, "The merciful One recited the Qur'an, created the human being and taught understanding discrimination. The sun and moon move in measured orbits while the stars and trees bend low in prostration. The skies God raised up and firmly set the balance, that you should not arrogantly upset the balance" (Surat Rahman 55:1–8). This whole cosmic harmony is created by God as the merciful One, al-Rahman. Being is brought forth through mercy as from oneness, there emerges a network of differentiation, diversity, multiplicity and contradiction.

The only way to preserve the cosmic balance is to not consider one's self weighty. The fine web of being is already in perfect balance, the scales are even, and to consider yourself weighty is to upset the balance. Arrogance is the root of all discord, evil and oppression. Consider a mirror! It is merely a slab of metal that has a polished surface. As metal, it has weight and density but is dark and dull. Its polished surface has no weight of its own but displays the radiant image of all that is around it. Disregard your own apparent weight and you will find your self light upon light. To show us the way, didn't Prophet Muhammad say, "If only the Lord of Muhammad would never have created Muhammad!"[132]

By nullifying the ego, we let the true image of God show through all that we sense and experience. As the false consciousness of ego dissolves, the true conscience of God resolves within the mirror of our hearts. To live in this way is an ever-deepening process of transformation, called mercification. We appeal to God's mercy, become merciful ourselves, and enact mercy toward others. In harmony with the divine Other, we mercify this world just as rainfall aquifies the parched earth, transforming it into verdant fields and vivid flowers.

This is the path of the Prophet Muhammad, who embodied to the utmost perfection how mercy is to be performed. God speaks to him through the Qur'an, "We have not sent you but as mercy to all the worlds. Say, 'It has been revealed to me that your deity is One, so will you all be in worshipful submission?'" (Surat al-Anbiya 21:107). Muhammad was sent not as a mercy but as mercy itself, the personification of God's quality of being the merciful One. He taught an outer religion: through that, he brought conflicting tribes, warring nations, and chauvinistic sects into the oneness of community. He also embodied an inner wisdom: through this, he brought envious individuals, powerless persons, and wounded souls into the wholeness of integrity.

The Prophet Muhammad initiated some of his companions and trained them in zikr, a way of remembrance, contemplation and awareness. They became spiritual teachers after him, establishing chains of illumination and conscience that linked the unfolding generations to his fountain of mercy. He may be gone in body, but he is still present in the still-resounding wave of transformation that is mercification, which he set in motion. The Qur'an invites us to submit to this wave and let it carry us along, for it gives us the power to have divine work carried out through us, despite our faults and failures. "O servants of God who have transgressed against their own souls, never despair of God's mercy for God forgives all sins—indeed God is the forgiving One who forgives, the merciful One" (Surat al-Zumar 39:53). This invitation is the cure for all despair.

Photo 17: Tomb of Pir Rasheed

This invitation comes to each person in a unique form. For me, this invitation came in the form of Pir Rasheed. He is my door of mercy through mercy to mercy. He is the door showing me a way out of the flaming darkness of egoism, revealing a passage through the dense, depressing wall of worldly distraction. His frame is frail, yet beyond him is light and beauty and tranquility. The merciful door swings wide open, if you only grasp its handle and gently pull.

APPENDIX:
IMPORTANT DATES IN THE ISLAMIC CALENDAR MENTIONED IN THIS BOOK

Muharram 1 Start of the Islamic New Year
Muharram 5 ʿUrs of Baba Farid al-Din Ganj-e Shakar
Muharram 10 ʿAshura

Safar 9 ʿUrs of Shaykh Burhan al-Din Ghareeb
Safar 21 ʿUrs of Pir Rasheed, Sayyid Muhammad Rasheed al-Hasan Jeeli Kaleemi
Safar 28 ʿUrs of Shaykh Yahya Madani

Rabeeʿ al-Awwal 7 ʿUrs of Shaykh Muntajab al-Din Zar Zari Zar-Bakhsh
Rabeeʿ al-Awwal 12 Milad al-Nabi or Birthday of the Prophet Muhammad
Rabeeʿ al-Awwal 13 ʿUrs of Shaykh ʿAla al-Din ʿAli Ahmad Sabir
Rabeeʿ al-Awwal 14 ʿUrs of Khwaja Qutb al-Din Bakhtiyar Kaki
Rabeeʿ al-Awwal 15 ʿUrs of Sayyid Muhammad Zia al-Hasan Jeeli Kaleemi
Rabeeʿ al-Awwal 24 ʿUrs of Shaykh Kaleemullah Shahjahanabadi

Rabeeʿ al-Sani 11 ʿUrs of ʿAbd al-Qadir Jeelani (day known as Gyarween Shareef)
Rabeeʿ al-Sani 18 ʿUrs of Hazrat Nizam al-Din Awliya
Rabeeʿ al-Sani 21 ʿUrs of Sayyid Muhammad Hasan Jeeli Kaleemi

Jumadi al-Awwal 17 ʿUrs of Sayyid Badiʿ al-Din Zinda Shah Madar

Jumadi al-Sani 16 ʿUrs of Baba Fakhr al-Din Pahari

Rajab 6 ʿUrs of Khwaja Muʿin al-Din Chishti
Rajab 27 Miʿraj al-Nabi or Ascension Night of the Prophet Muhammad

Sha'ban 14–15 Shab-e Barat or Night of Forgiveness
Sha'ban 20 'Urs of Baba Sharaf al-Din Pahari

Ramadan 14 'Urs of Sayyid Muhammad Fakhr al-Hasan Jeeli Kaleemi
Ramadan 17 'Urs of Shaykh Naseer al-Din Chiragh-e Delli
Ramadan 27 Shab-e Qadr or Night of Power

Shawwal 1 Eid al-Fitr or Feast of Opening the Fast
Shawwal 6 'Urs of Khwaja 'Usman Haruni
Shawwal 17 'Urs of Ameer Khusro

Dhu'l-Qa'da 3 'Urs of Shah Khamosh
Dhu'l-Qa'da 11 'Urs of Shaykh Nizam al-Din Aurangabadi
Dhu'l-Qa'da 16 'Urs of Hazrat Gesu Daraz

Dhu'l-Hijja 6 'Urs of Yusufayn, Yusuf and Sharif al-Din Chishti Kaleemi
Dhu'l-Hijja 10 Eid al-Adha or Feast of Sacrifice

GLOSSARY

Abdal: hidden saints, of whom there are always a certain number in the world and who keep the world in balance; when one dies, another steps into their place, so they are known as *abdal* or "those who substitute for each other."

Abjad: the numerical value of letters, such that word or phrases encode a symbolic number (for example, *bismillah al-rahman al-raheem* "In the name of God, the merciful One, the compassionate One" has an abjad value of 786). This system originated in Phoenician and was adopted into Aramaic, Hebrew and Arabic, and from there into Persian and Urdu.

Adab: good manners and respectful conduct; a famous Sufi adage says that "All of Sufism consists of good *adab*."

Ahl-e hadees: a modern sect of Sunni Muslims in India who reject interpretive traditions; they insist on literal interpretation of Qur'an based only on *hadees* reports, thereby claiming to follow the Prophet Muhammad's original teachings; they are often called Salafi or Wahhabi in other regions.

Ahl-e nisbat: people with a Sufi connection, meaning those Muslims who participate in Sufism; see *nisbat* below.

'Alam-e misal: "imaginal realm," an intermediate realm between this phenomenal world and the purely spiritual world of divinity; the soul can experience spiritual forces in the form of sensations and images through this imaginal realm, such as occurs in dreams, visions or prophetic revelation.

Ameer: a noble title, given to court poets to mark their royal patronage; Ameer Khusro Dehlavi and Ameer Hasan Sijzi enjoyed this title, though they were also Sufi poets.

'Amil: "practitioner," a religious teacher who turns prayer into incantations or amulets for practical benefits, like healing, or social success or warding off evil.

'**Ashura:** the first ten days of the Islamic year and a time of spiritual atonement; it culminates on the tenth day of the month of Muharram, when Imam Husayn was martyred.

Astana: "noble threshold," meaning a building housing a powerful entity, such as a saint's residence or a king's court; the small building housing the tombs of Pir Rasheed's ancestors is called "The Kaleemi Astana."

Awliya: "God's friends," a term for Muslim saints and Sufi masters; though it is a plural noun (singular *wali*), it is granted as an honorific nickname to highly revered individuals, such as the famous Chishti Sufi, Nizam al-Din Awliya.

Ayat al-kursi: "Verse of the Throne," a very profound and cosmic verse of the Qur'an, which Muslim recite for protection and security; it is Surat al-Baqara 2:255, and speaks metaphorically of God's throne and footstool.

Azan: "call to prayer," chanting aloud that God is greatest, that there is no god but God, and Muhammad is the Prophet of God, then calling the people to lead a successful life through prayer.

Baba: "father," an honorific and endearing title given to Sufi teachers.

Bansuri: bamboo flute, an instrument in Hindustani classical music that was adopted from Indian folk music and associated strongly with Krishna.

Baraka: "blessing" from God that gives health, prosperity, protection and fulfillment; divine blessing can come through others, such as the saints and prophets.

Barzakh: "medium" an intermediary place, referring to something that doesn't exist itself but rather exists as the meeting of two realms; in Chishti meditation practices, one's Sufi master is referred to as the medium between one's personal existence and the spiritual world beyond.

Bay'at: "initiation," referring to the ritual of "taking the hand" of a spiritual teacher and pledging allegiance, to begin training in a Sufi order.

Bhai: "brother," meaning fellow disciples of a spiritual guide (technically *pir-bhai*, or brothers who share the same Pir as father-figure); a female disciple can be called *pir-behen* or "spiritual sister."

Bibi: "lady," a term of a respected female; especially for Fatima, the daughter of Prophet Muhammad, the wife of Hazrat 'Ali and mother of Imam Husayn.

Bid'a: "innovation," introducing new practices into a religion that are not in accord with the essential principles of the religion.

GLOSSARY

Buraq: "Swift as Lightning," the name for the legendary steed that carried the Prophet Muhammad during his ascension through the heavens to the throne of God.

Burqa: a concealing garment worn to cover the head and body, often considered the most modest form of dress for Muslim women in India.

Buzurg: "great," meaning a person with a powerful and enlightened soul, such as a saint or elder.

Chilla: "forty," meaning a spiritual retreat lasting typically for forty days; it is sometimes applied to the place in which a famous saint made such a retreat.

Dargah: "royal court," meaning the shrine housing the tomb of a revered Sufi, which is a place of visitation, healing and intercession.

Dastar: "turban," an Islamic tradition and a display of religious authority; Chishti Sufis tend to wear turbans of yellow color, and the turban-tying ceremony—called *Dastar-Bandan*—is a mark of recognition by the community that a person has matured or become a leader.

Dhamar: song for the spring time in Hindustani classical music, associated with the Holi festival when Krishna plays with his lovers.

Din: "religion," meaning one's moral obligation, as the mediating force between this ephemeral world (*dunya*) and the eternal spiritual truth (*haqq*); it is often included as part of Muslim personal names.

Du'a: "petition," a kind of prayer, to ask for some favor from God; it is informal and personal, as contrasting with the ritual prayer called namaz.

Durud: "praise," a kind of prayer, to ask for blessings upon and connection to the Prophet Muhammad.

Fana: "obliteration," a spiritual state of reducing the ego to nothing in order to enjoy the fullness of being sustained through another's being; it is often translated as "annihilation" or "nullification." In Sufism, there are stages of fana: obliteration in the personality of one's Sufi master, then obliteration in the persona of the Prophet Muhammad, then obliteration in God.

Faqeeh: "jurist," one who makes judgments about the legal dimensions of the Islamic *sharee'a*.

Fatiha: "opening," referring to the first chapter of the Qur'an, called Surat al-Fatiha; it refers to a ceremony in which these verses are recited, along with durud and *du'a*, in honor of a deceased Sufi, often before eating a meal to commemorate his memory (and thus it refers also to the meal itself!)

Fatwa: "decision," legal ruling given by a Muslim jurist about some controversy.

Fitra: "nature," referring to human nature or the original state of God's creation (see Surat al-Rum 30:30); in Islam, it is believed that the original human nature is pure, sinless and aware of God's presence through a primordial covenant (see Surat al-A'raf 7:172).

Gabriel: the archangel, known also as Jibra'il or Jibreel, who bears revelation from God to humanity; Islamic tradition refers to Gabriel as *al-ruh al-ameen* "the most-trustworthy spirit" and *ruh al-qudus* "the holy spirit."

Gaddi-nasheen: "Successor" to a Sufi leader, or literally "One who sits on the seat" that a saint has established; a common title for descendants of Khwaja Mu'in al-Din Chishti who care for his dargah in Ajmer.

Ghazal: "love lyric," a kind of poem expressing the passion, longing, rapture and despair of a lover; composed of rhyming couplets, it depicts the beloved who could be interpreted as a person or idea or God.

Ghusl: "washing," a bath to cleanse the body of any ritual impurities, including to prepare a corpse for funerary rites and burial.

Hadees: "report," an oral tradition of what the Prophet Muhammad said, did or felt; these oral reports were slowly written down several generations after the Prophet's death to form a crucial part of Islamic tradition and law.

Hadees qudsi: "holy report," an oral tradition in which the Prophet Muhammad reports what God said in his consciousness; these reports are not part of the literal speech of God comprising the Qur'an, but constitute an important element of Sufism.

Hal: "momentary state," meaning trance or rapture that alters one's consciousness, rendering one open to spiritual realities that are ordinarily inaccessible to the senses.

Halal: "allowed," meaning food or income that is pure and wholesome; rules for determining what is allowed are detailed in Islamic law.

Haram: "forbidden," the opposite of *halal*.

Haqq: "truth," on the relative level it means doing what is right in a given situation (such as respecting someone's rights) while on the absolute level, *al-Haqq* is among the ninety-nine names of God, meaning the true One.

Haqeeqat: "reality," the spiritual truth that is obscured by sensory experience in this phenomenal world, but which is accessible by cultivating awareness.

GLOSSARY

Hazrat: "presence," a title of honor and reverence for a spiritual authority; often applied to Sufi teachers, Muslims saints and Islamic leaders.

Hijri: "year after the exile," referring to the Islamic calendar that begins with the flight of the Prophet from Mecca to Medina in the year 622 CE. The Hijri calendar is a purely lunar calendar with 12 months, each beginning with the new moon, such that the Hijri year has approximately eleven less days than the solar year of the Gregorian calendar; most 'urs dates move in forward year by year in relation to the Western calendar (see the appendix on important dates in the Islamic calendar).

'Ibada: "worship," meaning any action through which one submits to the divine will, whether it is through engaging in ritual or caring for others.

Iftar: "breaking open," a meal that breaks one's fast, especially at sunset during the month of Ramadan.

Ijaza: "permission," when Sufi masters permit one to transmit their teachings or practices to others.

Ikhlas: "purity," meaning the purity of a sincere heart; Ikhlas is also the name of the 112th chapter of the Qur'an which is essential to Sufism, referring to the purity of firm belief in radical monotheism.

'Ilm-e laduni: "knowledge by intuition," refers to spiritual knowledge that comes by intuition, inner awareness and inspiration rather than by intellect, learning or tradition; such knowledge is the basis of sainthood and mystical experience, as mentioned in the Qur'an (Surat al-Kahf 18:65).

'Ishq: "love," irresistibly strong emotion of passionate love that drives people to do what is beyond reason and custom; in the Chishti Order, the heat of passionate love is superior to the coolness of sympathetic love or *muhabbat*.

Jabarut: "realm of God's qualities," meaning the fabric of spiritual forces that compel the world to take the form that it takes.

Jalali: "wrathful," the qualities of might, power and wrath that are expressed in many of God's divine names, and which are reflected in the characteristics of some people.

Jamali: "beauteous," the qualities of gentleness, attractiveness and grace that are expressed in many of God's divine names, and which are reflected in the characteristics of some people.

Jama'at-e Islami: "The Islamic Party," a modern reform movement that follows Maulana Maududi, who formed a fundamentalist political organization in India and Pakistan; they accept modern technology but oppose Western secular culture, and reject Sufism as a superstitious heresy.

Janaza: "funeral," rituals for Muslim who dies, including cleaning and wrapping the body, procession of the body from home, special communal prayers at the mosque, and prayers at the burial.

Jihad: "struggle," grappling with conflict in order to find the truth; in a *hadees*, the Prophet Muhammad taught that the lesser outer struggle is to fight for justice, while the greater inner struggle is to overcome the forces of temptation that are inside each person's psyche.

Ka'ba: "square shrine," the ancient cube-shaped black shrine in Mecca considered to be the "House of Allah" which the Prophet Muhammad appointed as the center of the Islamic world and the direction to turn in prayer; see *qibla*.

Kaleemi: the name of a Sufi Order, the branch of the Chishti Order that comes through Nizam al-Din Awliya through Shaykh Kaleemullah, and from him to many contemporary Sufi teachers in India and the wider world.

Kalima tayyiba: "the wholesome words," a statement of direct, simple and uncompromising belief that "there is no god but God, and Muhammad is the Prophet of God" or *la ilaha illa 'llah, muhammadun rasulu 'llah*; this credo forms the basis of zikr and meditation practices in Sufism.

Karbala: a place where Imam Husayn, the grandson of the Prophet Muhammad was martyred for the sake of truth and justice; Husayn is considered a spiritual master for Sufis, a hero for Sunnis, and an infallible leader for Shi'is.

Khannas: "creeper," the force of temptation that whispers in the breast of each person, as mentioned in the Qur'an (Surat al-Nas 114:4); Sufis understand Khannas to be the name of Satan's child, who circles around the human heart inside each breast.

Khanqah: "hospice," a gathering place for Sufis; it consists of a hall large enough for spiritual devotions and often includes rooms for disciples to make retreats or live permanently; often a khanqah grows around the home of a Sufi master or his tomb after he dies.

Khatam: "seal," a ritual performed in a group gathering, in which reciting Qur'an and chanting zikr is done in a set formula, before reading out the names of all the saints in the *silsila* from the Prophet Muhammad to the current Pir, thereby setting a seal the relationship from past to present; Pir Rasheed's community would recite this wazeefa weekly, in one way for his Chishti *silsila* and in another way for his Qadiri *silsila*.

Khadim: "servant," one who does *khidmat* by serving a saint or caring for people who come to visit a saint whether living or dead.

Khaleefa: "successor," one who has authority to teach others as the follower of a spiritual teacher; the delegated authority is called *khilafat* and usually is granted after initiation and training.

Khadim: "service," meaning keeping company with a Sufi master, or also more generally helping other people; in the Chishti Order, service to others (*khidmat-e khalq*) is the highest form of worship.

Khuda: "lord," a Persian name for God or Allah.

Khwaja: "master," a Persian name for a sage or spiritual teacher; the founder of the Chishti Order, Muʿin al-Din Chishti, is often called Khwaja-e Khwajagan or "Master of Masters."

Kimas: the sciatic nerve that runs behind the knee; putting pressure on this nerve affects the heart.

Lahut: "realm of God's essence," meaning divine being that can be expressed only in negation, that is beyond all names, qualities, forms and effects.

Lataʾif: "subtle centers," nodes of energy along the spine that serve as the points of contact between the spirit and the body; this term is the plural of the Arabic term *lateefa*, which is analogous to the Sanskrit term *chakra*.

Madrasa: "place of learning," an Islamic school or university where Islamic sciences are taught, including Qurʾan recitation, Islamic law, math and astronomy and other natural sciences, and sometimes Sufism.

Majlis: "assembly," a gathering of Sufis for teachings or devotions.

Majzub: "divinely distracted," a kind of holy fool whose reason has been overwhelmed by strong emotional attraction to God.

Malakut: "realm of angelic forces," through which God's messages and intentions come into the world; angels are understood to be entities of light.

Malfuzat: "oral teachings," a record of the spoken teachings of a Sufi master; this became a central genre of Sufi literature in the Chishti Order starting with Nizam al-Din Awliya in the 14th century.

Manqabat: "laudation," a kind of poem, to praise a spiritual hero; poem or song that extols the virtues of a Sufi leader, especially Hazrat ʿAli.

Ma'rifa: "mystical knowledge," a kind of knowledge that is awareness of existential being or spiritual truth, rather than knowledge based on sensory perception, rational calculation, intellectual learning or received custom; sometimes called *gnosis* in English.

Matam: "mourning," especially ritualized sorrow expressed in lamentation and beating the chest.

Matlabi: "selfish."

Maulana: "master," an Arabic honorific title for a teacher or spiritual guide.

Mazhab-e 'ishq: "religion of love," an orientation in some Sufi Orders toward love as the pure experience of God's oneness and the supreme expression of devotional life.

Mazhar: "manifestation," especially meaning an image or feeling through which one senses the presence of God, one of whose names is *al-Zahir*, "the manifest One."

Mehfil-e sama': "celebration of music," a gathering of Sufis to listen to devotional music as a ritual of worship; this is the technical term for what is practiced in India as "qawwali."

Mulk: "realm of phenomena," the domain of cause and effect that we misinterpret through common sense, such that we pretend to possess and own things in it, especially our own ego.

Mulla: "teacher," an honorific term (simplified from *maulana*) for a religious teacher.

Muraqaba: "contemplation," method of silent mental control, using visualization or conceptualization; contrasted to zikr or meditation using chanted words.

Mureed: "seeker," a disciple of a spiritual teacher.

Murshid: "guide," a spiritual teacher; synonymous with Pir.

Na'at: "depiction," a kind of poem, to praise the Prophet Muhammad by depicting his physical beauty, describe his spiritual majesty, and extol his ethical virtues.

Nafas: "breath," the flux of inhaling and exhaling through which one senses the life of the soul, awareness of which can refine the soul.

Nafs: "self," the ego or human psyche that is energized when the spirit blows through the body; in Sufism, the nafs is of varying levels depending upon its spiritual refinement, as described in the Qur'an.

GLOSSARY

Namaz: "adoration," a kind of prayer that is fixed to specific times (five times daily according to the passage of the sun) and set to defined postures; this is the Persian and Urdu name for the basic prayer ritual for all Muslims, also called *salat* in Arabic.

Namaz-e awabeen: "prayer of those who turn to God," a supererogatory offering of six cycles (*rak'at*) of ritual prayer (*namaz*); most Muslims offer this additional worship after sunset prayer, but some offer it before noontime prayer.

Namaz-e istikhara: "choosing what is best," a prayer to ask God's help to choose what is best when facing a difficult or perplexing decision.

Namaz-e jum'a: "congregational prayer," on Friday at noon-time when Muslims attend prayer in a mosque and listen to a sermon; in India, it is usually only men to attend congregational prayer.

Namaz-e tasbeeh: "prayer of glorification," a supererogatory offering of four cycles (*rak'at*) of ritual prayer (namaz) very slowly, while reciting "glory to God, praise to God, for God is greatest" extensively during each of the postures.

Nasut: "realm of humanity," the consciousness of being human (*insan*) which calls us to ethical living that rises above selfish concern for the individual body and individualistic ego.

Nazrana: "offering," a monetary gift, usually of small financial value but of large symbolic value, given in appreciation of a musical, poetic or didactic moment as a way to approach a spiritual teacher.

Nisbat: "relationship," one's spiritual connection with a Sufi teacher, living or dead.

Niyaz: "supplication," gesture of begging for a wish or need to be fulfilled; in Sufi practice, this means a sacrifice or a meal that is given in charity to those in need, so that one's own need might be met by God.

Parda: "separation," especially in regard to gender; it can manifest in screening off a special "women's quarters" in a house or gathering place, or in covering up the body out of modesty; see also *burqa*.

Pir: "elder," a spiritual guide; it is synonymous with murshid and shaykh.

Pir-bhai: see *bhai*.

Piranima: "Pir's consort," the wife of a Sufi teacher or a female authority in Sufism.

Qalandar: "renouncer," a kind of ascetic who renounces the world by defying ritual conventions; Qalandars were radical Sufis who took a path of extremism and challenged social norms, even within flexible Sufi organizations.

Qaseeda: "ode," a kind of poem, to praise a hero; it consists of rhyming couplets that boast of the virtue, strength and generosity of a spiritual patron.

Qawwal: "vocalist," one who performs qawwali.

Qawwali: "delivering an articulate message," the art of singing devotional poetry in Sufi gatherings; the term is found in Persian and Indian Sufi communities, but the style of singing is particularly robust in India, where Sufi poetry is adapted to Indian courtly music by families descended from a group of musicians trained by Ameer Khusro in the 14th century.

Qazi: "judge," an authority in Islamic law who is appointed by the ruler to adjudicate legal cases and specify punishments.

Qibla: "direction to face," turning in a particular direction to express orientation toward God; in ritual prayer (namaz), this means turning to face the direction of the Ka'ba, and in Sufi devotion, this means considering one's Pir to be the most important location in the world.

Qur'an: "ever-recited," the speech of God as revealed to the Prophet Muhammad and written down as the Islamic scripture; Muslims believe that the Qur'an is God's speech, eternal and atemporal, as revealed to the Prophet in Arabic through the intermediary of the angel Gabriel, that is inimitable and preserved from loss, error and corruption.

Qutb: "axis of the world," an honorific title for a saint, especially one high in the spiritual hierarchy; it is also used in personal names and royal titles.

Raga: "musical mode," in Hindustani classical music there are seven basic notes in an octave, which can be raised, lowered or omitted in ascending and descending order to create different musical modes; each raga is related to a mood, time of day, or season of the year.

Ramadan: the ninth month of the Islamic lunar calendar, a sacred month of fasting and charity.

Rawzat: "garden," especially a sheltered garden inside the walls of a palace; an honorific name of a mausoleum, and also the garden of paradise.

Rebab: a plaintive musical instrument with strings over a leather-covered resonator; in some regions (Arabia, Turkey, North Africa and Southeast Asia) the strings are played with a bow and in other regions (Afghanistan and

GLOSSARY

Central Asia) they are struck with a plectrum; in India, its neck was widened to accommodate resonating strings, to become both the *sarod* (plucked) and the *sarangi* (bowed).

Ruh: "spirit," the divine breath that animates all existence; spirit is singular in that it comes from God and also plural in that it gives life to different beings.

Sajjada-nasheen: "one seated on the prayer-carpet," signifying the successor to a spiritual teacher who inherits the seat, relics, and institutional authority of a Sufi master.

Salam: "greetings," a kind of poem, to offer greetings of peace and blessings upon the Prophet from afar.

Sama': "listening," the art of interpretive listening to devotional poetry set to artful music; often translated as "audition" in English.

Sandal: "sandalwood perfume," especially a fragrant paste made of sandalwood power mixed with rosewater and 'attar essential oils, which is used to anoint the tomb of saints on the anniversary of their deaths (see 'urs).

Sarangi: upright viol, an Indian instrument with three gut strings played with a bow and thirty-six delicate metal resonating strings; its name means "a hundred colors" because it has no frets and imitates the subtleties of the human voice, and thus often serves as the accompaniment to intimate song styles like *khayal* and *thumri*, in addition to Sufi and Sikh devotional music.

Sawt-e sarmadi: "eternal voice," the resonance of the divine presence within the phenomenal world, which can be heard by those whose awareness is refined by meditation and zikr.

Sayyid: "leader," those with an Arab family pedigree traced back to the Prophet Muhammad through his daughter Fatima and her husband, Hazrat 'Ali; many Sufi masters are *sayyids*, though not all those with *sayyid* genealogy are Sufis or live up to their spiritual potential as descendants of the Prophet's family (the feminine is *sayyida*).

Sehri: "early meal," the food eaten before dawn during Ramadan fasting.

Shab-e Barat: "Night of Forgiveness," during the night of the fourteenth of Sha'ban when the moon is full, Muslims believe God is especially attentive to forgiving those who ask; many stay awake all night in prayer, visit the graves of the deceased to beg forgiveness for them, and fast the next day.

Shab-e Qadr: "Night of Power," the holiest night of the year for Muslims, in which the Qur'an as divine speech is believed to descend into the phenomenal world so that it can be expressed in human discourse; it is one of the last odd-numbered nights in Ramadan, often observed on the 27th night of that month (since it is uncertain that there will be a 29th night to the lunar month).

Shahid-bazi: "playing the witness game," contemplating a beautiful person as meditation on the beauty of God's creation which gives witness to God's own beauty.

Shagird: "student," one who learns from a master according to the strict norms of traditional apprenticeship; especially a student of music or other traditional arts.

Sharbat: "drink," a thirst-quenching delicacy made from flavored milk or syrup.

Sharee'a: "religious way," the social and ritual norms that make up religion, specifically the Islamic religion, as an outer comportment in life.

Shathiyat: "ecstatic utterances," a kind of spiritual boast spoken while in rapture, when the ego is nullified and only the divine presence remains to speak.

Shaykh: "elder," a person with authority; in Sufism, it means a spiritual guide.

Shaykh al-Islam: "authority of the faith," a person whom the Muslim community looks to for ethical and spiritual guidance; Nizam al-Din Awliya called his Sufi teacher, Farid al-Din Ganj-e Shakar, by this title, but the Muslim rulers of India made it into an official position appointed by the government.

Silsila: "chain," the path of initiation that links a Sufi to her or his spiritual teacher, and through him to a great saint, and through him to the Prophet Muhammad, and through him to God; this path is systematized as a Sufi Order.

Suluk: "path," the way of spiritual training in a Sufi Order.

Sunna: "exemplary behavior," the pattern of behavior established by the Prophet Muhammad, as known through the actions of his followers and the oral reports about him that they passed down; it also refers to optional prayer, in addition to the obligatory namaz, which the Prophet Muhammad used to make.

Tableeghi: "missionary," a modern Islamic movement that is moderately fundamentalist; they follow Maulana Ilyas, a Sufi who moved away from spirituality into social reform and communalism.

GLOSSARY

Tahajjud: "late-night vigil," a time of prayer and meditation in the hours just before dawn; many Sufis advocate waking up during this time for quiet devotions.

Talqeen: "instruction," when a Pir or spiritual guide instructs a disciple in how to recite zikr.

Taqwa: "awareness," meaning the constant awareness of God's presence and guidance; it is sometimes translated as "fear of God."

Tarbiyat: "training," that a Pir gives to disciples on how to practice Sufism in a particular *tareeqat*, often for many years; training may be given by the same Pir who gives initiation or by a different Pir, depending on circumstances.

Tareeqat: "spiritual way," meaning a Sufi Order, the method employed by a community of Sufis based on the teachings of an eponymous saint; for instance, the Chishti Order is a Sufi *tareeqat* with a distinct method of spiritual training based upon the life and teachings of Khwaja Mu'in al-Din Chishti, as systematized by generations of his followers in India.

Tasawwur-e shaykh: "visualizing the teacher," by imagining the form of one's spiritual teacher as a way of connecting to him and the chain of teachers while practicing meditation or other devotional acts.

Tasbeeh: "prayer beads," a string of 99 beads used to easily keep count of repeated words used in zikr; often compared to the "rosary" of Catholic devotion, though Buddhists and Hindus also use such beads for devotion.

Thumri: "love song," a genre of Hindi poem associated with Indian dance and gestures of loving devotion; originally an erotic genre sung by courtesans, these songs came to be adopted by Muslim and Hindu mystics as authentic expressions of love for the divine beloved.

Umm: "source," is a term for one's mother or the source of anything that exists.

'Umra: "sacred visitation," travel to Mecca to circle the Ka'ba and visit the sacred sites, but during any time outside of the Hajj pilgrimage time; it is sometimes called the "lesser pilgrimage" in contrast to the Hajj.

'Urs: "night of union," refers to a wedding night when the bride, after extensive longing and patient endurance, is finally united with her beloved; Sufis applied this term to the anniversary of the death of a saint, which is celebrated as the time of the pure soul's union with its divine source.

Ustad: "teacher," the master of a craft who teaches others with a bond of traditional discipline and reverence, especially in music, poetry or other arts.

Wahdat: "oneness," as in *wahdat al-wujud* or "oneness of being," a philosophical and mystical school of thought which asserts that only God is real and all other existing things—including human beings—are ephemeral and thus illusory.

Wahhabi: a modern sect of fundamentalist Muslims, who follow the anti-Sufi teachings of Muhammad ibn Abd al-Wahhab; they hold power in Saudi Arabia and from there, influence Muslims globally, even in Hyderabad.

Wajd: "rapture," the ecstasy of finding one's true being as nullified in God's own being; for Sufis in the Chishti Order, this experience is most accessible through music and sung poetry, though it can occur also through worship, meditation and spontaneous insight.

Wujud: "being," the fact of existence and the force that brings all the cosmos to life; see *wahdat*.

Waqf: "endowment," property that is given to God and dedicated to charitable purposes; rulers or rich people gave land as endowments to Sufi Orders or other religious institutions to materially support spiritual endeavors.

Wazeefa: "duty," a devotional formula that one recited regularly, as a spiritual duty while hoping for some reward; it is similar to wird.

Wilayat: "sainthood," the power bestowed on a person through intimacy with God; the terms also became applied to the region in which a saint's power was operative, meaning the extent of a person's influence.

Wird: "litany," a devotional formula that is chanted or read silently, usually bestowed by the founding saint of a Sufi Order.

Wuzu': "cleanliness," meaning one's state of ritual purity, maintained by washing after changes in one's bodily state.

Zakat: "purity," keeping one's earnings clean by giving a portion in charity before keeping wealth for one's own needs; Chishti masters generally did not earn or store wealth for themselves, so this term came to mean giving of one's time and spiritual attention rather than one's money.

Zikr: "remembrance," techniques for remembering God's presence, though meditation using a pronounced word, phrase or breath.

ENDNOTES

1. Jalal al-Din Rumi, *The Masnawi Book 2*, trans. by Jawid Mojaddedi (New York: Oxford Univeristy Press, 2007), verses 615 and 684–487.
2. Walid Salih, *The Formation of the Classical Tafsir Tradition: The Qur'an Commentary of al-Tha'labi* (Leiden: E.J. Brill, 2004), 116; the hadees report is recorded in Ahmad ibn Hanbal's *Musnad*.
3. Bruce Lawrence (trans.), *Morals for the Heart: Conversations of Nizam al-Din Awliya recorded by Ameer Hasan Sijzi* (Mahwah, NJ: Paulist Press, 1992), 113–114.
4. Lawrence, *Morals for the Heart*, 113.
5. In literature published in India, his name is often transliterated according to older colonial-era conventions, as Syed Mohamed Rasheed-ul-Hasan Jeeli-ul-Kaleemi.
6. Narendra Luther, *Legendotes of Hyderabad* (New Delhi: Niyogi Books, 2014), 162.
7. Watan, Sayyid Iftikhar 'Ali Shah, *Bustan-e Tasawwuf Ya'ni Diwan-e Watan* [Rosegarden of Sufism, being the Collected Poems of Watan] (Hyderabad: Minar Book Depot, n.d.), 56—for the full poem, see note 125.
8. Kugle, *Sufi Meditation and Contemplation: Timeless Wisdom from Mughal India* (New Lebanon: Omega Publications, 2012), 57–59; see also Kugle, "The Brilliance of Hearts: Hajji Imdadullah Teaches Meditation and Ritual," in Barbara Metcalf, ed. *Islam in South Asia in Practice* (Princeton: Princeton University Press, 2009), 221.
9. Lawrence, *Morals for the Heart*, 164–5.
10. Mushtaq Ilahi Faruqi, *Naghmat-e Sama'* [Tunes of Sufi Music] (Karachi: Educational Press, 1972), 30.
11. Kamgar Husayni, *Majalis-e Kaleemi o Ahsan-e Shama'il* [The Malfuzat of Shaykh Kaleemullah] Urdu transl. (Aurangabad: Dargah Nizam al-Din Aurangabadi Press, 2003), Introduction.
12. The poem in Persian: *Az kansa-ye rebab ma-ra ni'mati raseed / shud aftab har keh az-u zarra chasheed.*

13 Meraj Ahmed, *Surud-e Ruhani: Qawwali ke Rang* [Spiritual Melodies: Delight of Qawwali] (New Delhi: n.p., 1998), 77.
14 Kamgar Husayni, *Majalis-e Kaleemi o Ahsan-e Shama'il*, 303–304.
15 Muhammad Husayni Gesu Daraz, *Risala Ra'aytu Rabbi fi Ahsani Suratin* [Epistle on the hadees report "I saw my lord in the most beautiful form"] (Gulbarga: Sayyid Muhammad Husayni Gesu Daraz Tahqiqati Academy, 2003 forth printing), 34.
16 Waheeda Naseem, *Shahan-e Be-Taj* [Kings Without Crowns: the Sufis of Khuldabad](Khuldabad: Alamgir Book Depot, 2009 second printing), 6. In this poem, Naseem mentions many eminent Sufi personalities; some she mentions who are not detailed later in this book include Jalal al-Din Ganj-e Ravan "The Dispenser of Treasures" (a Suhrawardi and the first Sufi who first settled on the Khuldabad hills), and Baha al-Din Ansari Langot-Band "Bound in a Loincloth" (a Shattari Sufi who later settled outside of Daulatabad), and Azad Bilgrami (a great Sufi scholar in the 18th century and India's finest poet of Arabic verse).
17 Mushtaq Ilahi Faruqi, *Naghmat-e Sama'* (Karachi: Educational Press, 1972), 110; Ahmed, *Surud-e Ruhani*, 113.
18 This poem is often sung in qawwali and is popularly attributed to Maulana Rumi; its first line in Persian is *"Har lahze bi-shakli but-e ayyar bar amad, dil burd o nahan shud"* (Every moment in a new form that beloved idol shows up, steals the heart and then disappears).
19 On Muntajab al-Din's life, see Carl Ernst, *Eternal Garden: Mysticism, History, and Politics at a South Asian Sufi Center* (Albany: SUNY Press, 1992), 101–102 and 235–236; in Urdu, see Muhammad Abdul Hayy, *Gulistan-e Khuldabad* [The Garden of Khuldabad: its Sufis and Scholars] (Khuldabad: private printing, 2001), 109–115; Naseem, *Shahan-e Be-Taj*, 57–74.
20 Abdul Hayy, *Gulistan-e Khuldabad*, 121.
21 Abdul Hayy, *Gulistan-e Khuldabad*, 120–121, quoting from *Ahsan al-Aqwal*, a 14th century record of the oral discourses of Shaykh Burhan al-Din Ghareeb.
22 'Abdi is the pen-name of the author of *Ma'arij al-Wilayat*, a famous Persian compendium of Sufi biographies from India; see Abdul Hayy, *Gulistan-e Khuldabad*, 113.
23 Gesu Daraz, Muhammad Husayni, *Yazdeh Rasa'il* [Eleven Treatises], Urdu trans. by Qazi Ahmed Abd al-Samad (Lahore: Sirat Foudation,

n.d.), 187–189; from the fifth treatise entitled "The Being of Lovers" [*Wujud al-'Ashiqeen*].

24 Faruqi, *Naghmat-e Sama'*, 40–41 gives the Persian Ghazal by Ahmad-e Jam: *"Manzil-e ishq az makane digar ast / mard-e ma'na ra nishane digar ast."*

25 *Kalam-e Zia az Sayyid Muhammad Zia al-Hasan Jeeli Kaleemi* (Hyderabad: Maktaba Rahmaniya, 1401 AH), 4–7. This account was written by Sayyid Muhammad 'Abd al-Qadir Jeelani, son of his disciple named Maulana Sayyid Muhammad Anwar al-Rahman.

26 The most accessible biography of Shaykh Kaleemullah is: Zia Inayat Khan (ed.), *A Pearl in Wine* (New Lebanon, NY: Omega Press, 2001), 303–306.

27 K. A. Nizami, "Chishtiyya," *Encyclopedia of Islam* (new edition, Leiden: EJ Brill, 1960–), 2:55.

28 Ernst and Lawrence, *Sufi Martyrs of Love: the Chishti Order in South Asia and Beyond* (New York: Palgrave, 2002), 28–29.

29 Kaleemullah, *Tasnim al-Tawhid*, published in an anonymous English translation as *Tasmin-ul-Tauheed or The Unity of God* (Madras: Hoe and Company, 1909).

30 Husayni, *Majalis-e Kaleemi o Ahsan-e Shama'il*, 28–29.

31 Faruqi, *Naghmat-e Sama'*, 24-25. The phrases in quotation marks

32 Kugle, *Sufi Meditation and Contemplation*, 87–88.

33 Kaleemullah, *Tilka 'Ashara Kamila*, Arabic text with Urdu translation (Delhi: Astana Book Depot, 1406 AH); and Kaleemullah, *Siwa al-Sabil*, Arabic with Urdu translation (Delhi: Astana Book Depot, no date); and Kaleemullah, *Ma La Budd-e Kaleemi*, Arabic with Urdu translation (Delhi: Astana Book Depot, no date). His other works are listed in Zia Khan, *Pearl in Wine*, 305.

34 *Kalam-e Zia*, 101–102.

35 *Kalam-e Zia*, page 102–103.

36 *Kalam-e Zia*, page 103–104.

37 'Abd al-Jabbar Khan Malkapuri, *Mahbub Dhu'l-Minan fi Takira-ye Awliya-ye Dakkan* [The Beloved Who Bestows Gifts, a Memorial of the Saints of the Deccan] in Persian (Hyderabad: Matba'-ye Rahmani, 2001) 1:272–274.

38 Muhammad Isma'il Qadiri Multani, *Tarikh-e Sufiya-ye Kiram o Salatin-e Dakkan* [History of the Noble Sufis and Rulers of the Deccan], (Hyderabad: Student Book House, 2013), 1:21–23.

39 Murad 'Ali Tali', *Tazkira Awliya-ye Hyderabad* [Memorial of the Saints of Hyderabad] (Hyderabad: Minar Book Depot, 1969), 1:12–13; and Multani, *Tarikh-e Sufiya-ye Kiram*, 1:8–13.
40 Tali', *Tazkira Awliya-ye Hyderabad*, 1:14–15.
41 Multani, *Tarikh-e Sufiya-ye Kiram*, 1:101–102.
42 Multani, *Tarikh-e Sufiya-ye Kiram*, 1:103–104.
43 Bible, *Book of Psalms* 118:22, and also *Gospel of Matthew* 21:42.
44 Multani, *Tarikh-e Sufiya-ye Kiram*, 1:103 offers a photograph of this cave, but does identify its location; however, oral legends from the neighborhood of the dargah of Husayn Shah Wali correspond exactly to the story recorded by Multani and the cave in its book's photograph is identical to the one near at Husayn Shah Wali.
45 Faruqi, *Naghmat-e Sama'*, 202.
46 The couplet in Persian is: Karavan-am hama bi-guzasht ze maidan-e shuhud / ham chun naqsh-e kaff-e pa nam o nishan-am baqi-st.
47 Ahmed, *Surud-e Ruhani*, 143. Only the final couplet is given here, but for the whole song, see footnote 117.
48 Anthony Wild, *Coffee: A Dark History* (New York: Norton, 2005).
49 *Kalam-e Zia*, 134.
50 Ruth Vanita and Saleem Kidwai (eds), *Same Sex Love in India: readings from literature and history* (New York: St. Martin's Press, 2000): 145–156; see also, Kugle, *Sufis and Saints' Bodies* (Chapel Hill: University of North Carolina, 2007), 181-220.
51 From *Anis al-'Ushshaq*, translated in Schimmel, *Mystical Dimensions of Islam* (Chapel Hill: University of North Carolina, 1975), 290.
52 Papan-Matin, *Beyond Death: The Mystical Teachings of 'Ayn al-Qudat Hamadhani* (Leiden: Brill, 2010); see also, Nasrollah Pourjavady. (trans.), *Inspirations from the World of Pure Spirits: An English Translation of the Sawanih, the Oldest Persian Sufi Treatise on Love* (London: KPI, 1986).
53 From *Abhar al-'Ashiqeen*, translated in Schimmel, *Mystical Dimensions*, 291.
54 Schimmel, *Mystical Dimensions*, 291–292.
55 Kugle, "Sultan Mahmud's Make-Over: Colonial Homophobia and Persian-Urdu Poetics" in Ruth Vanita (ed), *Queering India: same-sex love and eroticism in Indian culture and society* (New York: Routledge, 2001): 30–46.
56 *Morals for the Heart*, 354.
57 *Morals for the Heart*, 103.

58 Zia Nakhshabi, *Silk al-Suluk*, [Stages of the Path] Urdu translation (Lahore: Nawal Kishore Press, no date), 41–2.
59 *Kalam-e Zia*, 122.
60 Kugle, *Sufi Meditation and Contemplation*, 61–66; see also Kugle, "The Brilliance of Hearts," 220.
61 Kugle, *Sufi Meditation and Contemplation*, 97–101.
62 Kugle, *Sufi Meditation and Contemplation*, 63–64.
63 Malkapuri, *Mahbub Dhu'l-Minan*, 1: 312–313.
64 *The Teaching of Hazrat Inayat Khan*, Vol 8A, chapter "Power of Silence." AS found online at http://hazrat-inayat-khan.org/php/views.php?h1=30&h2=37
65 *Diwan-e Shah Khamosh* (Hyderabad: Students Book House at Charminar, no date), 3-22 provides his biography in Urdu; his given name was Sayyid Muʿin al-Din Husayni.
66 *Diwan-e Shah Khamosh*, 18.
67 *Diwan-e Shah Khamosh*, 61–62.
68 *Diwan-e Shah Khamosh*, 75–76.
69 Faruqi, *Naghmat-e Samaʿ*, 21–22. This book makes a mistake in writing *sajda* instead of *hazhda* when the poem speaks of "18,000 worlds"—in Islamic thought, eighteen thousand is the conventional number of the varieties of living beings or the multiple universes in existence.
70 Muhammad Akram Quddusi, *Iqtibas al-Anvar Tazkira-ye Masha'ikh-e Chishtiya Sabiriya*, [Spreading the Light, on Biographies of the Shaykhs of the Sabiri Chishti Order] Urdu trans. by Capt. Wahid Bakhsh Sial (New Delhi: Farid Book Depot, 2004), 498.
71 Quddusi, *Iqtibas al-Anvar*, 498.
72 Quddusi, *Iqtibas al-Anvar*, 497.
73 Quddusi, *Iqtibas al-Anvar*, 498–99; pages 497–509 give his whole biography. This is how one source, *Mirat al-Asrar*, tells his story. A later souce, *Sayr al-Aqtab*, tells it in a different variation, in which Sabir was impatient for Jamal al-Din to read the document when he arrived at night, so he blew onto a lamp and lit it into flame. Seeing Sabir's reckless penchant for miracles and his fiery temper, Jamal al-Din tore up the succession document to save the capital of Delhi from Sabir's wrathful nature.
74 Ahmed, *Surud-e Ruhani*, 374.
75 For a rendition of "Take my Boat Across the Waters" by Ustad Rasheed Khan see http://www.youtube.com/watch?v=JmP-e5DeAOc;

for a rendition by Ustad Naseeruddin Sami see http://www.youtube.com/watch?v=sNsdg_uzscw; for a rendition in qawwali style by Ustad Neelay Khan, see http://www.youtube.com/watch?v=fFOAEUgL1jg.

76 The poem in Hindi and Persian reads: Sansar har ko puje, kul ko jagat sarahi / Makka main koi dhunde, Kashi ko koi jayi / Guiyan main apne pi ke payan padun na kahi / man qibla rast kardam bar simt-e kaj-kulahi.

77 Faruqi, *Naghmat-e Sama'*, 106–107; Ahmed, *Surud-e Ruhani*, 78.

78 Ahmed, *Surud-e Ruhani*, 77.

79 In India, it is considered auspicious to give an odd number of rupees as a token of appreciation, either 101 or 1001 or such odd number.

80 A popular song by the modern poet, Andaleeb Shadani.

81 Malkapuri, *Mahbub dhu'l-Minan*, 2:782.

82 Malkapuri, *Mahbub dhu'l-Minan*, 2:783.

83 Faruqi, *Naghmat-e Sama'*, 167–8; Ahmed, *Surud-e Ruhani*, 118.

84 Firoozeh Papan-Matin, *Beyond Death: The Mystical Teachings of 'Ayn al-Qudat al-Hamadhani* (Leiden: E.J. Brill, 2010), 187 and 210.

85 Amrit Rai, *A House Divided: The Origin and Development of Hindi/Hindawi* (Oxford: Oxford University Press, 1984), 174, 182 and 191. Urdu scholars in Hyderabad like Hafeez Qateel disputed the traditional attribution of this early Urdu text (in Deccani dialect) to Hazrat Gesu Daraz, and conjectured that it was written by his later followers in the Deccan and attributed to him out of respect.

86 Sayyid Akbar Husayni, *Jawami' al-Kalim* [Most Comprehensive Speech, being the Malfuzat of Gesu Daraz], Urdu translation by Mu'in al-Din Darda'i (New Delhi: Farheen Publishing Company, n.d.), 318.

87 Faruqi, *Naghmat-e Sama'*, 207-208. Ahmed, *Surud-e Ruhani*, 93; See also Qureshi, *Sufi Music*, 23.

88 Faruqi, *Naghmat-e Sama'*, 67. The way this poem is sung is noticably different from how it is published in Ameer Khusro, *Kulliyat-e Ghazaliyat-e Khusro* [Collected Ghazals of Khusro in four volumes] (Lahore: Packages Limited Publishers,1973), 2:481–2, ghazal 294.

89 Malkapuri, *Mahbub dhu'l-Minan*, 1:277–278. Multani, *Tarikh-e Sufiya-ye Kiram*, 1:151–155.

90 Malkapuri, *Mahbub dhu'l-Minan*, 1:272–273.

91 Malkapuri, *Mahbub dhu'l-Minan*, 1:274.

92 Malkapuri, *Mahbub dhu'l-Minan*,1:275. The Qutb Shahi king relented and built another reservoir further from the main city that he named

Ibrahim Sagar which watered a new settlement he called Ibrahimpatan (the Town of Ibrahim).
93 Kugle, *Sufi Meditation and Contemplation*, 67–68.
94 Faruqi, *Naghma-e Sama'*, 229.
95 *Waridat-e Kamil—Diwan-e Sayyid Shah Shaykhan Ahmad Qadiri Shattari* [Inspired Words, the Collected Poems of Kamil] (Hyderabad: Kamil Academy, n.d.), 103–104.
96 Faruqi, *Naghmat-e Sama'*, 22–23.
97 The couplet in Urdu is: Sanam ham dair ham but ham brahman ham / kare kis ki puja charhe kis ko chandan ham
98 Watan, *Bustan-e Tasawwuf Ya'ni Diwan-e Watan*, 26.
99 Yahya al-Nawawi, *Fourty Hadith* (Dar al-Ilm, 1982), 32; this is from the second hadees report called "The Hadith of Gabriel." For an astute explanation of its importance, see Sachiko Murata and William Chittick, *The Vision of Islam: Foundations of Muslim Faith and Practice* (Ann Arbor: Paragon House, 1994), 277.
100 Kugle, *Sufi Meditation and Contemplation*, 67–68; quote is from *Kashkul-e Kaleemi* or "The Alms Bowl of Shaykh Kaleemullah."
101 Kugle, *Sufis and Saints' Bodies*, 123–180. Ghaus is the Indianized way of transliterating his name, but it can also be written as Ghawth, following the modern scholarly way of representing the Arabic script.
102 Joyce Flueckiger, *In Amma's Healing Room: Gender and Vernacular Islam in South India* (Indian University Press, 2005).
103 The *hadees* recounted by Nizam al-Din Awliya is very similar in meaning to a famous report in Yahya al-Nawawi, *Fourty Hadith*, report number 36.
104 Lawrence, *Morals for the Heart*, 95.
105 Zia Inayat Khan, *A Pearl in Wine*, 313.
106 Sarfaraz Niazi (trans.), *Love Sonnets of Ghalib* (New Delhi: Rupa Press, 2002), 181–185; this ghazal is also sung in qawwali, as in Ahmed, *Surud-e Ruhani*, 226.
107 Niazi, *Love Sonnets of Ghalib*, 86–92.
108 *Dala'il al-Khayrat* is a book on offering durud or *salawat*, meaning blessings and peace and benedictions upon the Prophet, for each day of the week. This book was written by Shaykh al-Jazuli in Morocco, and it became famous throughout the Muslim world as the most intricate and beautiful book of durud.
109 The durud in Arabic is: Allahumma, salli 'ala sayyidina Muhammad bi-qadri hubbi-ka fi-hi, wa zidna, ya mawlaya, hubban fi-hi. Wa bi-jahi-hi

'inda-ka farrij 'an-na ma nahnu fi-hi. Salla Allahu 'alayhi wa 'ala ali-hi wa sabhi-hi wa barik wa sallim. La nas'alu-ka, ya rabbana, radd al-qada' wa-lakin-na nasa'lu-ka al-lutf fi-hi. Ameen.

110 Faruqi, *Naghmat-e Sama'*, 27–28.
111 Faruqi, *Naghmat-e Sama'*, 113; Ahmed, *Surud-e Ruhani*, 72–3. Khwaja 'Usman was actually from Harwan, a place near Nishapur in Iran, but people in India pronounce his name Harwani as "Haruni."
112 The Urdu couplet is: Mai se nasha se mujhe gharaz nahin / in guna be-khudi chahiye rat din.
113 These verses are sung in qawwali, but they appear to not be a ghazal; perhaps they come from Maulana Rumi's *Masnawi* rather than *Diwan-e Shams-e Tabrezi*.
114 Faruqi, *Naghmat-e Sama'*, 200; Ahmed, *Surud-e Ruhani*, 84.
115 Ahmed, *Surud-e Ruhani*, 51.
116 The Persian poem by Maulana Jami is: Ya Muhammad ba man-e be-sar o saman madade / Qibla-ye din madade, ka'ba-ye iman madade.
117 Faruqi, *Naghmat-e Sama'*, 88; Ahmed, *Surud-e Ruhani*, 71.
118 Ahmed, *Surud-e Ruhani*, 143.
119 The Urdu poem by an unknown author is: Ya Jeelani shainullah / al-madad bi-idhnilllah.
120 *Diwan-e Hazrat Mu'in al-Din Chishti* [Collected Poems of his Holiness Mu'in al-Din Chishti] (Lithograph; Lucknow: Munshi Nawal Kishore Press), 48. Ahmed, *Surud-e Ruhani*, 40.
121 This poem cites the Qur'anic phrase "Am I not your Lord?" to denote the moment when God faced all human beings directly, in the spiritual world before their material manifestation (Surat al-A'raf 7:172). This is called "the primordial covenant" and it forms one of the basic concepts of Sufism: all human beings have shared the intimacy of God's presence and have born witness to God's lordship before their creation, and each must now strive to remember the resonance of that moment, which forms the basis of faith. See Carl Ernst, *Sufism: The Shambhala Guide* (Boston: Shambhala Publications, 1997), 184–5.
122 Ahmed, *Surud-e Ruhani*, 70.
123 The durud in Arabic is: Allahumma salli wa sallim wa barik 'ala sayyidina Muhammad, al-fatih li-ma ughliqa wa al-khatim li-ma sabaqa, wa al-nasir al-haqq bi'l-haqq, wa al-hadi ila siratika 'l-mustaqim, salla allahu 'alayhi wa alihi wa ashabihi haqqa qadrihi wa miqdarihi al-'azeem.
124 Watan, *Bustan-e Tasawwuf Ya'ni Diwan-e Watan*, 56.

125 The Urdu poem by Sayyid Ahmed Barelvi is: Mustafa jan–e rahmat pe lakhon salam / sham'-e bazm-e hidayat pe lakhon salam. Translated here are the first four couplets and the final couplet of this long *qaseeda* that runs about 150 couplets.
126 *Kalam-e Zia*, 79–80.
127 Faruqi, *Naghmat-e Sama'*, 123.
128 Malkapuri, *Mahbub Dhu'l-Minan*, 2: 1139–1140.
129 Faruqi, *Naghmat-e Sama'*, 159; Ahmed, *Surud-e Ruhani*, 43.
130 Surat Muhammad is the 47th chapter of the Qur'an.
131 Yahya al-Nawawi, *Fourty Hadith*, 56; this is from the thirteenth *hadees* report.
132 Gesu Daraz, *Jawahir al-'Ushshaq* [The Essence of Lovers, a commentary on a Treatise by Shaykh 'Abd al-Qadir Jeelani] (Hyderabad: 'Ahd Afareen Press, n.d.), 5.